A COMPANION GUIDE
TO THE GOSPEL OF THOMAS

A COMPANION GUIDE TO THE GOSPEL OF THOMAS

A Guide to Inner Presence, Self-understanding and Fullness of Personal Expression

Christine Folan

AEON

First published in 2024 by
Aeon Books

Copyright © 2024 by Christine Folan

The right of Christine Folan to be identified as the author of this work has been asserted in accordance with §§ 77 and 78 of the Copyright Design and Patents Act 1988.

Christine Folan has asserted her right under the Copyright, Designs and Patents Act 1988 to be identified as the author of this work. All rights reserved, including the right of reproduction in whole or in part in any form. No part of this publication may be reproduced or transmitted or utilised in any form or by any means, digital, electronic, mechanical, photocopying or otherwise, without prior written permission of the author.

British Library Cataloguing in Publication Data

A C.I.P. for this book is available from the British Library

ISBN-13: 978-1-80-152-123-9

Typeset by Medlar Publishing Solutions Pvt Ltd, India

www.aeonbooks.co.uk

I am indebted to Mark M. Mattison for his interpretations and for his kindness and generosity in allowing free use of these.

CONTENTS

INTRODUCTION ... xix
   A journey with the *Gospel of Thomas* ... xix
   My personal journey with the *Gospel of Thomas* ... xxi
   Please note ... xxii
   The companion guide to the *Gospel of Thomas* ... xxii

CHAPTER 1
The beginning ... 1

CHAPTER 2
Seek and you will find ... 3

CHAPTER 3
One kingdom, one living father ... 5

CHAPTER 4
Each moment our world is made anew ... 7
   Amanda's story ... 8

CHAPTER 5
Knowing creation — 11
   My story — 12

CHAPTER 6
Guidance for living an authentic life — 15
   Do not lie — 16
   Do not do what you hate — 16
   My story — 17

CHAPTER 7
Know the light and darkness of human nature — 19
   Carol's story — 21

CHAPTER 8
Choose wisely that which you value — 23
   Jason's story — 24

CHAPTER 9
Treasure your spiritual seeds — 27
   Janet's story — 28

CHAPTER 10
Seek only truth — 31
   My life story — 32

CHAPTER 11
Find the meaning of life — 37
   Jessie's story — 38

CHAPTER 12
Choose wisely which teacher you follow — 41
   My story — 43
   Truth is a pathless land — 44

CHAPTER 13
I am, thou art — 45
   David's story — 46

CHAPTER 14
Dangers of the spiritual ego — 49
   My story — 50
   Reflections — 51

CHAPTER 15
Understand the source of all life — 53
   Omnipresence — 53
   Omnipotence — 54
   Omniscience — 54
   Worship your Father — 55
   My truth — 55

CHAPTER 16
Live by your own truth — 57
   Anne's story — 58

CHAPTER 17
Experience the presence of Christ — 61
   The story of the risen Christ — 63
   Please note — 63

CHAPTER 18
One continuum of life, no end, no beginning — 65

CHAPTER 19
The value of parables and symbols — 67
   The tree — 68
   Olga's story — 69

CHAPTER 20
Recognise *your* mustard seed — 71
   Preparation of soil — 72
   Removal of stones and weeds — 72
   Soil needs the ability to absorb water — 72
   The properties of the mustard tree — 72
   My story — 73

CHAPTER 21
Discover, value and protect your uniqueness — 75
   Humanity's story — 77

CHAPTER 22
Become whole, become holy — 79
   Diane's story — 81

CHAPTER 23
One united wholeness — 83
   Dreams — 85
   Sophie's story — 86
   Sophie's dream — 86

CHAPTER 24
Become a person of light — 89
   Joan's story — 91

CHAPTER 25
Claiming our other self — 93
   Noah's story — 94

CHAPTER 26
Judgements — 97
   Naomi's story — 98

CHAPTER 27
Understanding the Sabbath — 101
   My story — 102

CHAPTER 28
The journey of humanity — 105
   A story of empathy — 106

CHAPTER 29
The wonderment and opulence of spirit — 109
   Mickey and Danny's story — 110
   Mickey's story — 110

CHAPTER 30
Understanding oneness   113
    Please note   113
    Ivana's story   114

CHAPTER 31
Look deeper   117
    My own true story of the day I discovered the real,
       yet hidden, Anna   118

CHAPTER 32
Seek the highest awareness within yourself   121
    Tilly's story   122

CHAPTER 33
Let your life be a living example   125
    Thomas Merton   126

CHAPTER 34
Choose your teacher with discernment   129
    Addendum   130
    My story   130

CHAPTER 35
Build a strong belief in yourself   133
    Mary's story   134

CHAPTER 36
Be alert to trivia   137

CHAPTER 37
Be not afraid   139

CHAPTER 38
The illusion of emptiness   141

CHAPTER 39
Beware false teachers and prophets   143

CHAPTER 40
Root yourself and your life in God 145
   Jill's story 146

CHAPTER 41
Abundance is available to all who seek 147
   My story 148

CHAPTER 42
Be aware of your motivation 149

CHAPTER 43
A product is not separate from its source 151

CHAPTER 44
Judge not the manifestations of God 153

CHAPTER 45
We produce our own life-harvest 155
   Paula's story 156

CHAPTER 46
Be as innocent as a child 159
   Steve's story 160

CHAPTER 47
Which part will you serve? 163
   Howard's story 165

CHAPTER 48
Healing the fragmented psyche 167
   Becky and Jason's story 168

CHAPTER 49
Discover and develop your unique consciousness 171
   Pamela's story 172

CHAPTER 50
Owning and expressing our divine identity 175
   Elaine's story 176

CHAPTER 51
The new world is already present — 179

CHAPTER 52
Look to that which is present, here, now — 181

CHAPTER 53
Seek the truth within myths, rituals and symbols — 183
  Linda's story — 184

CHAPTER 54
Understand true poverty — 187
  Emily's story — 187

CHAPTER 55
Place god before all others — 189

CHAPTER 56
Look deeper, beyond the human façade — 191
  Fred's story — 192

CHAPTER 57
Blessings of our harvest — 193
  Sandy's story — 194

CHAPTER 58
Work diligently to discover the truth of life — 197
  Charlie's dream — 198
  The dream itself — 198

CHAPTER 59
Seek your truth in this life — 201
  Gerry's story — 201

CHAPTER 60
Stay conscious and awake — 203
  Luke's story — 204

CHAPTER 61
Become whole, become enlightened — 207
  Jenny and Peter's story — 208

CHAPTER 62
Protect divine mystery — 209
    Amelia's story — 210

CHAPTER 63
Live fully in the moment — 213
    Julie's story — 214

CHAPTER 64
The banquet is already prepared — 217

CHAPTER 65
Do not kill the messenger — 219

CHAPTER 66
Find the cornerstone of your life — 221

CHAPTER 67
Know yourself — 223

CHAPTER 68
Loved and blessed beyond measure — 225
    Dawn's story — 225

CHAPTER 69
Have the courage to be true to yourself — 227
    Adam's story — 228

CHAPTER 70
Be authentic — 231
    Joanna's story — 232

CHAPTER 71
Only truth is eternal — 235

CHAPTER 72
The fulfilment of your needs is within you — 237

CHAPTER 73
Harvest the spiritual crop — 239
    Ivy's story — 240

CHAPTER 74
Seek within yourself   243
    Oliver's story   244

CHAPTER 75
Becoming one, becoming whole   247

CHAPTER 76
Protect that which has eternal value   249
    Jan's story   250

CHAPTER 77
Finding divine presence in all situations   253
    My story   254

CHAPTER 78
Seek truth where it rests   257

CHAPTER 79
Blessed are those who have discovered the truth   259

CHAPTER 80
The relatedness of all life   261
    Sharon's story   261

CHAPTER 81
The secret meanings of wealth and power   265
    Alan's story   266

CHAPTER 82
Spiritual fire   269
    Daisy's story   269

CHAPTER 83
Spiritual light   271
    Scientists   273

CHAPTER 84
Discover the fullness of being   275

CHAPTER 85
The truth of life and death ... 277
   My story ... 277

CHAPTER 86
True identity ... 279

CHAPTER 87
Soul ... 281

CHAPTER 88
Insights and opportunities ... 283
   Suzy's story ... 284

CHAPTER 89
Discovering oneness ... 287
   An example of unity in nature ... 288

CHAPTER 90
Our divine resources ... 289
   Tina's story ... 290

CHAPTER 91
Learn how to seek ... 293
   Simon's story ... 294

CHAPTER 92
Persist in your search for truth ... 297
   Ella's story ... 297

CHAPTER 93
Protect that which is revealed to you ... 299
   My story ... 300

CHAPTER 94
Truth is freely revealed to all who seek ... 303

CHAPTER 95
Freely share that which you have ... 305
   Nature's story ... 305

CHAPTER 96
Value hidden talents — 307
    Containing the ever-present human ego — 308
    Sir Captain Tom's story — 308

CHAPTER 97
Stay conscious and alert — 311

CHAPTER 98
Know the powerful shadow — 313
    Vera's story — 315

CHAPTER 99
Recognise your true kinfolk — 317

CHAPTER 100
Three facets of a conscious life — 319
    Give to Caesar that which is Caesar's — 319
    Give to God the things that are God's — 320
    Give me what is mine (give to Christ that which is Christ's) — 320
    The inner Christ — 320
    My story — 320

CHAPTER 101
Know the true giver of life — 323

CHAPTER 102
Remain vigilant to those who would inhibit your journey — 325

CHAPTER 103
Know thy self — 327

CHAPTER 104
The awakened Soul — 329
    Interpreting symbolic representations — 330

CHAPTER 105
Do not compromise divine creation — 331

CHAPTER 106
Know and express the wholeness of being ... 333

CHAPTER 107
Return to God's embrace ... 335

CHAPTER 108
Be the inner Christ ... 337

CHAPTER 109
Discover the legacy within ... 339

CHAPTER 110
Understand true wealth ... 341

CHAPTER 111
Trust the living presence within ... 343

CHAPTER 112
Choose well whom you will serve ... 345

CHAPTER 113
The Kingdom of God is before you ... 347

CHAPTER 114
Wholeness of Soul ... 349
   Types of energy ... 350

CONCLUSION ... 351

BIBLIOGRAPHY OF SUGGESTED READINGS/STUDY ... 353

INDEX ... 357

INTRODUCTION

A journey with the Gospel of Thomas

The *Gospel of Thomas* is a collection of 114 sacred texts (or codices; each codex here is a saying, an affirmation or advice) which, together with several other ancient writings, are collectively known as the Nag Hammadi Scriptures. These Coptic writings were discovered in 1945 by two Arab peasants in an area of Egypt known as Nag Hammadi. The ancient papyrus texts were originally bound in leather and concealed in large earthenware jars, possibly around 150–200 AD. Although there is some dispute about the exactness of these dates, there seems to be general agreement in the astonishing earliness of these writings.

When the two Arab brothers took the ancient and fragmented texts home to use as burning material, they had no idea of the potential financial value of the papyrus they held in their hands. Nor had they any concept of the interest these priceless writings would eventually generate worldwide.

It seems, however, that *someone* had recognised their worth when one of the texts was discovered to have been secretly, and illegally, traded on the Egyptian black market. The world of antiquities was now alerted to this precious discovery.

The remaining texts were to begin a tortuous and contentious journey, subjected to lengthy legal battles regarding ownership. This was partially settled in the early 1950s when some texts were placed in the Coptic Museum in Cairo, where these fragments still remain and can be viewed on the museum's website. Some were purchased by, and placed in the care of, The Jung Foundation in Zurich.

The final part of this story reads like an Agatha Christie novel. It covers the intense rivalry that existed between an international group of scholars who sought the rights to translate the remaining texts from the original Coptic language into English. In addition, there was the highly contentious issue as to who held the rights to copy and to publish them. Great personal prestige would come from working with these texts, not to mention the significant financial reward that may be attached to their ownership.

Following many lengthy legal and political battles, the first completed English translation of the Nag Hammadi Scriptures was made available to the general public in the mid-1970s.

Several traditional Christian interpretations followed. These were largely written in ecclesiastical terminology and quite biblical in their approach. For many laypeople, their meaning remained obscure.

I have, therefore, chosen a more visceral approach in this book, which offers a sensitive and effective way of 'seeing' the texts' hidden messages. I have also added some authentic life stories which, I hope, demonstrate their relevance to contemporary life.

My intention in writing this book has been to illustrate the profound messages that are held, often quite obscurely, in these codices. As a practising therapeutic counsellor, and also a committed seeker of Spiritual Truth, I have been able to recognise the advice and guidance described in these very early life-lessons. Their contents still have profound relevance for today's contemporary world, some 2000 years later.

Scientific dating of the original texts, although open to debate, seems to agree that the Nag Hammadi Scriptures came into being between 150–200 AD approximately. These scriptures hold Christian teachings that predate the version of Christianity we have today.

To see the original codices and ecclesiastical translations, you can access the *Gospel of Thomas* at: www.biblicalarchaeology.org.

Mark M. Mattison's interpretations are also freely available at www.gospels.net (NB the 's' after gospel).

My personal journey with the Gospel of Thomas

My attention was drawn to these precious texts in 1990; in particular, the *Gospel of Thomas*. On my many readings over the years, the writings made little sense to me. However, something about their uncorrupted message would not let me go.

Intuition told me that hidden within these sacred texts was something of the greatest and most authentic spiritual value. I was driven to find the uncontaminated truth of early Christian teachings. I wanted to wrestle and dig deep within myself for *my* understanding. I wanted no other's opinion, no other's intellectual or learnt interpretation.

Because the original translation was carried out by ecclesiastical scholars, the terminology is biblical and an understanding as to how this teaching can benefit everyday life has remained beyond the reach of most laypeople. My intention in recording my interpretations was originally for my benefit only. However, several people expressed an interest in how the *Gospel of Thomas* can provide guidance in living their life well in current times and I made my interpretations available to them. These were well received. And so the idea was born that I should make my interpretations more widely available to those who are interested.

The chapter headings in the book are my own abbreviated translations/understandings of the teachings, and what follow are my interpretations of the underlying message, along with various true stories which emphasise the message.

* * *

In this book, I share my discernment with the sole intention of showing that an authentic Christian understanding can be found within every one of us, should we choose to seek it. We each have our own version of Truth. The *Gospel of Thomas* gives us permission and freedom to explore, to seek, to struggle with our inhibitions and, perhaps surprisingly, to face our fears about owning our unique version of Truth! I believe these writings are deliberately obscure, and at times repetitive, so we will search deep within ourselves for our own truth and meaning; that we will seek, until we find, that which is pertinent and personal to our unique character.

Everyone, I believe, has a contribution to make in life, whatever their calling happens to be. If spiritual understanding is your life's quest, you need no other person to teach you. Your inner Christ awaits your awakening interest and your commitment to discovering *your* Truth.

The sayings contained in the *Gospel of Thomas*—other than the necessary translation into English—are unadulterated. The translations were taken from the original texts and predate much of the Christian doctrine that exists today.

What follows is my interpretation of them.

The *Gospel of Thomas* is, I believe, a manual about the practical application of spiritual principles. It challenges us, not only to make sense of these texts in our own unique way, but to actually live them, day by day.

Please note

In order to protect privacy and confidentiality, names and identifiable details have been changed in the writing of the authentic life stories.

The companion guide to the Gospel of Thomas

The *Gospel of Thomas* came into existence approximately 2000 years ago. It was written at a time when life for many people was harsh and heavily controlled by undemocratic laws. Punishments for infringements were swift and ruthless. Crucifixions and floggings were common place and rebellions rapidly and brutally suppressed.

Humanity was in need of a completely new approach to living. It is my belief that the *Gospel of Thomas* came into being as a counter to the powerlessness experienced by the majority of the population. Although approximately 2000 years old, its wisdom is still relevant and pertinent to our current times.

To gain the most from this Companion Guide, it is suggested that it be used as a workbook and studied in conjunction with the *Gospel of Thomas* manuscript, which is freely available at www.gospels.net/thomas.

* * *

CHAPTER 1

The beginning

And he said, 'Whoever discovers the meaning of these sayings won't taste death'.

Those who find meaning in these sayings have begun the journey of their Soul.
    The truth of Eternal life will become known to them.
    Nothing is hidden from those with eyes to see and ears to hear.

CHAPTER 2

Seek and you will find

Jesus said, 'Whoever seeks shouldn't stop until they find. When they find, they'll be disturbed. When they're disturbed, they'll be ... amazed and reign over the All'.

My interpretation of the text in this codex is that our Soul Journey consciously begins with an awakening to a disquiet within oneself. We feel unsettled, troubled and uncertain of what ails us. This is a challenging time when life feels shallow and no longer satisfying. We begin the search for something of greater value.

In our seeking, we follow many false trails. In my experience, this can be a difficult and lonely period as meaningless pursuits are undertaken and discarded. It is a time for self-compassion when an inner change, deep within us, begins to occur. Nurtured by Infinite Love, we are guided towards a greater Divine awareness.

We slowly awaken to a new understanding of 'emptiness'. We discover a space within ourselves of eternal and fathomless depths. A space where Divine Spirit can make its presence known. Although nothing tangible within us has actually changed, our willingness and capacity to experience has changed.

The awakening soul slowly opens to the wonderment of Wisdom and Truth, which have been waiting since eternity. We grow in conscious awareness of pathways that have always been present. Now, however, we have the eyes to 'see'.

Suggested reading

Goldsmith, J.S., *The Gift of Love* (1975).

CHAPTER 3

One kingdom, one living father

> Jesus said, 'If your leaders tell you, "Look, the kingdom is in heaven", then the birds of heaven will precede you. Rather, the kingdom is within you and outside of you. When you know yourselves, then you'll be known, and you'll realize that you're the children of the living Father. But if you don't know yourselves, then you live in poverty, and you are the poverty'.

This codex teaches of the Omnipresence of God.

My interpretation of the text is that we grow to understand there is no place in the skies called 'heaven'; there is no place in the depths of earth known as the 'underworld'.

The Kingdom of Heaven is present in all space, in all lifeforms, at all times. God is omnipresent.

An infinity of everything will become available to all those who seek.

Those who do not seek live in spiritual poverty and are themselves impoverished by their own lack of awareness.

We are each blessed with the power of choice. We can strive for spiritual understanding or we can reject that which is within us.

We each have the gift of personal authority in our life-expression. This choice is our birthright.

Suggested reading

HH The Dalai Lama, and Cutler, H.C., *The Art of Happiness* (1999).

CHAPTER 4

Each moment our world is made anew

> Jesus said, 'The older person won't hesitate to ask a little seven-day-old child about the place of life, and they'll live, because many who are first will be last, and they'll become one'.

This saying teaches that we must seek to be without preconceptions and respond to each moment with the innocence of a child.

Throughout our lives, we accumulate knowledge about ourselves, other people and the world in which we live. Some of this may be useful but a great deal is irrelevant—misleading, perhaps even false.

Memory can be a mixed blessing with much of it detrimental to our life-journey. When we believe life will follow its habitual patterns, we prevent something new from occurring. Situations that are actually fluid, and relationships which are evolving, can become fixed and fossilised by our pre-set minds.

Codex 4 teaches us to approach each point in time with an open heart. To greet each moment as a new moment, a clean slate on which something completely new can be written and experienced.

When we expect life to follow the same recurring pathways, we have already decided how the outcome will be. We have prevented ourselves from allowing something new to unfold for us.

When we become aware of the awesome power that *we* command over our lives, we will understand that our life-path need not be an inevitable repetition of difficulties. By seeking the newness of every moment, we consciously become the chief architect of our lives.

Undoubtedly, this approach to living takes work, self-examination and serious commitment. It can, however, lead to a life of authenticity and joy, rather than a repetition of the 'same old stuff'.

Only we, ourselves, can choose to make such a change.

We do this by:

- Learning to *be* fully present in this and every 'now' moment.
- Learning to *think* with clean and positive expectations.
- Learning to *experience* with uncontaminated and accurate vision.

Amanda's story

(All the stories I share with you are true)

It would be foolish to claim that personal control of our lives is easily won. It is not. It takes much commitment, courage and tenacity to come to recognise the many hidden and habitual expectations which blight our lives.

Amanda's father was an unkind and angry man who treated her and her mother harshly. She had been raised with no other close male relatives. Consequently, and understandably, she believed all men were made in the same mould as her domineering father. Amanda's adult expectations of men were pre-set in childhood and entirely unconscious.

In her 40s, a nervous breakdown forced her decision to begin a therapeutic journey with a trained psychotherapist. Slowly, she began to unearth a vast store of untruths about herself and her expectations of *all* men. Although, in some situations, her beliefs were undoubtedly accurate, her blanket belief that all men were bullies, was not. Amanda was shocked to realise that she, quite unconsciously, never expected kindness from any man.

As she reflected on her teenage years, it became clear she had always discounted the attentions of any man who was kind and considerate. She was attracted *only* to those men who expressed the same toughness as her father. From an early age, Amanda unconsciously manifested her internalised expectations. Unsurprisingly, she married a man who was selfish, violent and lived only for himself.

During therapy, she grew to understand the self-created drama in which she had been living much of her adult life. She was shocked to discover she was not truly 'living', but repeating the historical experiences of her childhood over and over.

As Amanda gained a clearer vision of herself, she began to understand her past mistakes. She grew to realise she could choose to have better, happier relationships. In practical terms, she began to put aside her presumptions when she assessed men. She learnt to be more balanced and accurate in her assessments. She learnt to take the time to become receptive to better possibilities. She was no longer living a repetitive and carbon-copy life.

As she learnt to joyfully anticipate newness, she truly became 'alive'.

She became an undivided character, expressing herself as 'a single one', complete and whole with *all* her faculties functioning cooperatively on her behalf.

She eventually came to understand that life is a process of learning about ourselves and the ways in which we can allow something wholesome and creative to unfold.

Suggested reading

Anonymous, *Christ in You* (1910).

CHAPTER 5

Knowing creation

> Jesus said: 'Know what's in front of your face, and what's hidden from you will be revealed to you, because there's nothing hidden that won't be revealed'.

Divine Energy is the substance and essence of all creation. Its presence is all around us, right here, right now. Our human journey requires that we come to understand and know this truth.

Each individual life is fulfilled by the Power and Wisdom of God, manifested *largely* according to our own expectations. We unwittingly select the manner in which Divine Energy becomes depicted—perceived—as our life-stream, in much the same way a baker selects the mould for his loaf of bread.

We are co-creators with God. When we understand our shared responsibility, we can seek the knowledge to make wiser, better choices.

This codex states that spiritual knowledge is available to all and hidden from no one. It is, however, our prerogative to seek. Through meditation, contemplation, study and commitment, we gradually become in tune with Divine Presence. To develop and learn to express these truths is, in my opinion, our primary task whilst on earth.

Believing that heaven is possible only at the point of death, is, I believe, a misunderstanding. We are already in heaven! It is already here, within ourselves.

Codex 5 suggests that when we begin our soul journey into spiritual understanding, Truth is revealed to all who seek. There are no secrets, no teachings, no doctrines which are preserved solely for the 'chosen few'. All those who desire to know and understand, will be shown. Everything will be revealed.

My story

Having lived a conventional life until my 40s, a time came when I felt unsettled, troubled and dissatisfied. Looking back, I see that the falseness of my life, the hypocrisies I witnessed daily and the sheer boredom of a repetitive life, were inconsistent with the person I was gradually becoming.

In my 20s, I had followed a certain New Age Christian movement. For several years I thankfully immersed myself in its teaching. Gradually, however, I needed something more, perhaps a different approach, but I had no idea what that might be and I had no idea how to find it.

During those difficult times, I felt totally alone, bereft and empty of all human solutions. I now see that, slowly, an ability developed within me to connect with the 'Still small voice' of God. I had, at last, become receptive to something new.

Unexpectedly, an experience came completely out of the blue in the form of a spiritual teacher, namely Rafael. He was Cuban by birth and resident in Washington, US.

I read an announcement in a small spiritual magazine that Rafael would shortly be giving his first class in the UK. His teaching would be based on the philosophy of Joel Goldsmith, founder of The Infinite Way. The five-day course was open to all. As I read the notice I wept tears of gratitude and joy—this was what I had been waiting for. And so began perhaps the most intense period of my life.

This teacher, over a period of three years, profoundly changed me, and consequently my life, for ever. It was never a personal relationship but an intense teacher/pupil bond. I owe Rafael more than I can convey. He was demanding and challenging with all the students who attended his bi-annual classes. He understood that we must be shaken out of our cosy and comfortable spirituality. He demanded that we seek deeper truths which lay hidden within the consciousness of each one of us.

God had sent me someone who would confront my misperceptions and challenge the ways I hid from facing Truth. This proved to be an extremely painful period of my life. Much of what I had held dear, I realised, was 'missing the mark'. Rafael, despite his deep dislike of travel, came to the UK several times during that intense three-year period.

The same group of eight dedicated students gathered each time for a period of five days. Every day, long periods were spent in shared Silence. There, I believe, I developed a heightened sense of Presence. From early morning to late evening, time was committed to seeking the Inner Christ; that which is perpetually and lovingly present, but remains largely unnoticed by many.

Rafael taught us the essential nature of daily meditation practice and dream analysis. We also became aware of the necessity of processing the many personal issues that inevitably arise during such heightened experiences. These were exhausting and yet strangely exhilarating times!

Over a period of three years, I had been lovingly led to a place *within myself* where I could experience the profoundness of Divine Being. My mind had been sufficiently cleansed of dross to be aware of Rafael's authentic message. I did not have the maturity to fully understand what was happening then, but it seemed I had no choice but to go along with the process, wherever that may lead.

After three years, came the final class. At the time, none of us realised this. Rafael, however, did know! He never said any goodbyes. He simply believed his job had been done and it was now up to each one of us to put his teaching into practice.

I never saw or heard from him again.

* * *

So began the next stage of my spiritual journey. With my inner reference points demolished by the directness and intensity of Rafael's approach, I felt I had been scoured from the inside out. With Rafael gone from our lives, there was now no one to turn to except the Silence of the Inner Kingdom.

Within a matter of days, following Rafael's return to the US, I began to experience the profoundest sense of Divine Love. I was beginning to truly *know* Divine Presence, both in an internal and an external way.

I thank God with all my heart for the gift of Rafael. His tough approach had forced me to let misperceptions and untruths die. Only then could the Inner Divine Truth enter my consciousness, to become known and experienced.

Knowing there is something eternally precious deep within *each of us*, gave me the tenacity to stay and endure the process.

This codex reminds us that nothing is ever hidden; that all wisdom, power and love are present everywhere, at all times. What is required of us is the willingness and the courage to receive our Divine Message; to allow ourselves to be immersed, fully, in Presence; and to endeavour to live that Truth to the best of our ability.

Suggested reading

Tolstoy, L., *The Kingdom of God is Within You* (Chapter 3; 2010).

CHAPTER 6

Guidance for living an authentic life

> His disciples said to him, 'Do you want us to fast? And how should we pray? Should we make donations? And what food should we avoid?'
>
> Jesus said, 'Don't lie, and don't do what you hate, because everything is revealed in the sight of heaven; for there's nothing hidden that won't be revealed, and nothing covered up that will stay secret'.

The disciples ask for guidance as to how they should conduct their lives, how they should pray and the foods they should consume. Jesus conveys that there are no rules about eating and fasting.

He does, however, stress that we must live by two specific commands:
Do not lie.
Do not do what you hate.
The fulfilment of these tasks, although seemingly simple, is not easy to achieve. It requires a sincere commitment to the task of self-scrutiny and self-knowledge. It demands courage to face not only the inevitable dark side of one's own nature, but the courage to make changes within oneself.

During our life, we absorb a great many 'messages' from external influences. The most persistent inner 'voice' will be the one we unconsciously act upon. Yet, when consciously examined, we many discover it is rarely the voice of our own personal truth.

We frequently, and erroneously, accept opinions, beliefs and directives from outside sources without personal scrutiny; much of our own Truth remains hidden and unlived.

Do not lie

To lie means to be less than truthful, both with oneself and others. How frequently we tell a 'white lie' supposedly to protect another, when actually our hidden motive is to protect ourselves from the other's pain or anger.

Many live a life of pretence, masquerading as someone different to who they truly are. In believing we are not 'good enough', we fear rejection and try to be the person whom another wants or needs us to be.

It is only when we have the courage to examine ourselves and our intentions that we discover the extent of our disingenuous behaviour. It is only then that we realise the lies we live in order to be someone different to who we really are.

It can be difficult to make the shift from lying to expressing our authenticity. Others often have a great deal invested in the 'games' we play. We may feel that being fully our self will cost us dearly in the loss of relationships.

However, continuing to act out the role that has been foisted upon us does us great harm. We are living a lie.

We must challenge our self to be conscious of these harmful traits and destructive behaviours. The support of therapy, I believe, is necessary as we make a shift to an authentic life. Although essential to our well-being, it takes courage and tenacity to make these changes.

Do not do what you hate

This teaching emphasises the error of doing that which we hate. Inner discomfort will always guide us away from mistakes and lead us towards the rightful path for which our true self yearns. We must find the courage to act in ways that honour and respect the real person we are.

When we continue to do things we hate, we reject our true identity and we leave the world bereft of our particular gifts and attributes. Every authentic person has great value. Only we ourselves can express who we really are.

Together, we are one humanity. We make one whole and complete picture, each piece having equal value to the Whole.

* * *

As a result of damage to our psyche in our younger years, many of us live with a limited sense of self-worth. This concept can be identified as 'The Wounded Child'. During our early years, we unconsciously adapt, developing the intention of becoming more loveable to others.

Eventually, however, the repressed true self begins to express itself and demand recognition. This can cause great turbulence to the personality and can happen at any age.

Sadly, troubled people are often medicated to induce a false calmer state of being. In my opinion, these eruptions should be welcomed and the person supported as the authentic self painfully emerges from its tightly restricted prison.

Lacking awareness of our many deep-seated battles, each generation passes on the same psychological injuries to the next generation. Self-delusion has become so endemic in Western society that we have largely lost connection with the real person we are each born to be.

This, I believe, is the thrust of Socrates' statement 'Know Thyself'. He says we must develop the discernment to fully know our true selves and discard beliefs and ways of being that are not in accord with who we really are.

My story

In my middle years, my psyche forced me to heed difficult and powerful feelings that were shaking my personality. I was deeply unhappy, directionless and something within me was demanding attention. I felt compelled to break out of the confines of my narrow and restricted life. A new life awaited my acceptance and my courage.

At the time common sense said that to leave a very comfortable life was madness and to break away from the 'safety' of my prison was extremely risky. I also knew I could not rely on any external support. I was (humanly) on my own.

The day I packed my belongings and moved into a small flat heralded the beginning of a new life based on Truth. As I closed the door on one life and opened the door on a new one, I experienced within myself a depth of love, power and support that I had not previously known. I knew I was now on my rightful path. It may prove to be difficult, and it certainly did, but I was no longer living a lie.

After several months I turned to therapy for help. This was the second 'best' decision I made. Although my financial position was in poor health, amazingly and unexpectedly there was always enough money to keep me afloat.

Therapy was like switching the lights on in a darkened room. Very quickly I began to better understand myself and my distress. It became clear that, from the tender age of 5, I had lived a lie. I had become skilful at keeping the family peace. I had intuitively learnt how to avoid inducing angry and unbearable outbursts from my father. I had learnt to be watchful and to act in ways that soothed his temper. I grew into the protector of my fearful mother and my anxious grandparents. I lived the life my father demanded of me. Driven by anxiety, I never argued, rebelled or complained. I had learnt to completely smother my true self. I lived a complete and utter lie.

Over time, therapy guided me towards the discovery of the real me. It was not an easy journey but gradually, as my true self emerged from her inner cocoon, a new life opened up for me.

In the passage of time, I trained as a therapist and began to help others in the quest to discover, and begin to live from, the 'real self'.

Some 30 years later I am still deeply moved by the mysterious workings of Divine Love and Blessed Providence.

Gradually, it became possible for me to endeavour, to the best of my ability, to live according to the guidance contained in the *Gospel of Thomas*.

Suggested reading

Berne, E., *Games People Play* (1964).

CHAPTER 7

Know the light and darkness of human nature

> Jesus said, 'Blessed is the lion that's eaten by a human and then becomes human, but how awful for the human who's eaten by a lion, and the lion becomes human'.

Our bodies carry the evidence of the great journey the human race has travelled. As a species, we have evolved from primitive lifeforms and, over millennia, have adapted to optimise our chances of survival. Although the human body contains many examples of these adaptations, what is less tangible is the evolution of the human psyche.

Codex 7 reminds us that we still carry many of the survival instincts from our animal ancestry. Our historical animal nature, part of which is identified in the original text as the lion, has remained largely untamed within us. It is, I believe, perhaps closer to the surface of expression than we care to admit. The first day of the January sales is an example of the animalistic self-first instinct which is immediately triggered at the prospect of gain or loss!

Whether it is deprivation of the trivia of life or deprivation of life/love itself, our powerful impulse is to protect ourselves and those close to us. We easily feel threatened by the 'outsider' and often choose to perceive the world in terms of 'me versus the other'.

This saying teaches that we must humanise our animal instincts. We do this by consciously accepting and learning to embrace them. To deny, reject or fear them, leaves them outside our control, often wielding enormous and unconscious power. When we choose to understand and integrate these natural energies, we can consciously learn to use them wisely. With the assistance of professional therapy, we are capable of transforming selfish aggressive energy into a powerful force for good.

Religious teachings have tried to address this unacceptable and hidden aspect of our bestial nature by commanding that we cease judging and love all as brothers and sisters. These are wonderful aspirations but far less easy to implement than is implied. The courts and prisons around the world testify to the power of the selfish and largely uncontrollable 'me only' energy.

Unfortunately, as Christianity has unwittingly proven, to *will* oneself to love all others is simply not possible. Most of us cannot, by a sheer act of will, force ourselves to love those we find distasteful, violent and/or different. Such unconditional love is possible only when we have attained the *ability* to love all.

In addition, this saying cautions about the power of ego-pride, which is synonymous with the lion. This destructive energy can overwhelm our conscious will, leaving us isolated from our Divine Self.

Much of Christian teaching has demanded from us that which, I believe, is almost impossible for most people to achieve. Unsurprisingly, the number of weekly church services and Christian worshipers are fast diminishing. Without the additional 'tools' of regular self-introspection and trained therapeutic support, I believe the beauty, eloquence and power of Christianity will eventually be lost. I cannot think of a sadder demise for one of the world's greatest teachings.

Life demands a great deal from us in these current times. *Relevant* support and guidance is perhaps more necessary now than it has ever been. At present, it seems to me that Christianity is asking more of its followers than its outdated rhetoric can support. In my opinion, it is no longer providing the teaching and direction so necessary for today's modern self-realising seeker.

It would seem that Eastern religions, with their prescribed focus on the internal energies, have begun to fill that void in the Western world. I believe Christianity still has an important role to play, but it must offer what ordinary people find relevant to their lives and their world.

Carol's story

As a young woman, Carol could be quick to express anger. She relished the sense of power it gave her. She felt vindicated in her judgements and actions, believing she was entitled to express her feelings. In truth, she was expressing behaviours she had learnt in childhood from her mother. She was easily consumed by her 'inner lion' which was often powerfully and seriously out of control. Thankfully, Higher Powers within her brought forth a lesson she would never forget.

* * *

One summer day Carol was trawling the High Street looking for a parking space. She was beginning to feel irritated. She needed to park. The 'lion' in her was primed, ready for action. When a space became available, a small car gently and slowly pulled in front of Carol into 'her' space. Indignation rose and she vigorously demanded the right to park. The 'interloper' restarted her engine, quietly pulled out of the space and disappeared down the street. The satisfying surge of lion-power lasted as Carol went about her business.

An hour later, however, her attention was drawn to the 'interloper's' car, now parked further down the same street. Shame filled Carol as she noticed the driver, a young mother, lifting twin boys from their tiny car seats into a specially adapted buggy. Both boys were very young and both disabled. The mother had been trying to park close to the clinic where the boys were receiving specialist treatment.

That incident taught Carol more about her inner self than any spiritual or psychological book could ever have done. She had been brought face-to-face with the power of self-centred animalistic behaviours. She had 'met' the aggressive lion within herself. She was taught a vital lesson about love, cooperation and kindness.

As a direct result of the shaming experience, Carol began therapy. She gradually learnt to recognise, identify, understand and come to terms with the latent animal power within each of us. She discovered that this energy cannot be suppressed purely by willpower. It must be made conscious, humanised and ultimately used for good. Over time she learnt to make productive use of that vast reservoir of power which resides within each and every one of us.

This saying is also a reminder to be awake to the many daily lessons that come our way. We are all presented with endless opportunities for self-learning, cleansing and maturing of our innate powers. Only then can we become a channel for the expression of Divine Love.

* * *

Over time Carol also learnt to forgive others when mistakes are made. Each of us is on the path of learning. Each of us is discovering our enormous inner potential and the great complexities of our humanness. We cannot discard any of our innate powers. We can, however, choose to understand, integrate and harmonise them for the betterment of each other and for the natural expression of Divine Love and Compassion.

* * *

In my experience, the state of complete and unconditional love is possible only on rare occasions and under exceptional circumstances. Long-term commitment to regular daily meditation seems to prepare the way for some remarkable outpourings of Love. This type of experience, I believe, happens entirely of its own volition and is not within our power to invite. We can, however, prepare the way by bringing all disparate parts of ourselves into cooperative harmony. Only then can Real Love find its own expression *through us.*

Although these exceptional spiritual experiences seem to fade as quickly as they come, I believe each one leaves a tiny imprint of its presence and a lingering experience of profound Love. It is my belief that this 'lingering' has a gradual, accumulative effect.

Understanding and accepting all aspects of oneself ends self-judgement. We then desist from projecting onto others what are really our own issues. This allows us to be more present and consciously attuned to the infinite Presence of God in all people. In the modern world, we often choose to be too busy, too caught up in external matters to give our inner peace a chance to grow and be fully present. However, only during those times of inner peace can we be open to the flow and expression of Unconditional Love.

Suggested reading

Martin, J.S.J., *Becoming Who You Are: Insights on the True Self from Thomas Merton and Other Saints* (2006).

CHAPTER 8

Choose wisely that which you value

> He said, 'The human being is like a wise fisher who cast a net into the sea and drew it up from the sea full of little fish. Among them the wise fisher found a fine large fish and cast all the little fish back down into the sea, easily choosing the large fish. Anyone who has ears to hear should hear!'

I believe the 'fine large fish', mentioned in the text of this codex, symbolises the discovery of our true identity. It means coming to the realisation of God's Presence within ourselves, each and every moment. It represents that inner Knowing of our enduring God-Self. To catch the large fish means 'catching' the full understanding and awareness of that fact.

It also means being able to say, feel and know, not only that 'I Am a Child of God', but also that *'You* are a Child of God'.

Modern life is busy and full of distractions. We take for granted the tsunami of information that can besiege us through modern technology. Some of this may be useful and accurate. Much, however, can be false, perhaps even dangerously invasive. Showered with unrequested information, the precious internal sense of peace has, for many, been 'drowned-out'.

This saying of Codex 8 could not be more relevant to the times in which we live. It urges us to seek only the Large Fish in life. To internalise only that which will bring lasting spiritual nourishment. To show discernment for how, and with whom, we spend our days on this earthly plane.

Time is precious. It easily slips away. Perhaps we need to consciously value our time on earth as a gift, something of the greatest value to be used with discernment and appreciation.

This codex also asks that we remain conscious and alert to the Little Fish, too; i.e. the distractions of life that easily entice us away from spiritual growth. Valuing that which will enhance our sense of spiritual well-being, will allow Divine Love, Wisdom and Potency to flourish during our lifetime. Only we ourselves can make that choice to seek the Large Fish.

* * *

Finding time for quiet reflection and contemplation is becoming ever more difficult. For some, it seems almost impossible. However, I believe we can choose to find space and time for what will give us the greatest spiritual nourishment.

A daily practice of 'Being in the Silence' quietens the mind and brings our attention to that which is already within us. As we develop an enhanced receptivity to the inner Still Small Voice of God, we become a channel of Divine Creation which will be revealed in our own unique way.

Committed and persistent self-scrutiny gradually allows 'space' within oneself for wisdom, love and potency to unfold. The heightened sense of connectedness to all life will eventually lead to an enduring awareness of God's Perpetual Presence in all creatures, including oneself.

Jason's story

Jason caught his Large Fish when he met his spiritual teacher at a Buddhist retreat centre. The Buddhist monk was on an extended visit from Nepal and was offering daily silent meditation practice and teachings. Jason immediately recognised the valuable opportunity being offered to him. This was his Large Fish. For some considerable time, Jason had been seeking spiritual direction. Now, he believed, his yearnings had been provided for.

The monk freely gave his time to all those who requested his spiritual support. Jason immersed himself in this precious opportunity. Not only did he participate in the twice-daily meditation practice, he also attended classes based on the teachings of the Buddha.

This offered regular immersion in the consciousness of the Pure Self. It was, Jason believed, the most precious gift he could have been given. Recognising his Large Fish when it came his way, he was able to discard much of the life-trivia that no longer served him well. He had a cleaner and clearer space within himself to ingest the great wisdoms of the world.

These Truths were now his, possibly for eternity.

Suggested reading

Merton, T., *New Seeds of Contemplation* (1972).

CHAPTER 9

Treasure your spiritual seeds

> Jesus said, 'Look, a sower went out, took a handful of seeds, and scattered them. Some fell on the roadside; the birds came and gathered them. Others fell on the rock; they didn't take root in the soil and ears of grain didn't rise toward heaven. Yet others fell on thorns; they choked the seeds and worms ate them. Finally, others fell on good soil; it produced fruit up toward heaven, some sixty times as much and some a hundred and twenty'.

As spiritual beings participating in a human experience, our journey has two distinct parts, one spiritual and one human. Each has the potential for its own individual journey. The ultimate intention, I believe, is the eventual interaction and blending of our spiritual qualities together with our human characteristics. This eventually enables the development of a unique expression of Soul.

* * *

In the scientific world, the double helix is the symbolic representation of a person's unique identity, known as their DNA (Deoxyribonucleic acid).

In the spiritual world, this same model could be used as an analogy for the wholeness of each individual being, whereby:

- One strand of the DNA represents our inner source of Divinity, the wellspring of *universal* wisdom, truth, love and power.
- The second strand represents our humanness, which expresses our *individuality* in the world.

In the double-helix model, the two intertwining strands appear, metaphorically, to be linked by bars. Looking with 'spiritual attention', the link-bars could represent the soul, whose purpose it is, I believe, to blend both Human and Divine elements of our Being.

Considered this way, the double helix could also be understood as a symbolic representation of the wholeness of each human being: universal spiritual potential blending with individual human possibilities, interacting and blending together to create a unique Soul. I believe Divine intention is for each of us to be a distinctive, solitary and unrepeatable expression of God in human form.

* * *

Codex 9 suggests that by placing our efforts and our attention—*our seeds*—into the fertile ground of an awakened consciousness, we will reap the rewards in the actuality of our life. We are given every assistance when we are sincere in 'planting good seeds' into the 'good soil' of an awakening consciousness. The choice is ours to make; the rewards are ours to experience.

Janet's story

The village in which Janet lived offered no opportunity for spiritual discussion, meditation and learning. As a sincere 'seeker' and meditator, it was suggested that perhaps she could fill that vacuum. She was shocked. Although aware of a need for something of this nature, it had never occurred to Janet that perhaps this task was hers to fulfil.

At the time she was consciously on her own unique spiritual journey, and had been for several years. But this was *her* bumbling journey. How could she help others when she was still unsure of so much?

She took no action for several weeks. Fear and a sense of complete inadequacy fogged any decision. Gradually, however, although the fear remained, a gentle awareness developed that perhaps this task really *was* waiting for her to fulfil it.

Janet decided to place a small advert in her local paper about a meditation group. She made a commitment to herself that if anyone should respond, even just one person, then she could be sure this was the Will of God and that somehow the courage to complete the task would come to her. Within a few days of publication, 19 people had responded. She was deeply shocked. The old internal message of 'not good enough' rushed to the surface. She was thrown into despair at how to fulfil this task which had so clearly been assigned to her.

Through meditation, a plan for a six-week course began to unfold. With thought and personal consideration, she decided there would be six weekly topics, each one based on the guiding principles that had served her well for many years. Twenty minutes of silent meditation would begin each meeting. She would introduce spiritual readings that would illustrate the spiritual principle selected as that week's topic. Sixty minutes of shared discussion would allow for exploration of these ideas. A closing meditation would end the meeting. The applicants would be divided into two separate groups, as much for Janet's ability to cope as for the common sense of logistics.

Over several months the two groups were gradually whittled down to one group of eight women. This group continued to meet weekly for the next ten years. Each woman learnt to bring her own fledgling sense of inner Divinity. They all, including Janet, learnt a great deal from the shared discussions. They also learnt to respect and appreciate each person's individual response to the variety of topics. Not only did this broaden their spiritual understanding, it also developed a tolerance for different opinions. It was one of the most significant and defining experiences of Janet's life.

* * *

Codex 9 clearly states that our efforts must be planted in fertile ground if we are to flourish. Janet's experience demonstrates that often God challenges us, not solely for the benefit of our own development, but also for the benefit of others. We will never be asked to do what is beyond us; we will never be asked to 'grow seeds' which are impossible.

However, developing the ability to wait until we are able to sense/feel what is 'asked' of us, will give us the reassurance that we will only be directed to 'plant our seeds in productive soil'.

* * *

I believe therapy is beneficial for most people. It helps us to distinguish between our understandable fears and our avoidance issues. It gives us self-awareness and helps us develop the tools to live a more courageous and fulfilled life. As we become more skilful at making better choices, our inhibitions begin to diminish.

Wayne Dyer, who was an author and motivational speaker, was often heard to say, 'Don't die with your music still in you!'

Do not shrink from 'planting your seeds' in the most life-enhancing position. Every soul has its unique 'music' to play. The world may be waiting to hear your unique Truth.

This saying asks that we use our life to the very best of our ability. I believe we are each assigned the task of contributing our uniqueness to the 'whole'. That we 'plant' our seeds, not solely for the benefit of ourselves as the 'sower', but also for the glory of Divine Power as the 'grower'.

Suggested study

Dyer, W.W. (DVD) *The Shift* (2009).

CHAPTER 10

Seek only truth

> Jesus said, 'I've cast fire on the world, and look, I'm watching over it until it blazes'.

Jesus brought a new teaching into the world that would challenge much of Orthodox Judaism. He was not afraid to confront what he believed to be hypocritical and untrue. He sought to banish many of the rules and edicts that had evolved from the time of Moses. Jesus's message of forgiveness would challenge the vengeful culture of the Old Testament, which condoned 'an eye for an eye', 'a tooth for a tooth'.

The notion of setting the world ablaze, mentioned in the text, can be understood as a metaphor for renewal. In nature, forests spontaneously ignite when their undergrowth becomes too dense for new life to germinate. As vegetation above ground is destroyed and a charred and empty landscape remains, it seems all is lost. However, a time of regrowth naturally and spontaneously begins. That which had appeared as utter devastation becomes nature's opportunity to renew the forest. It is a period of valuable revival.

At the time of Jesus, humanity required such a regeneration. The world was in need of a radically fresh approach to life and living. A new era was to begin, an epoch where the values of love, compassion and personal responsibility would be prioritised over slavish adherence to the questionable dictates of religious leaders.

* * *

Codex 10 encourages us to confront whatever is outdated and no longer helpful in our own lives. It suggests we eradicate impositions that limit our personal growth. That we 'set ablaze' all that is inauthentic for ourselves and create space for the germination of our own unique and individual truth.

To do this, however, requires an authentic awareness of oneself, one's personal beliefs and a willingness to discard that which is no longer valid in one's life. We also need to truly understand our hidden emotional vulnerabilities and motivations, which can have the power to restrict and inhibit us. This can be a challenging period as we develop the courage to abandon ideas and ways of being that may have shaped our lives, perhaps even our culture.

An accurate discernment of our innermost feelings can be a reliable guide to our personal truth. Our heart, when free of past hurts, will always lead us in the most helpful direction. Our task is to develop the skill of listening to our internal Truth. This demands that we develop a sensitivity to our personal integrity and allow space for something completely new to unfold within us. The world may be waiting for your truth to be revealed!

My life story

My spiritual journey began in a small way at the age of 16 when I was given *In Tune with the Infinite*, written by R.W. Trine. I loved the book's gentle Christian message and it was a constant companion for many years. It comforted me through challenging times and, I am sure, laid down spiritual seeds for future growth and renewal.

In my 40s 'the forest ignited' when I became overwhelmed by unhappiness and despair. Life seemed wrong. I needed to find a new direction. I craved the inner peace which Trine describes so beautifully in his book. I sought help and solace in Christian churches, groups and organisations. They each left me feeling miserable and even more alone. I was enduring the barrenness of 'scorched earth'.

Eventually, I turned to Buddhism. The welcome I received was warm and non-intrusive. I found their silent meditation practice deeply nurturing. Through their generosity of spirit, I became a committed meditator. I shall be ever grateful to that eclectic mix of people who, without judgement or censure, provided the nourishing soil that allowed for the germination of my own Truth. I have continued to sit in solitary, silent meditation twice a day ever since.

There was to be discovered, however, another side to my spiritual growth. As in all aspects of human life, there are two parts, each defining the other. Spiritual growth is no different. One aspect of our true self experiences/feels/intuits the presence of God. This is achieved through the activated 'eros' aspect of our nature.

Its opposing 'logos' side, of equal importance, provides meaning, explanation and understanding of those experiences. These energies are totally non-gender related and are present in everyone. One part, however, will usually be more dominant. Our task is to develop our more latent aspect. Over time, with committed personal effort, the two opposing parts can slowly begin to integrate, informing and cooperating as one whole.

When wholeness becomes established, we possess not only the potential for Divine outpourings, but also the ability to understand them. We will not just be an observer of Truth but also an active and conscious participant in the Divine Plan.

* * *

Although Buddhism had given me the means of experiencing the Divine through meditation practice, its philosophies and explanations were not compatible with my true self. I continued to read countless books on theology, past religions, current religions, eastern religions, and esoteric understandings. I am sure each one provided a stepping stone in the right direction but, once again, I was on the loneliest of paths. I had not found my natural spiritual home and seemed unable to find a sanctuary to 'lay my head'.

Meditation, throughout, remained a deeply meaningful support and I found some level of peace when I made a choice to simply accept my situation. I decided to be satisfied with my treasured books and my times at peace with God. It seemed that somehow I was at variance with accepted practices of shared worship and perhaps one day I would understand what I was getting so wrong.

When eventually I discovered a spiritual teaching that totally resonated within me, I realised that nothing had ever been wrong. Just as the soil in the charred forest waits for the rain to activate germination, my seeming barrenness had been a time of preparation. My truth could only come to me when I had sufficient inner 'emptiness' to allow consciousness to germinate and grow into *my* Truth.

* * *

Jacob Needleman's book, *Lost Christianity*, had sat in my large bookcase for several years, its words dismissed as totally inaccessible to me. Only when my consciousness had been 'set ablaze' and cleansed of rhetoric, could I begin to appreciate the book's profound message. I still weep with gratitude for the day I was compelled, once again, to pick up that book.

As I began to devour its ancient teachings I knew that finally I was ready to experience a resonance between my truth and the writings of Father Sylvan, a remote and largely unknown teacher, described and quoted in Needleman's book. The scant few pages of Father Sylvan's work, which Needleman had acquired by some mysterious source, have remained some of my most treasured writings.

The understanding I have taken from Father Sylvan's writings relates to the development and purpose of the soul. This, he states, is present within everyone, but only in potential until it is consciously activated. The soul can be described as a bridge between the human experience and inner Divinity. A two-way communication between both needs to develop, each informing the other. When one seeks to express God, the soul must open and receive Divine Truth. Only then, can this manifest as oneself and one's life.

As we become an avenue of Divine expression, we grow to be the true Child of God that we are, right now, even when we are not aware of it!

Some 30 years on, I am still learning from and assimilating Father Sylvan's message. Since Truth is infinite, I guess that journey will never end.

Codex 10 advises that we set alight and empty ourselves of all that is old and borrowed from others. That we discard outdated rhetoric.

As the forest must first disintegrate to survive, so we need time and space for our own disintegration and eventual regeneration. Our life purpose, I believe, is to allow for the development of the authentic Soul so that our spiritual life may flourish.

Then, I believe, we begin to express our inner Divine Uniqueness, that which only we, and we alone, can express.

When this happens, not only do we ourselves benefit, we each add something of unique value to the entirety of human consciousness.

Suggested reading

Johnston, W., *The Still Point* (1970).

CHAPTER 11

Find the meaning of life

> Jesus said, 'This heaven will disappear, and the one above it will disappear too. Those who are dead aren't alive, and those who are living won't die. In the days when you ate what was dead, you made it alive. When you're in the light, what will you do? On the day when you were one, you became divided. But when you become divided, what will you do?'

We are challenged by this teaching to find the real meaning of heaven. It is not a destination that we arrive at, but a state of consciousness that we attain. Much of humanity is ignorant and blind to this fact, unaware that we are already totally immersed in the presence of Divine Spirit.

In the distant past, humanity accepted 'dead' teachings. The *Gospel of Thomas*, however, brings a different message. It states that we should discard old, inaccurate and redundant teachings that no longer serve us well. It asks that we seek and ingest Truth which is alive, fresh, full of relevance and meaning.

We are asked to consider the changes in ourselves and our lives when we discard 'dead' teachings and move into the Light of Truth. All life is One. Heaven is the state of consciousness where we know that fact. This saying asks us to consider what we will do and what we are willing to change when we are in the light of truth.

Now is the time to truly know and respect all expressions of the One Divine Life Force.

Jessie's story

Some years ago, Jessie attended a five-day residential retreat based on the ideas of Carl Gustav Jung, the eminent psychiatrist and psychoanalyst. Ten people attended, all previously unknown to each other. Each day consisted of teachings, exercises, some therapeutic artwork and two one-hour meditation practices. Two experienced Jungian therapists facilitated what proved to be an extremely intense experience for all present.

In that rarefied atmosphere, cocooned from the distractions and demands of the outside world, the group began to collectively experience a depth of oneness that was pure and yet impersonal. Jessie later recalled that she experienced a state of love which projected itself outwards to all life, a place of no separate selves, just an experience of one life, one love.

On the third night of the retreat, Jessie had a powerful dream. One so intense that, many years later, she could still recall every detail. She had also been 'shown' a short poem in the dream, which had no meaning for her.

The retreat offered group time for dream work but, disappointingly, Jessie could find no conscious links to her life, either within the poem or in the dream's images. It was a perplexing and unsatisfying situation. However, on the final day of the retreat, Mary, a quiet and timid woman, asked to speak.

With great difficulty, Mary explained that she believed Jessie's dream had actually been a message for herself. As the dream had been described to the group, Mary had begun to connect with its message. On hearing the words of the poem, she had no doubt it was for her. Unfortunately, she had been too shocked to openly 'own' it before.

Through many tears, Mary told the history of the poem. She explained it had been written by her grandmother shortly following Mary's birth. It had always been a treasured and significant acknowledgement of the enduring love they had shared.

Recently, following the grandmother's death, her cottage and all its contents had been bequeathed to Mary. The message in the dream had clearly conveyed that Mary should sell this property. The funds would enable her to realise her desire to become a school teacher. Lack of finance had previously prevented this from happening. Although her grandmother's legacy could remove her financial anxieties, Mary had been unwilling to part with the property. The memories it held seemed too precious.

The dream's message was very clear. It was time for Mary to move on! Her memories were within herself and would always remain with her. The cottage was nothing more than a symbol. The real love was in her heart.

For reasons unknown, Mary had not been able to receive this important dream for herself but Divine Love and Power had found a way. Not only did Mary leave the retreat with courage and permission to take the next big step in her life, she had experienced the extraordinary power and wisdom of *Oneness*.

One retreatant, totally unknown to her, had been able and willing to be a channel of love for another. An example of beautiful Oneness in all its potency!

Suggested reading

Kornfield, J., *A Path with Heart* (1993).

CHAPTER 12

Choose wisely which teacher you follow

> The disciples said to Jesus, 'We know you're going to leave us. Who will lead us then?'
> Jesus said to them, 'Wherever you are, you'll go to James the Just, for whom heaven and earth came into being'.

Codex 12 is limited in concrete information. The naming of James the Just in the original text required me to study all I could find about this enigmatic man. Reliable facts are few. However, the consensus of opinion indicates that Jesus valued James above all others, believing he had grasped the Eternal Message. Jesus stated that those disciples in need of leadership should go to James. It is my opinion that Jesus intended they should go *only* to James and avoid seeking help from the priests.

Information is limited on James's understanding of the new teaching. I will, therefore, restrict my interpretation in this piece of work to that which resonates as true for myself. The Secret Book of James, contained within The Nag Hammadi Scriptures, has also been my guide.

* * *

Until the time of Jesus, Jewish worshipers had slavishly followed the guidance of priests. It was believed that an intermediary was necessary to liaise between God and His subjects. This rendered the lay person impotent against the power of the clergy. James would seem to have stated that such instruction was unnecessary and that we all have the potential to commune directly with God. Not only was this a controversial teaching, it also denied the priesthood their status and, potentially, their livelihood. This could ultimately redress the balance of power away from the church towards the ordinary people.

Undoubtedly, the ability to commune with God needs to be fostered and developed. It has been my experience that the sensitivity required is entirely possible for those who truly desire it. We have, I believe, a spiritual 'muscle' that needs deliberate and persistent attention through regular meditation. The purpose of the soul is to grow attuned to the perpetual and authentic presence of God; to personally experience eternal love, guidance and wisdom.

> Our awakened soul experiences our life force as directly from God.
> Our awakened soul feels the breath of God breathing life into our being.
> Our awakened soul knows the impossibility of being outside God's love.
> It is our knowing of these truths that is the attribute of Soul.

Our relationship with our inner Divinity is a deeply personal matter. Sometimes that communication is clear but often it is not. I believe it is more honourable for me, and me alone, to wrestle directly and daily with that ambiguity.

The more we trust in the permanent reality of the inner Presence, the more we trust in its constant guidance. Our path is already prepared. We need no other to interpret God's message. Trust who you are. Trust that you are a beloved Child of God, perpetually held within the Love, Power, Wisdom and Care of God.

Undoubtedly, the pressures of modern life frequently carry us away from Soul Awareness. It is, therefore, essential that we have a degree of clarity about our emotional wounds. These easily distort our perception and our truth. For this reason, I believe therapy is an important, perhaps even essential, asset to our spiritual journey.

My story

Without tangible awareness of God's Infinite Presence, we can lack confidence in ourselves and our abilities. We may easily be fearful of difference and uncertain of newness. We can shrink from unfamiliarity.

Recently, I responded to an advert offering places on a silent seven-day retreat. This was to be facilitated by a well-established Christian organisation whose quarterly newsletter I had been receiving, and enjoying, for four years.

Over a period of years, I had participated in several extended silent retreats, each one in a traditional Christian retreat house. I found the silence and the warm hospitality both greatly nourishing and deeply supportive. With this background I applied for a place on the contemplative retreat, confident this would be an enriching experience.

My application was surprisingly met with fear and rejection. Having been completely open about the diversity of my spiritual journey, I seemed to have unwittingly aroused suspicion in the mind of the organiser. During a phone conversation in which I was asked to provide more details about myself and my spiritual history, it became clear they considered me 'unsuitable' for their retreat. It was stated that my presence 'may be unfair' to other retreatants. The fact that the retreat was entirely silent and that I was a committed meditator, left me wondering what they feared I might do!

I never asked for an explanation. I came to understand that I had been guided away from attending something that, in action, did not live up to its teaching. I felt deeply saddened by the encounter. It said much about the hypocrisy within some Christian circles and the lack of genuine understanding regarding Jesus's message. It seemed the organisers had little idea of the true Oneness of life and judged those who had explored a variety of paths to God as 'unsuitable'. It felt as if, in their eyes, only one route was acceptable.

This confirmed for me that high-ranking credentials in ecclesiastical circles are man-made and offer no certainty of an authentic ability to guide me towards my Inner God.

As James the Just advised: seek only your unique pathway to God. We can never be outside of God's Loving Embrace. Listen to, trust and follow the Inner Divine Guidance.

Truth is a pathless land

A silent retreat is a symbolic enactment of Oneness where individuals can come together in wholeness. Whatever a person's journey may be, all paths will lead eventually to our Divine Centre.

If we are 'followers', we tread another's path, we follow *their* truth. Gurus, teachers and leaders are essential in the early stages of our journey but a time must come when we plough our own furrow.

Our purpose is ultimately to discover our intimate and deeply personal connection with God.

My difficult encounter with the contemplative group reinforced my belief that only our inner Divine Self can ever be our certain guide. We must give no other the power to direct our spiritual journey. Inner Divine Presence is our authority; trust the Still Small Voice which forever awaits our attention. We may frequently make mistakes but forgiveness is always ours. We are always practising! It is solely our intention on which we are judged.

James the Just dismissed the validity of external sources. We all have the potential to have a relationship with our inner God. Only on that, can we fully rely.

Suggested reading

Krishnamurti, J., *This Light in Oneself: True Meditation* (1999).

CHAPTER 13

I am, thou art

Jesus said to his disciples, 'If you were to compare me to someone, who would you say I'm like?'

Simon Peter said to him, 'You're like a just angel'. Matthew said to him, 'You're like a wise philosopher'. Thomas said to him, 'Teacher, I'm completely unable to say whom you're like'.

Jesus said, 'I'm not your teacher. Because you've drunk, you've become intoxicated by the bubbling spring I've measured out'. He took him aside and told him three things.

When Thomas returned to his companions, they asked, 'What did Jesus say to you?' Thomas said to them, 'If I tell you one of the things he said to me, you'll pick up stones and cast them at me, and fire will come out of the stones and burn you up'.

In this saying, Jesus showed great caution regarding his revelations. He chose to share secret truths with Thomas alone, taking him away from the other disciples.

Even for us, in modern times, to speak our truth can be risky, especially when we are still uncertain of our beliefs. We are like young saplings, fragile and vulnerable to unfavourable conditions. Our truth is our most precious possession. We should treat it with great tenderness and care. Even Jesus chose to keep secret his most contentious understanding.

This saying suggests that we speak our truth only with caution and sensitivity. Many will have little or no understanding of our words.

In the text of this saying, Jesus shows concerns regarding the disciples' understanding of his teaching and asks how they perceive him. He is dissatisfied with their answers. He knows he is offering them something of much greater value than that of a messenger, philosopher or teacher. In truth, he is God Incarnate and he recognises that all people have the same potential. Thomas is the only disciple he challenges and corrects. Perhaps this confirms that Jesus believed in the potential of Thomas for greater knowledge.

We can only surmise what those secret truths may be. However, it is my opinion that Jesus may have spoken of the Divine Personhood present in all people. That the presence of life, in all beings, is proof of the Eternal Selfhood in all.

I feel certain that such a frank disclosure would have been blasphemous in those bygone days. I am also sure that, even in our current era, many would still consider this to be an outrageous statement.

For me, however, this is truth. Our life is God's Life. Our spirit is God's Spirit. When we are able to quieten our busy minds, we will find God waiting in our innermost depths. Our struggle is with the imperious ego whose power has reached unacceptable proportions. The ego must find its proper and appropriate place within the wholeness of the Self. Its intended purpose is to function in the service of God, to be the player in the journey of life, aiding our growth towards our Divine Identity. Life is the school of the individuating Self. We graduate when we have come to *know* who we really are and can truly say, 'I Am'. We fully graduate when we can add to all others, 'You Are Also'.

As with every stage of our spiritual journey, it is for us to choose to accept our Divine Identity. This will never be imposed upon us. Although we may reject the gift many times, Eternity waits until we are ready.

David's story

Although my spiritual journey has been a lonely one, this aloneness has allowed me complete independence. The freedom that came in my middle years opened the path for me to go wherever God took me.

I have met many people of varying faiths over the course of my journey. However, my heart has always been with the authentic Christian message, but authenticity has been hard to find. Deep contemplative Christianity is not readily available in orthodox worship. In times of emptiness and disorientation, Buddhism has given me sanctuary with its straightforward message of the Pure Self. I owe enormous gratitude to those who, without judgement, offered me what I needed. They have been the epitome of the Good Samaritan. In my experience, Christianity in-practice still has much to learn.

Having greatly valued my own gift of freedom, David's story touched me. I could identify with the predicament that came along in his later years: as a young man, he had explored life to the full. At the age of 25, when Christianity called, he felt sure Jesus was directing his path to ministry. He wholeheartedly accepted the role that seemed to beckon. By the time of his ordination, David had a young family and willingly settled into the busy life of an inner-city vicar.

All was well until he reached those troublesome years of middle age when depression became a constant companion. He began regular psychotherapy in the hope it would lay old ghosts to rest and he could happily return to his normal life. What David had not anticipated was that therapy would release the yearnings of his younger self to pursue a more free, esoteric and contemplative form of worship. This approach was quite at odds with orthodox Christian practice. He began to find it increasing difficult to offer traditional Christianity to his parishioners.

Sadly, he refused to see this as a glorious intervention to seek a more personal and intimate relationship with God. Instead, he chose to see it as a psychotic illness. Eventually, he abandoned therapy and accepted the stifling regime of prescribed medication. The story he told himself was that his family still needed financial support and his yearnings were trivial and childish. This appeased his ego but damaged his authentic spiritual journey. We all have obligations, but David's family had outgrown the need for daily commitments.

Pressure from his family further compounded his fear of change. With insecurity overwhelming his courage, he turned his back on this precious opportunity to allow something extraordinary to develop from within himself. Sadly, his depression deepened and he became a much-troubled shadow of the man he was destined to be.

Our ego has many tricks it employs to protect its elevated and self-imposed position. When we understand the universal potentiality of the Divine Life, we can be certain we will never be directed to do or be something that will harm another. Those close to us may not appreciate change, but we can be assured that, whatever we are called to do, will also be in the best interests of all involved. Our egos, of course, will try to tell us differently.

* * *

Choosing the valuable assistance of therapy requires that we work with a therapist whom we can trust. At times, our ego will have tantrums. It is essential, during those times, that we stay with the process. There is much at stake, as David's story illustrates.

David's Divine Self was ready and yearning for expression. The 'I AM' of him was ready to 'BE'. Depression is exactly what it suggests: a pressing down, a smothering. He was experiencing sadness and grief associated with his inability to accept the Divine Gift which we are all ultimately destined to receive.

Suggested reading

Benner, J., *The Impersonal Life* (1969).

CHAPTER 14

Dangers of the spiritual ego

> Jesus said to them, 'If you fast, you'll bring guilt upon yourselves; and if you pray, you'll be condemned; and if you make donations, you'll harm your spirits. If they welcome you when you enter any land and go around in the countryside, heal those who are sick among them and eat whatever they give you, because it's not what goes into your mouth that will defile you. What comes out of your mouth is what will defile you'.

Here, Jesus challenges some of the accepted practices of the Jewish faith. It is my opinion that his objections hinge, not on the actual act of fasting, praying and charitable works, but on the hidden motives behind such behaviours. When the need to be 'seen' as pious and virtuous is our motive, such hypocritical actions are harmful to our spirit. He also states that what we say and do in life is of much greater importance than what we eat. Although Jesus focuses on the Jewish faith, this issue, I believe, is problematic for all faiths.

The spiritual ego is a very particular aspect of human behaviour which, over centuries, has accumulated enormous power. Like a track through a forest which has become ever deepened and widened with persistent use, the well-trod path of the spiritual ego is a real hazard to those seeking Divine Illumination.

This aspect of the human ego acts in a self-righteous manner and is capable of great intolerance and judgement. It is responsible for religious wars and has carried out terrible atrocities. Its power is of such magnitude that it can overwhelm and take control of personalities that are weakened by unresolved emotional wounds. The task for all who are consciously on the spiritual path is to face the presence of this potentially harmful energy in the collective unconscious. To be mindful of its existence; to be alert in oneself to feelings of self-aggrandisement, thoughts of spiritual superiority and the belief in one's right to condemn another's spiritual journey. These are indicators of a rising spiritual ego.

The effective contradiction to spiritual conceit is to know that we are all equal, wherever we are in the unfolding of our spiritual understanding. Regardless of our life-path, we are all, I believe, God made manifest. There is no one path more superior to another. Religion is entirely a man-made concept. Its usefulness lies in its intention to make sense of that which we can only experience. Its vulnerability lies in the consequences of division, separation, judgement and intolerance. Religion is simply an aid to discover meaning in the intangible. Many cultures and faiths have lost their purpose by focusing on formulised prayers and prescribed and ridged ways of worshipping.

My story

As a young woman, I watched my father gradually turn from a charismatic, intelligent and spiritual man into a demonic tyrant. In his younger years, he had had an understanding and sensitivity for deep spiritual truths. He resonated with the personal and contemplative type of Christianity found in the teachings of Joel Goldsmith. He was also a follower of an emerging Christian movement called 'Science of Mind', which advocated the need for personal psychological understanding.

My father ran group discussions and regular meditation sessions. People seeking a new way to God were drawn to him. In his locality, he became well-known for his spiritual knowledge and inspirational talks. He possessed a charisma that attracted men as well as women.

Within ten years, however, he had changed into a man I could hardly recognise. He had become arrogant and full of his own importance.

Discussion was not tolerated and those who dared to question his beliefs were made to feel grossly inferior. His intention to be the leader of a new spiritual pathway drove him to unacceptable lengths. He became prone to wild exaggerations about his achievements.

A false personality, full of hubris, began to emerge. He had lost the ability to distinguish truth from fiction. The worst of his behaviour was meted out towards my mother, whom he regularly and publicly humiliated, treating her with utter disdain. His classes and his writings remained in demand over several years. Gradually, however, his ability to control himself greatly diminished.

As age took hold, he retreated to a remote hideaway surrounded by several women who had fallen under his undeniable spell. Following the death of my mother, there was nothing more to hold me to my father. I thankfully never saw him again.

Reflections

For reasons still unclear to me I had always remained an observer, rather than a participator, in this saddening family drama. At the time I was in my early 20s, but I never fell under my father's spell. Although I had no knowledge of the spiritual ego, it became clear to me that something was dreadfully wrong when my father's actions became completely at odds with his teaching.

Under the protection of unseen forces, I believe I was able to watch and experience the power of this archetypal force from a distance. I was able to learn, first-hand, about the hypnotic power of the spiritual ego whilst remaining detached and protected. Eventually, this demonic energy not only destroyed my father and my beloved mother, it also destroyed my precious paternal grandparents.

* * *

Although my father would seem to have had a relatively sound upbringing, he carried deep emotional wounds. He had been over-indulged by a doting mother and criticised by a remote and domineering father. These two opposing parental styles had created a split personality with a fault line too deep for natural integration into healthy adulthood.

Believing he could never be good enough to gain his father's approval, he sought positive acclaim from the outside world, particularly from his spiritual followers. He became addicted to the hero worship that easily came his way.

In his youth, he had studied the new science of psychology and focused particularly on human behaviour and coercion. As a consequence, any threat to his elevated position was met with aggressive resistance. Sadly, therapy was not a part of regular life in those times. Had my father been able to take advantage of such help, he may have found ways to heal his split personality. As it was, the mingling of spiritual power with a fractured ego, produced a man who believed he had the God-given right to do whatever he wished.

In the early days of his spiritual quest, my father had learnt to say, 'I am an expression of God'.

He sadly refused to offer the same truth to all others. His emotional wounds would not allow him to bestow equal value on all people.

He chose to believe he was the sole son of God.

History tells of tyrants who quickly rose to power, their charisma carrying the naïve along with them. In such cases, evidence often shows an upbringing where power and compassion, instead of working together, are strongly polarised.

Suggested reading

Trine, R.W., *In Tune with the Infinite* (1965).

CHAPTER 15

Understand the source of all life

Jesus said, 'When you see the one who wasn't born of a woman, fall down on your face and worship that person. That's your Father'.

The Essence of God is Omnipresence, Omnipotence and Omniscience.

Omnipresence

God is the very source of all life. God is within us and is the wellspring from which Divine Providence flows. As Divine Provider, all needs, whether spiritual or material, are potentially present and available to each and every being. The more we consciously and deliberately open our hearts and hands to receive, the more will be given to us.

We need to have great patience and love for ourselves as we participate in the growth of human consciousness. For aeons, human civilisations have believed in the separation of God and human. We are now in an era where those long-held falsehoods are being challenged and corrected. We are learning that our very life force is God and we must invite Divine Energy to fill our lives and flow freely into our expressions.

Omnipotence

Our belief in limitation prevents us from experiencing the totality of our Divine inheritance. For thousands of years, humankind has believed that God is a separate Being and that we must cajole and bribe Him/Her/Them to take care of us. When we wipe those limitations and negativities from our consciousness, we will grow to trust the inner presence of Divine Love which holds back *nothing*.

We must seek the means, perhaps through therapy, of cleansing our psyche and ridding ourselves of its inherited and often inaccurate belief systems. This is not an easy task and, in my opinion, may require the persistence of several lifetimes! But we do not accept this challenge on our own. A vast wealth of unseen, but ever-present forces, support us throughout our journey into the Wholeness of Truth.

Omniscience

Omniscience means all knowledge. Science has helped us to better understand the forces of nature, the evolution of species, geology, earth itself and much, much more. Celestial activities, which so spooked our early ancestors and created the illusion of powerful external gods, are now understood, thanks to scientific exploration. We better understand how the universe functions, the laws that regulate it, the mathematics, the equations that show the vast complexity and the infinite wisdom of an intricate and intelligent order.

I would like to believe that a new era is in the making where the wisdom of science will integrate with the wisdom of the great Seers, the mystical poets and the authentic philosophers of past and present. I believe ancient mystical teachings were simply a different way of seeing and understanding much of which, today, science has shown to be true. Together, science and mysticism may inform the next step in humankind's evolution.

* * *

Of equal importance in our spiritual journey are the modern sciences of psychology and psychotherapy, which can aid the cleansing of our inner world. We need to find ways of discarding falsehoods which unhelpfully pass from one generation to the next and which unwittingly overshadow much of human life. We are, I believe, co-creators of our life, and manifest much of that which we anticipate.

Unfortunately, we are frequently unaware of the many unconscious expectations we project. These have become habitual and largely learnt from others. We see, touch, hear and sense that which we anticipate, consequently perpetuating our own illusions. Our consciousness largely remains firmly closed to Truth, which lies beyond the realm of the five human senses.

Worship your Father

The yearning to know God must come from within oneself. Only when we have a sincere desire to know deeper truths will we grow in sensitivity to receive them. Nothing is ever hidden from us, but without an openness and willingness to discover, we do not have the 'eyes to see'. As our minds and senses develop greater states of receptivity, discernment grows of that which has always been within us. This is the Divine journey into Infinity which has been prepared for us; a journey into our own internal and endless consciousness; a journey that will never cease.

Jesus asks that we be alert to the Presence of the Father as the One source of life. He commands that we honour and revere that which is ever-present and recognise that we are the avenue for God's visible creation.

My truth

In Codex 15, Jesus limits his words.

All the words in the world cannot fully convey experiential knowledge of the Divine. God can only truly be known through personal experience. My spiritual story is very simple but the task of sharing this with others has often seemed beyond my ability.

Suffice it to say, I have come to know God through the conscious experiencing of Love, Wisdom, Truth and Beauty. In return, I have experienced Love beyond measure.

Perhaps, dear reader, I may encourage you to seek your own.

Suggested reading

Gibran, K., *The Prophet* (1991).

CHAPTER 16

Live by your own truth

> Jesus said, 'Maybe people think that I've come to cast peace on the world, and they don't know that I've come to cast divisions on the earth: fire, sword, and war. Where there are five in a house, there'll be three against two and two against three, father against [sic] and son and son against father. They'll stand up and be one'.

It is clear from this saying that Jesus intended to shake up the world. He believed his message was of such profound importance that the normal conventions and mores of life must be cast aside. He commanded that people live by their own inner truth, no matter how much conflict this may create.

My interpretation of Codex 16 is that we must have the courage to be the unique person we really are. The time has come to end the inherited and imposed practices which have held human consciousness captive for thousands of years. Undoubtedly this takes resolve, even in these modern and more liberal times. Although family pressures are weakening, other influences such as social media are taking their place. These also will have negative consequences if we choose to act in ways that conflict with our own conscience. We are advised to be extremely vigilant. When we allow external pressure to direct our lives, we have become robotic. We cannot experience Presence when our attention is absorbed by external demands.

The inner Divine Voice 'speaks' to us in many ways, teaching and directing our journey. Meditation, I believe, is the foremost pathway in developing the essential listening 'ear'. As the ever-present voice becomes more audible, clearer and more persistent, we begin to trust in the wisdom of its loving guidance. Our part is to develop commitment and resolve to live this sacred message.

Meditating with others who have long practised 'Being in the Silence', can be most helpful. The simple sharing of a quiet space, free of noise and distraction, is a gift to be treasured. Such an environment can aid the development of the 'listening ear'. In stillness and tranquillity, our sacred journey begins to unfold.

Our focus must be on that which aids the blossoming of our soul, not that which pleases others.

Anne's story

I met Anne on a seven-day retreat which was largely held in silence. We were a small group of eight people, all previously unknown to each other. The facilitator provided an hour at the end of each day for those who wished to talk and share. No subject was off the agenda and it quickly became a time of bonding.

Anne, however, remained silent, watchful and attentive. On the fifth day, she said she was at last ready to tell her story. She gave a most moving account of herself as a young woman who had struggled to find the courage to be the person she truly was.

As a young girl growing up in Ireland, Anne had had a great deal of contact with Catholic nuns who were both adored and revered by her family and the larger community.

From a young age Anne easily absorbed the family vision that it would be a great accolade for her, and the family, if she were to be accepted as a nun in the Catholic faith. She enjoyed the quiet yet substantial pride of her family as this eventually became a reality. Any misgivings she had during her training were dismissed as perfectly normal. Needless to say, in time Anne came to have great struggles with her life as a nun. She was told this was a challenge she must now accept. Her reward would become evident in heaven.

Peter, the young priest allocated to support Anne's convent, was also secretly questioning his vows. Unsurprisingly, Anne and Peter became confidantes in their distress and, over time, fell in love. Supported by mutual courage and their love for each other, they chose to run away. They made plans in secret and one night escaped to England by ferry.

Very quickly they found work in a charitable organisation which supports the homeless. Temporary accommodation was provided for them, and their new life—eventually as husband and wife—began. In the early months of this new life, times were extremely difficult, particularly for Anne. They never doubted, however, that Spirit had intervened in their quest to follow their inner guidance. Eventually, they both trained as psychotherapists and remained actively engaged with the charity until Peter sadly died of a brain haemorrhage at the age of 59.

Anne attended our retreat a year after Peter's death. Her loneliness was quite palpable. The loss of her beloved husband had rekindled the deep loss she had felt at leaving Ireland and her birth family. She never for one moment regretted leaving the convent, but her actions had sadly ended her relationship with her parents. Although Anne had written to her mother many times and always remembered family birthdays, these gestures of reconciliation were returned to her unopened. As Anne told her story we supported her with many shared tears and much love.

This was one of the bravest stories I have personally encountered. Anne's deep relationship with her inner God had directed her to a different life, something more suited to her natural personality. The support Peter and Anne received in England was practical and emotional. Loving care and financial help also came their way. As Anne and Peter followed their inner guidance, their journey unfolded. They grew to be a deeply committed support for the many homeless people who passed through the refuge.

On reflection, Anne commented on the great fullness of Divine Support that had fulfilled their every need. She noted that, although breaking her vows had affected her deeply, God's direction had been quite unambiguous. She had never doubted the rightness of their decisions.

The final and most recent part of Anne's story had come as a result of actions by her sister, Mary. After much anguish, Mary had chosen to follow her own wishes and reconnect with Anne. This change of heart followed the death of their parents. Reconciliation was a great gift to both women and, I believe, a healing intervention by Divine Spirit. The two women, freed from family constraints, were able to renew their relationship and to be a great comfort and loving support for each other in their later years.

Anne's message to the retreatants was to always follow your heart, no matter how difficult it may seem. Listen for God's Still Small Voice. You will always be shown which 'road to travel'. In so doing, you and perhaps many others will eventually reap rewards beyond measure.

Suggested reading

Merton, T., *No Man is an Island* (1955).

CHAPTER 17

Experience the presence of Christ

> Jesus said, 'I'll give you what no eye has ever seen, no ear has ever heard, no hand has ever touched, and no human mind has ever thought'.

Jesus states that he has brought to humanity experience and knowledge of something previously unknown to the earthly world. It is my opinion that he brought awareness of a very real, yet hidden, identity which is present in all people. His purpose was to bring a change in human consciousness so that we may all come to know and, in time, express that fullness, joy and love which are integral to our inner Divine Self.

This earthly life, I believe, is a platform where invisible spiritual principles may be given visible form. Where we can choose to experience that which seems beyond, and yet integral, to human life. That which, although unseen, unheard and unfelt, can still become known through spiritual attunement.

Jesus brought the possibility of a change in consciousness, offering us greater opportunities. He taught truths which have always existed but have rarely been realised. Jesus, I believe, came to negate the limitations and falsehoods which have shackled humanity. He brought us the freedom to *be* and to express the fullness of an Inner Living Identity.

* * *

As the soul becomes more open and receptive to Divine Teaching, we become the means of a unique and creative expression on the earthly plane. A new chapter of our life has begun. We notice subtle changes, not only in ourselves but also in people's responses to us. The trinkets of this world no longer appeal as they once did. Our priorities naturally become adjusted to higher ideals and values.

We come to understand the responsibility we share with God in the creation of our own life experience. We begin to recognise that, unwittingly, many of the beliefs we hold are 'borrowed' from family and culture, simply a replica of that which has gone before.

However, when we acquire the ability to act from Soul, our life becomes a truly original expression. We become blessed with the opportunity to be 'reborn' as a unique Christ.

As new ways become embedded and embodied, our life experience changes. We may experience overwhelming feelings of great love for anyone and everyone. Compassion for others is readily present. A new and spontaneous joy settles around us. We come to know contentment just for its own sake. We may be surprised by truths and kindnesses that spontaneously pour forth from within ourselves. We can feel awestruck by intuitions and insightful truths that seem to voluntarily present themselves. We are becoming an instrument of God.

This is the birth of the Inner Christ, the beginning of a unique and truly Divine Identity. This is God expressing as oneself. We have become a very real and functioning Christ on earth. We have taken Christ as our second name.

Jesus said, 'In all truth I tell you, whoever believes in me will perform even greater works ...' (John 14:12).

In my opinion, whilst Jesus asks that we believe in his teachings, he did not mean that we be a replica of him. The word 'me' should be interpreted as the inner Christ/Divinity which resides in each one of us, awaiting the time of our 'rebirth'.

I believe Jesus came as an example of what we will, perhaps after many lifetimes, all become. He is very clear that we all have the potential to do greater work than he has. When we are 'clothed' in our Christhood, our tasks will come from the Inner Divine Spirit; our willingness to fulfil those tasks, however, must come from ourselves.

The story of the risen Christ

Healing

It is my belief that the healings performed by Jesus were made possible by his understanding of Divine Identity *in all people*. He had the ability to look beyond the mistakes, the difficulties of humanity. He 'saw' *only* the inner presence of God, which cannot create disease.

We human beings unwittingly create much of our own distress and disease. When we learn to acknowledge *only* the inner Christhood in all people, the purity of God then has the opportunity to be made visible.

In human terms, healing of body or mind has the possibility of taking place.

In terms of Christ's expression, disease has been denied all power.

Please note

This saying may be experienced as a highly contentious statement ... as I believe it is intended to be!

It challenges each one of us to 'wake up' to whatever is happening within our own world. It asks that we question and take personal responsibility for ourselves and our life.

Sadly, we now live in a culture of victimhood. This is deeply restricting to a full life-expression. Jesus, I believe, asked that we recognise our inner power and remove the habitual sense of disempowerment which is endemic in our modern world.

The truth, I think, is that we are perpetually immersed in God. Where we are in life, in our relationships, in our creative expression, is largely by the action of our own consciousness. We hold a great deal more power in our own hands than we realise.

Many turn away from the personal responsibility of making changes. Many of us have the means and the ability to do so, but feel debilitated by fear.

We do not need to dig deep for a 'tonne of courage', we only need to find the first 'cupful' *and use it!*

A well-known saying: 'How do you eat an elephant?'

'One piece at a time!'

Suggested reading

Lindeblad, B.N., *I May Be Wrong* (2022).

CHAPTER 18

One continuum of life, no end, no beginning

> The disciples said to Jesus, 'Tell us about our end. How will it come?'
>
> Jesus said, 'Have you discovered the beginning so that you can look for the end? Because the end will be where the beginning is. Blessed is the one who will stand up in the beginning. They'll know the end, and won't taste death'.

In the text of this codex, the disciples are concerned about how their lives will end.

Jesus seems to chastise them for their ignorance regarding death. He implies that they have learnt very little in their time with him and, in fact, have not even started their inner journey to truth. They seem to have no understanding that death does not exist and that there is nothing to fear.

I believe death is merely a change of consciousness, when our spirit evacuates the corporeal form and is released into a higher spiritual plane. Without support from the Divine Life Force, the physical body disintegrates. The eternal inner spirit, however, never dies.

It is my opinion that those with a mind closed to the possibility of further lives may not allow themselves to know life beyond this plane.

I believe there is no punishment, simply further opportunities to return and explore the earthly plane. I believe this can happen many times in our evolution. We are given as many opportunities as we need to 'open our eyes' to Truth.

Eventually, the defensive shell of the ego will begin to crack. Spirit needs only the tiniest chink in a person's armour for Divine Light to gradually illuminate consciousness. Then, their inner journey, rather than the outward journey, begins.

Suggested reading

Alexander, E., *Proof of Heaven* (2012).

CHAPTER 19

The value of parables and symbols

> Jesus said, 'Blessed is the one who came into being before coming into being. If you become my disciples and listen to my message, these stones will become your servants; because there are five trees in paradise which don't change in summer or winter, and their leaves don't fall. Whoever knows them won't taste death'.

Jesus states that those who come into the earthly plane with soul awareness are deeply blessed. They may have evolved through many lifetimes to a depth of consciousness where they understand the universality of Christ's Identity. Consequently, they experience a greater mastery of themselves and their lives. They understand the creative role for which each soul is intended. The earth is their playground for exploring and expressing Divinity. They are, indeed, blessed.

Jesus frequently uses symbols and imagery to convey his message. It is a method of communication which becomes more familiar as we deepen our understanding of Divine Wisdom.

Spiritual truths need to be known in two ways. First is a logical, reasoning 'knowing', which defines, rationalises and contrasts. Second is the intuitive 'knowing', which experiences and senses that which is beyond the reasoning process. Although one function is often more dominant, I believe it is necessary for our spiritual evolution that both parts are developed. This will gradually bring a much deeper and more profound understanding.

* * *

In my opinion, this parable refers to the spiritualising of our five senses in order to deeply experience the Eternality and Omnipresence of Christ present in all people. This enables, through study and contemplation, a growing awareness of Divine Energy as the substance of all forms.
Consequently:

1. With spiritual eyes, we will 'see' beyond the superficial and physical form to the inner Divinity which tangibly expresses life.
2. With spiritual ears, we will 'hear' greater depths and hidden meanings in life issues.
3. With spiritual taste buds, we will 'taste', 'savour' and be fulfilled by Divine Essence present in human experiences.
4. With spiritual nostrils, we will 'sniff out', or discern, the Truth of situations and discover solutions.
5. With spiritual touch/feel, we will intuit the hidden truth of persons, relationships and experiences.

The tree

I believe the tree, as used in this parable, can be understood as a representation of humanity which gives visible form and cognisable expression to the Presence of God. As the tree's roots are planted in the earth, its growth gradually fills earthly space and the branches reach for the heavens. It can be seen as a visible conduit of Divine Energy, linking the heavens with the earthiness of human life.

In addition, trees can be understood as a representation of Divine Providence. A tree freely gives shelter, sanctuary and sustenance to many creatures. It provides much of the necessities essential to life on earth. In the same bountiful manner, Divine Supply freely gives to each and every one of us without discrimination. Our part is to graciously choose to receive and accept.

Olga's story

Olga's book, *Entering the Circle* (see below), is an authentic, comprehensive and eloquent description of a mystical journey into ancient Siberian wisdom. As a qualified and practising psychiatrist, she was taken on a physical journey deep into the remote wilderness of Siberia. As she encountered the ancient wisdom of times past, she developed an ability to receive and perceive deep truths, all previously unknown to her.

I can recommend this book as an aid to breaking the false shackles of a narrow and limiting awareness. Olga eloquently endeavours to share with the reader, worlds she experienced beyond the norm.

Suggested reading

Kharitidi, O., *Entering the Circle* (1996).

CHAPTER 20

Recognise *your* mustard seed

> The disciples asked Jesus, 'Tell us, what can the kingdom of heaven be compared to?'
>
> He said to them, 'It can be compared to a mustard seed. Though it's the smallest of all the seeds, when it falls on tilled soil it makes a plant so large that it shelters the birds of heaven'.

The disciples are curious about the Kingdom of Heaven. Perhaps they believe it is a particular place to which they will eventually ascend. There is, in fact, no such place.

I believe heaven is a state of consciousness which is already present in embryo within each and every one of us. In the text of this parable, it is likened to the humble mustard seed, which must be planted in favourable conditions in order for it to flourish.

I believe this parable teaches that we should prepare 'our soil of consciousness' with committed learning and contemplation. As our 'seed' of awareness grows strong and becomes firmly grounded in Truth, the benefit will come not only for ourselves, but for others who share our world. It is possible that from the tiniest seed-awareness, we can develop a robust and strong capacity to tolerate difficulties. The parable adds that we will also become a place of shelter and sanctuary for others who also seek.

Preparation of soil

Life often brings difficult experiences which cause us to create a protective shell around our emotional heart. We must have the courage to loosen the crust that seems to give us protection but, in reality, prevents us from experiencing Divine Love. Therapy, I believe, is an efficient and effective way to heal our tender emotional wounds. The soul must be cleansed and made sensitive to the Word of God. Only then can we be an expression of Divine Creation.

Removal of stones and weeds

Our consciousness needs to be cleansed of defensive attitudes and the many false beliefs which interfere with our growth. The 'soil' of consciousness requires preparation and softening through introspection and therapy. These processes loosen the knotted emotions that restrict and inhibit our lives. As fears resulting from past hurts diminish, our soul softens to a fine receptive 'tilth' in which God can 'plant' His ideas, His tasks and His wisdom.

Soil needs the ability to absorb water

Without water, a seed will not germinate. Only when the soil is properly tilled can it receive and retain life-giving moisture. Likewise, our consciousness must be sufficiently open to receive the Holy Spirit, for which water is the symbol. The Holy Spirit freely and graciously 'waters our soul', giving life and expression to Divine Creation.

The properties of the mustard tree

Being hardy indicates that, once germination has taken place, the seed will continue to grow, even in difficult conditions. Likewise, Divine Providence waits for conscious awareness to break through our outer defensive shell. This is equivalent to the sprouting of the mustard seed. As our unique inner Being begins to flourish, our spiritual growth will continue. We begin to express our True Self. Our need for protection and shelter is perpetually provided for.

We are often required to wait for what seems an unreasonably long period for evidence of this growth. Waiting, however, develops and strengthens our resolve and trust in Divine Providence.

My story

The task of preparing my inner 'soil' has been a long one. The limited sense of self-worth that clung until my middle years, meant that my 'mustard seed' found little worthy soil in which to grow. When my eyes were 'opened' to the falsehoods from which I had lived my life, I set about 'tilling my soil' with earnest. It became clear to me that only I could create the conditions for my healing to take place. Only I could remove the stones and weeds that inhibited my growth.

My journey from sprouting seed to present day has required me to pursue several avenues of study and therapy in order to understand the emotional wounding which constantly eclipsed my soul. It has required a deep search into a variety of spiritual traditions in order to find my unique path to God. It has asked of me years of committed meditation and contemplation. It has required me to develop the art of listening to the Inner Divine Voice of God.

My journey has also been greatly assisted by many silent retreats. Some years ago I was 'guided' to a Christian monastery which had chosen to open its doors to seekers of all 'brands'. On a practical level, they offered clean, solitary accommodation, good and wholesome meals, large outdoor roaming spaces and two beautiful chapels in which 'The Silence' seemed to envelop me. Most of all, however, the monks offered a space of tranquillity and pure reverence for Divine Presence.

To arrive at this place, in its remote setting, felt like entering another realm. The awesome sense of a 'different world' was quite palpable. I have never stayed for fewer than eight days. The hardest part has always been the leaving and returning to 'normal' life. Even though I am aware that my heightened experiences came from within my own inner heaven, the monks' life of constant prayer and contemplation, made access to my inner space so much easier. Their willingness to just let me 'be' within their sanctuary is one of the most precious gifts my life-journey has brought me.

My intention in my translation of this parable is to show that all the requirements for our journey are already ours. Only when we have chosen to plant and grow seeds of awareness, will we recognise the many Divine Gifts that come our way. We then become a co-creator with God in Divine Expression.

Suggested reading

Morgan, M., *Mutant Message Down Under* (1991).

CHAPTER 21

Discover, value and protect your uniqueness

Mary said to Jesus, 'Whom are your disciples like?'

He said, 'They're like little children living in a field which isn't theirs. When the owners of the field come, they'll say, "Give our field back to us". They'll strip naked in front of them to let them have it and give them their field'.

'So I say that if the owner of the house realizes the bandit is coming, they'll watch out beforehand and won't let the bandit break into the house of their domain and steal their possessions. You, then, watch out for the world! Prepare to defend yourself so that the bandits don't attack you, because what you're expecting will come. May there be a wise person among you! When the fruit ripened, the reaper came quickly, sickle in hand, and harvested it. Anyone who has ears to hear should hear!'

In the text of this codex, Jesus is asked to describe his disciples. He portrays them as naïve children living within the consciousness, the 'field' or 'house', of others.

He says they must come to an awareness of this false persona, identified as 'the clothes' and shed their artificiality and copied behaviours.

They must also give back the 'clothes', by recognising and correctly attributing the source of those falsehoods.

Jesus states that they will need to be strong and vigilant at this stage of their journey. He warns that those around them will try to 'steal' their spiritual growth and halt the journey into their true selfhood.

It is also suggested that support from a wise companion who understands the potential dangers of this journey would be beneficial.

* * *

Much of our life story is created from the expectations and assumptions we have stored within our consciousness. This is largely an accumulation of what we have unconsciously absorbed from others: their beliefs, their hopes and their dreams. We also collect and build a complex library of our own experiences. We rarely analyse those events in our life. Perhaps we should!

The result is that we live a copied life. We become a follower—a duplicate—not an initiator of our journey. A time will come when we need to shed the artificial personality, our 'outer clothing', in order to find our unique individuality which already resides deep within us.

When we come to this realisation we must be at our most alert. It is a vulnerable time. To make the choice to change and become our true self means we gradually grow into a person that others may not recognise. Those with whom we share our life may find this a great challenge.

Undoubtedly, living by our own values, beliefs and aspirations can be immensely liberating. Jesus, however, warns that the external world may try to control and overlay the old monotony upon us. He teaches that we must be strong in our resolve and vigilant in protecting our fledgling True Self. It is our most precious possession, which can easily be 'stolen' from us.

* * *

It takes courage, and perhaps therapeutic support, to allow our real self to be revealed and to be lived in its fullness. A challenge may come from within our own psyche as our artificial and cloned persona senses a diminishing of its powers. This aspect of our ego will use any trick available to rein us back into its clutches. It will use fear to scare us, anger to challenge the need for change and sadness at the loss of the past. None of its predictions will be accurate, but to be forewarned of this potential internal battle will reduce the ego's capacity to halt our progress.

* * *

Sadly, the collective world view is, for the most part, scientifically based. This leaves little value for our intuition, our 'sixth sense' which, when understood, can be our most reliable guide to discovering our true self. We must also guard against the judgements and condemnation of others who would try to destroy our path to freedom.

Protection comes from knowing that we *will* be challenged, possibly by friends, family and most definitely by our ego. Strive to hug your 'knowing' to your heart and wait for the storm to pass, as it inevitably will.

Jesus states that when our consciousness begins to bear fruit, we must gather in the 'harvest' and store the tangible results. In other words, we must acknowledge and develop our own valid consciousness from the growth of our life-journey. Gathering a personal storehouse of authentic experiences and understandings will sustain and comfort us through testing and challenging times.

Not everyone is consciously on a path of spirituality. Even so, it is essential that we grow into our unique individuality and the person we were born to be. Our journey, if lived consciously, will lead us towards the discovery of our True Self. We must never remain a facsimile of someone else.

Humanity's story

Humanity can be symbolised—visualised—as one jigsaw puzzle made of approximately 8 billion individual pieces. When each unique life has become conscious and known, all individual pieces will be expressed within the totality of the human story. Wholeness will be made visible and understood by the completion of 8 billion discrete, yet interconnected, pieces: one complete Eternal Story, illustrating the value of each individual life; humanity developed from earth-bound individuals into One Divine Identity.

Should this ultimately occur, we will understand that:

- Each piece is essential to the wholeness of the earthly story.
- Each piece has equal value; no one piece has greater importance than another.
- Each piece is completely unique and distinct from all others.
- Should one piece be incomplete, it leaves the human picture unfinished.
- Only when every piece is in place can the whole human story be known and, perhaps, the earthly puzzle resolved.

This small parable shows the responsibility that we each carry. Until we discover and express our true uniqueness, the jigsaw remains incomplete and the Divine journey unfinished. With all our heart and soul, we must discover who we *really* are.

Seek *until you find. Live and* be *the real you.*

Suggested reading

Dobisz, J., *One Hundred Days of Solitude* (2008).

CHAPTER 22

Become whole, become holy

> Jesus saw some little children nursing. He said to his disciples, 'These nursing children can be compared to those who enter the kingdom'.
>
> They said to him, 'Then we'll enter the kingdom as little children?'
>
> Jesus said to them, 'When you make the two into one, and make the inner like the outer and the outer like the inner, and the upper like the lower, and so make the male and the female a single one so that the male won't be male nor the female female; when you make eyes in the place of an eye, a hand in the place of a hand, a foot in the place of a foot and an image in the place of an image; then you'll enter [the kingdom]'.

In this codex, Jesus teaches the disciples about a state of consciousness which will reveal the Kingdom of Heaven. He explains they must be in the same state of innocence in which babies exist. They should be without preconceptions and open to guidance and instruction from within their own Christhood. Just as a baby totally trusts in the nourishment of its mother's milk, the disciples must learn to trust Divine Spirit as the source of life-nourishment in all its forms. Only when they correctly understand the wellspring of life will they enter the Kingdom of God.

* * *

Our human language is largely composed of contrasts and comparisons through which we gain awareness. The polarity of night and day defines both. Wet and dry bring awareness of each other. Full and empty are made apparent by their difference. Diversity defines and sets the foundation of consciousness by which we come to know and make sense of the earthly plane. By adding subjective meaning, we build our personal manual for human life.

Jesus asks that we seek a greater wholeness which recognises the centre ground between polarities. We should not dismiss the pairs of opposites. Rather, we should focus on that which holds both extremes in tension. This demands a different way of observing, of noticing. We must come to understand that opposites are *always* two sides of *one* 'coin'. This denies power to the false earthly sense of separation and division.

We externalise in life that which we hold in our consciousness. What is inside us becomes expressed and visible on the outside. This is the true meaning of wholeness and oneness. Jesus asks that we remove the false notion of separation between inner and outer and, instead, recognise the centre which holds our inner and outer worlds in one continuum.

We are also commanded to unify the polarities of male and female energies within ourselves. These are *not* gender related but simply a traditional method of definition. Both energies are present in all people but can be expressed to varying degrees, usually with one more dominant. Our task is to develop and gradually integrate the more latent function into a position of equality and respectful balance.

The energy of rationality gives clarity, meaning, scrutiny and judgement. The energy of discernment teaches intuition, relatedness, and compassion for oneself and others. When the energy of rationality and the energy of discernment harmonise, we become a more complete human being. We will express judgement with kindness; we will apply scrutiny with understanding; we will categorise without criticism; we will allow intuition to inform perception.

When polarised energies achieve some level of acceptance and integration, the personality will find a better balance and will function as a greater whole. We will have the ability to observe 'the bigger picture' in which we are aware of not only our own needs but also the needs of others. We will no longer discriminate and judge harshly. We will treat all others as we would wish to be treated ourselves. In areas of conflict and discord, we will work towards an appropriate compromise. We will discover the 'middle ground'.

Jesus also teaches that we do not separate God and the physical body, but know Divine Spirit as the source of all physicality and, also, as the life that supports it: that our human hand is also the hand of God ... that our human foot is the foot of God.

He urges that we see, with our spiritual eyes, the presence and wholeness of God in all space, at all times. God is omnipresent. When we *know* and experience this truth, we will enter the Kingdom and become another Holy Christ.

Diane's story

Diane was an accomplished poet who had achieved some success with her undoubted creative talent. Although several pieces of her work had been published in the small local newspaper, she had accumulated an enormous collection of unpublished poems. She was always working on 'the next' poem and was pleased to fulfil any special request asked of her.

Although she achieved some acclaim, her greatest sorrow came from the strange attitude of her husband, Fred. In all of their 50 years together he had never read any of her work. Diane was a timid character who expressed very limited power when in her husband's presence. Although her creative energy had found expression in her writing, her assertive male energy, which yearned to publish a book of her poetry, was deeply suppressed. Unsurprisingly, as she grew older depression became another hindrance to her life-expression.

On the death of a relative, Diane inherited a small legacy. This, she felt, could be her opportunity to fulfil her aspirations of publishing her work. With the support of their daughter, she found a publisher who was willing to make her book a reality and the process was set in motion. Fred was aware of this exciting development but, sadly, refused any involvement or support.

On the day Diane was to pay her contribution towards the publishing expenses, she found that the joint bank account holding her legacy was almost empty. Fred had decided to 'surprise' Diane with a new car! Under the guise of love for her, he had deliberately and wilfully destroyed her plan. Diane's book was never published and she never wrote another poem. Within 18 months a cancerous tumour developed and she died the following year.

Diane had the power within her to make her dream a reality but she allowed Fred to control and overrun her life and steal her dream. We pay a great price when we choose to be complicit with another's interference in our journey.

Divine opportunity had provided for the harmonising of both of Diane's energies, her creativity and her rational desire to make her work visible. When this was denied, her demonstration became stagnant. Just as a static pond becomes toxic through lack of movement, so Diane's internal world became malignant, creating destruction in her body.

We must all work with the sincere intention of bringing our God-given assets to fruition. We must discover, develop and integrate the latent parts of ourselves if we are to manifest all that God has given us. We must be willing to express our inherent wholeness. We must allow no other to steal our rightful expression.

Suggested reading

Freke, T., *Rumi Wisdom: Daily Teachings from the Great Sufi* (2000).

CHAPTER 23

One united wholeness

> Jesus said, 'I'll choose you, one out of a thousand and two out of ten thousand, and they'll stand as a single one'.

To be chosen means to be offered the opportunity to become unified with Divine Spirit. By virtue of being born, we are already 'chosen'. We must, however, grow into a conscious awareness of that fact. Only then will we willingly open ourselves to be a Child of God on earth.

Jesus believed very few people were willing to receive his message. His teaching requires a particular focus and a strong commitment to the life-journey we have been offered. This is neither relevant nor appropriate for everyone. Certain aspects of our path would seem to have little spiritual application as we concentrate on the external facets of living.

However, our growth into the realisation of our Divine Son-/Daughter-ship is never a prescribed and linear process. It can be experienced as a meandering path, through many twists and turns, seemingly in no particular direction. We are all, I believe, destined to reach our ultimate purpose of unity with Divine Spirit. To achieve this requires that we become conscious of *all* aspects of ourself and grow into ownership and expression of that wholeness. Eventually, each one of us will learn to 'stand as a single one', as a complete wholeness of Divine Expression.

* * *

Jesus made this statement in Codex 23 some 2000 years ago and since that time human consciousness has, in many ways, changed. The idea of God as an integral aspect of our being, rather than an external separate God, has gained greater acceptance. The cause and the consequence of this change is that the collective unconscious has developed over the past two millennia. Mass education, particularly in the western world, has taught people to think for themselves, to assess and give due consideration to new ideas and concepts. Many are now less willing to accept theories and dictates from elders, without question.

Consequently, religions have lost much of their influence. Formulaic worship and rigid laws are no longer appropriate for those who have come to believe in an internal Divine Essence. Philosophies that speak of the inner void and the Universal Divine Soul have brought a timely gift to those who are sincerely seeking a more holistic and personal approach to the spiritual life.

We each stand on the shoulders of those who have conquered the collective resistance to owning our inner Divine Self. We benefit from those who have already journeyed towards the realisation of their true identity, no matter which direction their path has taken. We grow towards a collective humanity which consciously accepts that we are One Being expressed in billions of ways.

* * *

There are innumerable methods of leading us towards our centre of Oneness. One such technique is the use of a mandala. This is a pictorial symbol of the eternal journey into our Divine Centre. It is used in various forms and illustrates the diversity of the spiritual path. Its purpose is to bring clarity and order to what may seem like a chaotic life. It gives equal value to *all* the states, stages and aspects of our journey. It brings an appreciation of the great value of human life in all its diversity.

Typically, the design of a mandala will show an outer circle in which is contained a square with four entrances, one on each of its four sides.

Within the square is a type of maze, sometimes an inward spiral and sometimes irregular juxtaposed avenues, cul-de-sacs and dead ends. Its purpose is to give credence to the vast diversity of paths we may choose in order to gather experience and self-knowledge. Whichever mandala design is used, each one has a centre into which all paths eventually lead. The centre depicts the unification and shared Oneness with our inner God.

The four entry points into the maze, in my opinion, correspond with the four types of human functioning. These can be labelled as thinking, feeling, sensing and intuiting. We each carry within our psyche all four ways of expressing our humanness. One, however, will be dominant, with a second supporting. The third will be used to a limited degree and the fourth will contribute very little. It should be understood, however, that all functions carry equal value to human life and, I believe, will all ultimately be developed through various lifetimes.

The predominantly 'thinking' personality experiences and expresses life rationally, through logic. The predominantly 'feeling' personality is most aware of emotions and feelings. The 'sensing' personality considers that which is tangible to the five senses. The 'intuitive' personality attaches deeper meanings to that which is beyond the visible. All four functions can be turned inward to introspectively understand one's self. The awakening of each function is, I believe, essential to our ultimate Wholeness.

As all four functions come into 'one cooperative whole', we grow into a being of Oneness with all parts integrated. We will 'stand as a single one' with all aspects cooperating with and informing each other.

We are each an individual aspect of One Humanity; each of us will stand as 'a single one', expressing the One Infinite Life, in our own unique and precious way.

Dreams

Dreams are messengers of guidance and wisdom that help us to navigate the twists and turns of life. Dream symbols express truths that cannot easily be conveyed through words. They carry enormous power-packs of meaning for the dreamer. It is, however, a language that we must learn to interpret according to our own particular circumstances. Although some types of therapy can greatly assist and support us, it must be we ourselves who make the links between a dream and our life situation. Dreams give a voice to our own inner wisdom. They bring true clarity and, I believe, are worthy of our respect and attention.

Sophie's story

Sophie had consciously been on her spiritual path for many years. She was becoming despondent and uncertain of where her life was heading. She began to judge herself harshly and berated herself for missed opportunities and making inappropriate choices. Sophie's therapist suggested she create a personal and colourful mandala of her life in a large open format. He explained the basic layout of a mandala and asked that she show the highs and lows, the twists and turns, the ups and downs and the ins and outs of her life. He suggested that nothing should be censored. Whatever came to mind should be included. Sophie, being well-established in her therapeutic journey, was able to fully engage with this project. She was willing to give it all the time that was needed and to let her heart lead the way.

Over a period of several weeks, through the mandala drawing, Sophie became conscious of the connection, the oneness, between her inner world and her outer world. A picture of her life-journey became visible by her own hand. She became aware of the connection between seemingly random events and experiences.

She found a deep love and respect for herself. Those issues on which she had judged herself, she now recognised as valuable parts of her journey, part of her experience, part of her learning, part of her evolving consciousness. The notion of Oneness within herself, and Oneness with all others, was no longer simply a wonderful idea. The actuality of the One Life had now become a more tangible reality in her consciousness. She came to understand, through her mandala, how various seemingly unimportant aspects of her life had actually been central to her life-journey.

Then she had her dream, a dream which brought further reassurance of the rightfulness of her journey!

Sophie's dream

Sophie is on a train full of happy people, all chattering and enjoying the journey. No one but Sophie seems to be in a hurry to get to their destination, nor do they seem to be conscious of the journey itself. As the train travels along, Sophie moves towards the front of the train. There are people everywhere ... sitting on the floor, doubling up on seats and sitting on tables. Although she has to pick her way around lots of people and through many carriages, Sophie knows the whole atmosphere is happy and jolly. People are having fun! Although she feels separate from the crowd surrounding her, she is enjoying the atmosphere.

Sophie then finds herself alone, no longer on the train. She is outdoors, walking confidently up a flight of extremely wide, steep stone steps. She is approaching the vast entrance to a beautiful cathedral. The magnificent doors are wide open. She is aware that she is expected and is welcome. Her appearance and clothing are highly significant. She is wearing a very sophisticated and fashionable black dress. Her hair is extremely elegant under a large black full-brimmed hat. She is wearing black stiletto court shoes and is carrying a small white leather-bound bible. She is the ultimate image of sophistication. She exudes maturity and a self-assured feminine energy. She is to be married. There are no other people present. She is united in Oneness with her Inner God. This is the symbolic union of God and human.

It was a phenomenal dream, full of meaning. The message was very clear. Sophie's spiritual journey had been fast, conscious and had brought her to a place of deep spiritual understanding. She had developed maturity and a sophisticated understanding of creative energy. She carried a white Bible as a symbol of the purity of her Divine message. She was now forever consciously united with her Divine Spirit. They 'stood as a single one'. Her marriage to the Invisible God within herself was for eternity.

Sophie understood the profound message. She felt its wisdom in her heart. In her life-expression, she had begun to consciously and joyfully express her true ultimate purpose on earth. She now knew deep within her heart that she was united with God and could fulfil any task that was asked of her. She knew she would always be guided, protected and filled with the Holy Spirit.

She stood as a single one.

Suggested reading

Campbell, J., *The Hero with a Thousand Faces* (2001).

CHAPTER 24

Become a person of light

> His disciples said, 'Show us the place where you are, because we need to look for it'.
> He said to them, 'Anyone who has ears to hear should hear! Light exists within a person of light, and they light up the whole world. If they don't shine, there's darkness'.

A person of light is, in my opinion, someone who has developed a state of consciousness in which human life and spiritual life are understood as One. They have come to understand that through the process of living we each grow towards the discovery of our Divine Centre. Whilst appreciating the opportunity that life offers, a person of light also accepts its transient impermanence. They know that earthly manifestations are largely shaped by one's own choosing, whether consciously or unconsciously. These temporal and self-created outer appearances are formed from the Divine Stuff of God, according to our expectations and beliefs. A person of light knows that each one of us sees ONLY what we expect to see. We are 'blind' to other realities. We do not realise the infinity of possibilities available to us.

A 'Person of Light' knows that every living form, even a seemingly inert pebble, is a tangible manifestation of an idea brought forth from

Infinite Presence. They recognise the Holiness of all life. This knowing, in my opinion, is the meaning of Enlightenment. Its supreme value rests in its ability to cast the Light of Truth upon every facet of life.

* * *

In seeking to awaken our Inner Light, we must begin with the person we are at this very moment. We must learn to look within our own being and discover who we are. We must come to know our personal desires, tendencies, assumptions, prejudices and perceptions. Most of us have a limited awareness of our thoughts, feelings and actions. They are largely habitual and unconscious, often imposed by the society in which we live. Until we know ourselves, we cannot eliminate that which is inauthentic. We are each like a flower bulb whose characteristics remain hidden until the bulb is planted and given the opportunity to grow and become visible.

The Divine command to 'Know thy self' must be honoured if we are to fulfil our Divine destiny.

* * *

The journey of self-discovery can seem difficult as we are forced to confront that which we may find unacceptable within ourselves.

A person of light has courageously chosen to shine the torch of awareness within and has come to know their frailties, inconsistencies, fears and judgements. Society, and often religious doctrine, has cast shame and judgements on many normal human thoughts, feelings and behaviours. This imposition can cause internal conflict, distracting humanity from the real purpose of life. We can spend a lifetime erecting barriers of shame around our inner self. This can leave the True, Permanent and Divine Self locked outside of consciousness.

* * *

As a more accurate and realistic self-awareness grows, personal thoughts and emotions are recognised as nothing more than superficial chatter, like ripples on the surface of a lake. The 'ripples' are real, they exist, but they exist only in a temporal and non-permanent way.

A person of light denies power to those ripples by allowing them to float on by, like puffs of cloud that come and go.

It is my opinion that our personal journey into self-awareness progresses through many lifetimes. Our soul gradually becomes translucent and responsive to the Divine impulse of God. As we take up our unique Christhood, we become a source of Infinite Wisdom, Everlasting Love and Generous Potency. We express the profound and permanent love of God which has always been available, always present, always true.

A person of light has experienced, and intellectually understood, these truths. Their life is guided by Divine Principle. Once we awaken to this truth we can do no other than 'To Thine Own Self Be True'. It becomes almost impossible to act in ways that are unhelpful to ourselves and all others involved.

Joan's story

Joan epitomised my notion of a kind, non-judgemental and fun-loving woman who recognised everyone as a Child of God. I knew her well, perhaps more deeply than most others. During her lifetime she had experienced her fair share of human tragedies and difficulties but I never once heard her complain or criticise another. She simply dealt with each day as it came, doing her best to live by her chosen principles of non-judgement and kindness. The sentiment she expressed, when asked about her degree of tolerance, was that perhaps we would all act like those we condemn if we had had their life experiences. She believed we cannot judge another until we have walked in that person's shoes.

She was, however, no saint. She did, indeed, feel anger and resentment, but she chose to refrain from spontaneously, and perhaps erroneously, acting on those feelings. She had the strength and confidence to hold her emotions within herself and inwardly process them at an appropriate time. There was no pretence about her, she was fully human. She did not turn a blind eye, nor a deaf ear to unacceptable behaviours, but she waited for inner guidance to direct her response. In all the 49 years I knew her, I never heard her raise her voice. She deliberately sought to come to terms with her inner world, no matter what was happening around and to her.

To me, Joan was a Person of Light. Simply by being her true self, she exemplified a life lived by Divine Principles. Her example was visible to those with the 'eyes to see'. She cast the Light of Truth upon everyone she met. There were no exceptions. In return, she was deeply loved and respected by those fortunate to have spent time with her. She left a profound and lasting mark on the world.

I was with her as her death drew close. She was ready to leave this world but she was still thinking of others. She knew I had long carried a damaging resentment towards her husband, who, I believed had treated her badly. She wanted me to be free of this harmful judgement. Without specifically mentioning the issue, she simply squeezed my hand and quietly said, 'Let it go, Christine. For me, it was all just another experience'.

She was authentic, deeply loving and interested in others, right to her last breath.

A true Person of Light leaves the world in better shape than when they arrived. A life lived as an example for others is perhaps the greatest gift to offer the world.

I feel very blessed that Joan was, in fact, my mother.

Suggested reading

Goldsmith, J.S., *A Parenthesis in Eternity* (1986).

CHAPTER 25

Claiming our other self

> Jesus said, 'Love your brother as your own soul. Protect them like the pupil of your eye'.

The term 'sibling' in the translation of this codex refers, in my opinion, to a hidden aspect of our being. This vital part resides largely unacknowledged in the darkness of our shadow. It contains all the unlived parts of ourselves which we have chosen, consciously or unconsciously, to reject. Some of these hidden parts are those we believe to be unacceptable, shameful, unconventional, or perhaps too problematic to own. Unacknowledged, they are capable of causing turbulence to our mental and physical health as they demand expression in our life. When these issues begin to make their presence felt, it is imperative that we make a deliberate choice to come to know and befriend them.

This can be a demanding challenge for each of us and is, I believe, more successful when undertaken with the help of an experienced therapist. In the western world particularly, attitudes are changing. Old, rigid ideals regarding etiquette, convention, and prescribed ways of thinking, feeling and being, are weakening. As a society, we are becoming more willing to accept difference and diversity. Traditional norms are fast becoming redundant. Consequently, people are taking the freedom to follow their inner desires and live according to their true self. As the collective shadow loosens its hold on fixed notions of sexuality, gender, race and lifestyle, people are less likely to live a life of pretence and feel more comfortable in their own skin.

This is a time for inner integration and cooperation as seemingly opposing aspects in our psyche find a mutual compromise. A skilful therapist is able to hold the necessary middle ground where assimilation of the two sides can gradually take place. This brings benefits to the whole personality. As a greater balance becomes established, better physical and mental health and a greater sense of fulfilment are only the beginning of the considerable advantages that come from this shift in consciousness.

In practical terms, our previously denied 'sibling' begins to take its full and equal place within the psyche. For example, a fiercely logical personality may discover a tolerance for intuition. A self-centred person may become more sensitive to the needs of others. A quick-witted and assertive character may gain the ability to be reflective. A quiet and withdrawn individual may find value and joy in sharing time with others.

As our soul grows into wholeness, it begins to blossom. It becomes translucent and receptive to the Divine Impulse. We then begin a new journey as a true and authentic Child of God.

Jesus states that we must protect our sibling 'like the pupil of the eye'. The English Dictionary defines the pupil as 'the opening through which light passes'.

This makes clear that when we value and include our 'sibling', the consequential wholeness of our Being allows the 'light of consciousness' to flow through us and into our life-expression.

Through the pupil of the physical eye, the light of the *outer* world passes and makes the external visible and known to us.

Through the pupil of the soul, the *inner* Divine world is revealed and becomes individually and uniquely realised.

Noah's story

Noah was approaching middle age when his successful life began to feel empty and pointless. In his own words, it felt 'soulless'. Nothing outward in his life had changed. The dissatisfaction was entirely within. For many years he had enjoyed lecturing in engineering. He, his wife and family had enjoyed the financial stability that came with his chosen career. His unrest was sudden and so out of character that he was urged by his doctor to take a sabbatical and seek professional therapeutic help. Fortunately, no tranquillisers were prescribed.

Within the therapeutic relationship, Noah was given the time, freedom and support to explore his difficult feelings. Within several weeks of regular therapy, it became clear to Noah that he was now living a lie. Something within him had changed. What had previously given him great satisfaction and purpose, now felt pointless. In addition, he realised he felt trapped by his own success and it seemed impossible to make changes—he believed the consequences to his family would be too great. The sense of entrapment was the major cause of his depression as his feelings of powerlessness rendered him incapable of exploring new possibilities.

Noah, however, was a courageous man and he made a decision to persist with the therapeutic process until he fully understood his predicament. He gave himself permission to take the time he needed to fully explore these inner promptings. Only then would he consider his future.

As unexpressed feelings of frustration, anger and sadness rose to the surface of consciousness, Noah was shocked not only by their presence but also by their intensity. In the safety of a therapeutic setting, these feelings were allowed expression. Their voice and their valuable contribution were given the time and space to be heard. Gradually, Noah was able to comprehend the significance of these previously unrecognised feelings. He began to see for himself that, whilst they had caused his depression, they were a vital gift of awareness from his 'sibling'. They were the product of his emerging 'hidden self' that, until now, had remained dormant. They brought the impetus and the inner guidance that would help Noah to make productive and valuable adjustments to his life.

After a period of time, Noah found renewed confidence and a deep sense of rightfulness in a decision to end his current working regime.

He decided to follow his life-long desire to fully explore his love of music. This had been a part-time but enduring hobby since his teenage years. Now, in middle age, he decided to fully immerse himself in the direction that his 'sibling' was leading. His previously suppressed yearning to compose, teach and perform music was guiding him towards his personal bliss and wholeness.

Through the therapeutic process, he found great compassion for the hidden aspect of himself that had patiently waited for Noah to listen to its message. He shed many tears as he came to know and deeply love his 'sibling'. As the 'oughts' and 'shoulds' of his former life diminished, he was able to speak openly and honestly to his wife. He was shocked to discover that she, unbeknown to him, had always known music should play a more significant role in his life. She was sufficiently adult in herself to have no pangs of anxiety about this new direction and fully embraced the next phase of their shared journey.

As Noah 'followed his bliss' a new joy descended upon him. Undoubtedly, there were many bumpy patches along the way of integration, but openness to following his true path brought a deepening sense of fulfilment.

With his energy restored, he also found a greater appreciation for his former life. He realised, with gratitude, that his old conscious self—i.e. his ego—had carried him well through his first 50 years. It had contributed much to his own life, his family's life and the lives of many students who had chosen to study engineering.

Noah and his wife began to share this new musical life together. Not only was Noah's life enhanced by his courageous step, his wife also greatly benefitted. Noah had grown into a more wholesome and complete individual. He was on the road to expressing the unique beauty of his soul.

Suggested reading

de Mello, A., *Sadhana: A Way to God* (1984).

CHAPTER 26

Judgements

> Jesus said, 'You see the speck that's in your brother's eye, but you don't see the beam in your own eye. When you get the beam out of your own eye, then you'll be able to see clearly to get the speck out of your brother's eye'.

My interpretation of this codex is that it is about judging others. When we judge other people, we often expose issues that actually reside in ourselves; believing them to be unacceptable, we project them onto others. By unconsciously denying ownership of these perceived flaws, we endeavour to feel better about ourselves. We deflect self-judgement in the hope of avoiding the pain of criticism. We do not, however, escape the critique of our inner sensor, which knows the truth of our being! This adds further internal discomfort as we try to justify our judgements. It is in our best interests to face, and come to terms with, those parts of ourselves that we believe are unacceptable.

In a reverse way, this also applies to those whom we idolise and idealise. We often project qualities and talents onto others that, perhaps for lack of courage, we have refused to own and express in our own life. Being in awe of someone and attributing guru status to anyone can be a precarious venture. Greatly valuing another whilst denying our own worth can become unhealthy hero worship.

Therapeutically understood, projection can be a valuable tool in self-understanding. It winkles out those hidden and troublesome parts of ourselves which can cause great distress to our psyche. This is best used in the realm of professional therapy as we try to resolve those issues.

* * *

Jesus states that we must remove the beam from our own eye before we can comment on the speck in someone else's eye. He shows that our own flaws may be huge in comparison to another's blemish and, in fact, so obtrusive to our spiritual vision that we cannot see the truth of the one we judge. Only when we have owned our own flaws and issues may we be in a better position to help others.

Naomi's story

Naomi had grown up in a family which demanded that she and her two siblings, Peter and Felicity, live by strong and unrealistic Christian values. In their small remote community, their parents were idealised as good God-fearing Christians. This 'badge of honour', which they wore with considerable pride, hid their internalised sense of inadequacy and inferiority. They projected their need for validation onto their three children and demanded that their strict standards were adhered to. To ease the burden of their unacknowledged flaws they also projected the 'sinful' parts of themselves onto other 'flawed' parishioners. No one escaped their judgement.

The three children found their mother terrifying in her criticism, and their father remote and withdrawn. Unsurprisingly, Felicity and Peter grew up to be timid and compliant with all authority figures. However, within their small church community, Felicity found her power in adulthood and expressed it with the same ferocity as her mother. Peter never found a productive and happy path through life and became a recluse, living a frugal and lonely existence hidden away in the Welsh hills.

However, Naomi—the second daughter—had retained some degree of spirit within herself. She chose to study for a nursing degree. This was deemed a 'worthy' occupation by her parents and they reluctantly accepted that her training required her to move from home. She found the changes both terrifying and exciting. Sadly, and unsurprisingly, Naomi found it almost impossible to integrate with the other students. She was living out her parents' true emotional state of an inferiority which must be hidden at all times. This created an invisible barrier between herself and the other students.

Naomi's path began to change when psychology was added to the curriculum. She learnt quickly and began to better understand herself. Although this new knowledge was often difficult to bear, painful to accept and extremely challenging, she stayed the course. Great insight came to her with the realisation that her upbringing had taught her to focus only on the 'bad' in herself and others. Her eyes slowly opened to the damage this had inflicted on her younger self. As justifiable anger rose to the surface, Naomi's sense of impotence began to ease and the parental shackles loosened.

The solace, love and support she needed at this difficult time came in the form of a young man, also studying for a nursing degree. As attraction and eventually love drew them together, they were able to share their newly discovered understanding and help each other to break down some of the lies and hurts that had greatly restricted both their young lives.

Gradually, Naomi realised she no longer needed to follow her family's ideals. She could and would, choose her own. This was a great dawning for her. It was, however, only the beginning of a long road to freedom from many past humiliations and limitations.

In my opinion, parents carry a great responsibility for the future outcome of their children. The onus to encourage, treasure and support a child as they develop into their true self cannot be overestimated.

Suggested reading

Bradshaw, J., *Homecoming—Reclaiming & Championing Your Inner Child* (1991).

CHAPTER 27

Understanding the Sabbath

> 'If you don't fast from the world, you won't find the kingdom. If you don't make the Sabbath into a Sabbath, you won't see the Father'.

My interpretation of this codex is that we must seek to understand the Sabbath.

The creed of many religions states that the Sabbath is one particular day of the week when work ceases and attention is placed entirely on God. This traditional practice would seem to deny that the presence of God is within every living creature, each and every moment. In my opinion, it encourages the notion that God and human are separate.

Nowadays, people of various faiths are coming to know and experience Divine Presence as a hidden aspect of all beings. This more holistic awareness of Divine Energy, therefore, no longer limits our acknowledgement of Presence to one day of the week. When we understand that God is life itself, the daily experience of this truth is something we can strive for.

Contemplation and meditation are, I believe, methods of 'fasting' from the world. A conscious personal relationship with our inner God is our most precious possession and requires regular meditation to still the busy mind and calm the emotions. Contemplation, the act of pondering, develops discernment and understanding of Truth.

Jesus asked that we develop the spiritual habit of looking beyond outer appearances to the Divine Presence that is at the centre of all life. When we adjust our outdated perception of God and 'look behind' the external lifeforms, we will come to know every moment as a 'Sabbath' moment; every day is a 'Sabbath' day. Each day is yet another opportunity to practise the acknowledgement of Divine Presence.

We ourselves *are* the Presence of God. Even when we have no awareness of this Truth, it is still impossible for us to be separate from God! Sadly, though, we can act as if we *are* separate.

My story

Some time ago I attended a silent retreat at a Christian monastery in the south of England. This new venture had been instigated by the Abbot as a response to the emptiness he sensed in ordinary people with their lives. I felt fortunate to join the 20 people, most of whom were practising Catholics. A few, like myself, were seeking God through any means.

We were housed in an adjoining wing to the main buildings. A small number of monks took care of our needs. We were well-fed. We shared their religious services. We could roam the well-tended gardens and the chapel. We had access to the well-stocked library with its surprisingly large coverage of alternative religions. The silence was broken only with a short daily talk in which time for questions and answers was included. The whole week was an outstanding experience. The moment-by-moment reverence that was possible in such a place left a lasting impression of the perpetual presence of God within all life.

One daily talk in particular, however, stayed with me. An elderly monk told a simple but beautiful story about mothers and their hidden antennae which are attuned to the welfare of their child. He cleverly illustrated how a busy mother whilst out shopping, instinctively knows the whereabouts and well-being of her young child. Consciously, the mother is focused on her shopping. At a deeper level, she retains a powerful and protective link to her child. An inbuilt relationship of trust has been established, which serves the child well. The monk wished to explain that this special mother-and-child bond is a great example of how we need to experience our inner God. As the mother never loses 'contact' with the child, so we must endeavour to never lose the awareness of the perpetual inner Divine Presence.

Many world beliefs try to tell us otherwise and draw us into negation. Our task is to hold firm when doubts try to suggest otherwise. We can choose to ignore Divine Providence and Love—but we cannot be separated from them.

Suggested reading

Merton, T., *New Seeds of Contemplation* (1961).

CHAPTER 28

The journey of humanity

Jesus said, 'I stood in the middle of the world and appeared to them in the flesh. I found them all drunk; I didn't find any of them thirsty. My soul ached for the children of humanity, because they were blind in their hearts and couldn't see. They came into the world empty and plan on leaving the world empty. Meanwhile, they're drunk. When they shake off their wine, then they'll change'.

My interpretation of this codex is that Jesus seems to be in despair at the shallowness of human consciousness. He sees that people are intoxicated and seduced by worldly appetites and pleasures. Their attention is placed solely on their own needs and passions. They have been 'captured' by greed, self-aggrandisement and hedonistic tendencies. He sees people at all levels of society who live cruel, egocentric and arrogant lives with no thought for others. They have no 'thirst' for compassion, love and Truth. They have no desire for God.

Living such a life ensures they will depart this earthly plane having gained little of true value. When they awake to their shallowness, they will be full of sorrow. This awakening, I believe, may take many lifetimes.

* * *

Unfortunately, people frequently repeat harmful behavioural patterns which they have learnt from others and their environment. They spend their life perpetuating the same lack of care which they themselves have experienced. Such a cycle is difficult to break. In addition, retribution and revenge are still seen as justifiable outcomes for many people.

In this codex Jesus refers to humanity being drunk on indifference, people's hearts blind to love, their empathy non-existent. He sees that people allow themselves to be drawn into a soporific state where higher ideals are simply ignored.

However, this is not always the case. Some people turn away from the hurt of past experiences. They choose to refrain from repeating the hurts they have experienced, never inflicting the same treatment on another. Life has shown them how distressing bad experiences can feel.

They have gained empathy, perhaps for eternity. They have 'shaken off their wine' and woken up to the permanence, love and care of Divine Presence. They have learnt to 'do unto others as you would have them do unto you'.

A story of empathy

To be empathic is to understand how another person feels. When we metaphorically 'stand in their shoes', we feel their feelings and we understand their hurts. When we have a strong sense of empathy, we can do no harm to others. We may even feel remorse for any hurt we may have previously caused.

A new initiative within the justice system is gaining momentum to bring about a change in the way victims of crime and their offenders are treated. There is a recognition that victims are frequently left deeply traumatised by their experience, finding it difficult to move on, even when the offender has been apprehended and is serving their sentence. Inner resolution can be difficult for many victims to achieve.

The offender also can remain stuck in the behavioural patterns that caused the initial offence. Statistics show that little good comes from traditional custodial sentences; repeat offending is a common occurrence. In the last 20 years, there has been a growing awareness that we need a new system, something that will heal not only the victim, but also the offender. This new initiative is called Restorative Justice.

The efficacy of Restorative Justice, in some cases, is becoming accepted by a growing number of countries. The UK, Ireland, some

European countries and certain North American States are among those gradually introducing this as an alternative and very different way of lowering crime. In 2007 the United Nations produced a handbook containing guidelines for those countries wishing to include Restorative Justice within the options of their own justice system.

Although in the UK this method is slowly gaining momentum, at the present time (2022) it is considered suitable only in a very small number of cases which fall within strict criteria.

The purpose of Restorative Justice is to bring the victim and the offender to a place of mutual empathy through meetings and dialogue. Both parties must *freely* choose to take this path and the offender must have first acknowledged their guilt. It should not be underestimated the high degree of courage this requires from *both* parties.

Such a meeting takes place under very stringent conditions with two or more trained facilitators in attendance. If both parties are willing, a series of meetings *may* develop.

Victims often seek answers about why the offence has happened to them ... the 'why me?' question is common. Such a meeting gives the victim an opportunity to try to make sense of something that often seems senseless, random and deeply traumatising.

This process also offers the offender an opportunity to understand how the victim felt, and to learn about the consequences of their actions. I repeat: this takes a great deal of courage from both parties.

In time, with professional support, a degree of mutual empathy may develop. Statistics show that this often marks the beginning of a permanent healing for both victim and offender.

Various reliable sources have collated statistics which prove the efficacy of this method in some cases, *although not all*. Thankfully, society is slowly moving away from the old methods of retribution towards healing and reconciliation. When we have empathy for 'the other', we feel less aggrieved and more able to move on, whether we are victim or offender.

Changing criminals changes crime levels.
Healing victims heals lives.

To further explore the subject of extreme human behaviours, I recommend a very special book: *The Choice* by Dr Edith Eger (see below). Edie teaches from her own personal and harrowing experience in Auschwitz. Although Edie's story is extreme and very disturbing, she eloquently conveys her message that all experiences have much to teach each one of us. I will not explain more. Edie can speak far better for herself than I can. Her story, I believe, can help us all to find freedom from emotional trauma, no matter how bad those experiences have been. Understanding can release us from the trap imposed by deep hurts, anger and hatred.

Suggested readings

Eger, E.E., *The Choice* (2017).

For reliable information on Restorative Justice: www.restorativejustice.org.uk; and *The United Nations Handbook on Restorative Justice Programmes*.

CHAPTER 29

The wonderment and opulence of spirit

Jesus said, 'If the flesh came into existence because of spirit, that's amazing. If spirit came into existence because of the body, that's really amazing. But I'm amazed at how [such] great wealth has been placed in this poverty'.

In this codex, Jesus marvels at the power of spirit to manifest bodily flesh.

Equally, he marvels at the reciprocal arrangement whereby corporeal flesh offers the means of rendering spirit visible, tangible and knowable to those who seek God in all forms.

- The body provides hearing; the beauty of bird song; the joy of music, communication.
- The body offers a visible knowing of colour, beauty of form, height, depth.
- The body gives us discernment of taste and smell.
- The body allows for the joy, love and warmth of physical contact.

Mickey and Danny's story

Mickey was a self-employed potter, well-known and respected in his local area. He sold his distinctive artwork at trade fairs, summer fêtes and some specialised homeware/gift shops.

Due to family difficulties in the past, Mickey had become the sole carer of his 8-year-old son, Danny. Although he sometimes found this situation difficult, he was a very caring and adept father. They had a sound and honest relationship and Danny thrived.

Problems started when Mickey became unwell. An infection was attacking his body and his health quickly deteriorated. The medical profession tried everything at their disposal to help Mickey. Nothing worked, and his body began to fail and shut down.

A decision was made to try a new and untested drug. This was not without risk but the medical team felt there was nothing to lose—they had no other alternative.

It was deeply saddening for all concerned when this final option not only failed but seemed to exacerbate Mickey's condition. They were to discover, at a later date, that Mickey was allergic to this new drug and that it had, in fact, speeded up the decline of his organs. There was no blame. Everyone had done their very best with the information and medications available at that time.

During this difficult time, Danny had lived at the home of his best friend, Sam. There, he felt safe but he deeply missed his father. Now, with no life expectancy for Mickey, Danny was in an extremely vulnerable situation.

Mickey's story

Mickey knew he was very ill. He had been hospitalised for several weeks and was aware he was not improving. He was very worried about his beloved son. Although he knew and trusted the family that had taken on Danny's care, he was concerned about their ability to shoulder this extra burden for much longer. However, as there were no other responsible family members available, it was a very worrying situation.

* * *

Mickey slipped into a coma. He would later recount hearing someone say it was time to bring in the relatives and that the life-support machines were to be switched off. Simultaneously, Mickey described experiencing the deepest and most profound sense of love. He remembers feeling/thinking it would be so easy to let himself float away into this all-embracing love. But Danny's well-being was still paramount in his mind. He knew if he let himself go completely into this other realm, there was no one to take care of Danny permanently. There was no one who would love Danny as Mickey had always done.

He decided that he *must*, in Mickey's own words, 'get back' into his body. He must make the medical staff realise he wanted to live. He willed with all his might to make some movement. He willed and he willed and he willed. Incredibly, and astonishingly, a young nurse noticed a tiny flicker in Mickey's little finger! This surely was what we could call a miracle. From that moment on, Mickey began to slowly improve.

As a result of experiencing such intense love for Danny, Mickey had awakened to the perpetual experience of Divine Love which supports each and every one of us. Miracles DO exist within Divine Presence. We each experience them time and again but, sadly, they go unnoticed—we all lack awareness of the miracles, big and small, that occur each day in all our lives.

Mickey's healing began. In the acknowledged Presence of God, there is no sickness. Over many months Mickey slowly recovered most of his faculties, with the exception of his right hand. Although this compromised his ability to create his large signature pots, he discovered he had the aptitude for teaching pottery. Being well-known in his locality, he quickly gained a regular following of students. His new career not only paid the household bills, it also gave Mickey a new source of satisfaction. He discovered he truly enjoyed teaching and passing on his skills.

As for Danny, experiencing such selfless and devoted love from his father, he continued to thrive.

When called upon with trustful expectation, the permanent and active Divine Presence furnishes our every need.

Our part is to *know* with trusting expectation; to refrain from doubt; to acknowledge the permanence of Divine Love.

* * *

Spirit manifests the tangible form that we know and observe with our five senses. What we experience as solid matter is shaped by Divine Essence, mainly according to our will and expectations. Far greater possibilities are open to us all than we realise. Mickey proved that he, and he alone, largely controlled his body. He had the power to choose recovery and life. He had experienced one of the most profound spiritual truths available to each of us in this earthly existence.

We need to understand that in normal daily life we exist in a hypnotic state where we believe we are a victim of our own body and our circumstances. We are ignorant of the fact that we are the master of our life. Mickey, through absolute necessity, discovered his mastery. He found a reason to live: something—*someone*—that mattered more to him than himself. This is real love. Mickey chose, out of love for his son, to let heaven wait for another time.

Not one of us is without some form of impairment. We can choose, however, to overcome perceived negative circumstances which may be physical, emotional or intellectual. We may not find the power to transform our physical body as Mickey did, but we can all choose never to be a victim of our own consciousness.

Overcoming difficulties begins with our attitude. As a society we are quick to complain, to blame, to feel indignation, to demand compensation. Many seem to 'enjoy' the victim position. It would be more productive and helpful to ourselves, our families and our community, if we were to develop an attitude of thankfulness for what we DO have, rather than complaining about what we believe we lack.

We can do this by:

- *Choosing* to appreciate those with whom we share our life, instead of focusing on what is difficult for us.
- *Choosing* to value the circumstances of our life and looking for what goes well rather than focusing on what is problematic.
- *Choosing* to be aware of, and remember, the special gifts that life regularly brings our way.
- *Choosing* to be thankful for life itself.

It is within our power to become someone who appreciates value and expresses gratitude. Mickey's story can be our story. Having lived through the darkest of circumstances, he chose to value the resulting situation and, indeed, the experience itself. We each have the ability to do the same. Which will you choose?

Suggested readings

Alexander, E., *Proof of Heaven* (2012).
Eger, E.E., *The Choice* (2017).

CHAPTER 30

Understanding oneness

Jesus said, 'Where there are three deities, they're divine. Where there are two or one, I'm with them'.

Please note

There has been some ambiguity surrounding this saying, which has led to a reconstruction of the original translation and a referral to the Greek *Gospel of Thomas*. I have, therefore, worked with the reconstruction.

* * *

In this codex, Jesus states that when we believe in individual and separate lives, we do not experience God. We have failed to understand the true meaning of the One Divine Life. There is, in truth, only one Life Force which enlivens every form of existence in the entire universe. Each seemingly individual life is intended to express its own unique aspect of that One Life.

Our body is an example. It would seem to consist of many distinct parts: cells, blood, organs, bones, tissue, skin, hair etc. If we were to cut the body into its individual components, no life force could exist outside of that collective body. Each part must function according to its Divine 'blueprint'. It cannot be anything other than what it is. A heart can only be a heart, an eye can only be an eye. Each seemingly separate component has a vital and unique part to play within the whole.

Using this metaphor, we can understand that each person can only be that which God intends them to be, and for that we each must resolutely seek. It is unproductive to compare oneself with others. To be at our most fulfilled, and at our happiest, we must fully be who we are divinely intended to be. When we value our uniqueness, we will value all people.

When each part of our life/body/character is fulfilling its unique and rightful task, the fullness of Divine Oneness can flow. This is the place of heaven, where each part lovingly cooperates within the Whole.

* * *

Science has brought us extraordinary knowledge of the awesome world in which we live. It has taught us about inherent natural selection processes and the necessary evolution of diverse lifeforms. Due to scientific exploration, we have come to value how awesome our universe is and our place within it.

However, science can only observe what is observable. It cannot locate, nor explain, the intelligence that lies at the very heart of all life. Science shows us the *product* of invisible, infinite wisdom, it cannot inform us of it. We can only come to that knowledge through an inner personal experience. Meditation and contemplation prepare the way for the opening to everlasting knowledge of Ultimate Oneness.

Divine Presence is, and always has been, constant and unvarying. It is known to us by the faculty of soul. For this ability, we must strive with desire and commitment. When there is an understanding of the Oneness of life, *there* is God.

Ivana's story

Ivana lived on the outskirts of Dubrovnik, the coastal city of Croatia. When war broke out in Eastern Europe in the early 1990s, she found herself with two young children in the middle of a war zone. Bombing raids were destroying the infrastructure of modern life and they feared for their survival. She, together with neighbours and several strangers, decided to find temporary shelter within the walled city of Dubrovnik, a UNESCO Heritage Site protected by United Nation conventions. As such, they believed they would never be bombed whilst they lived there. Their trust in the enemies' scruples was sadly misguided, but that's a different tale.

Surprisingly, Ivana's story centres on the preciousness of her experiences through those terrifying times. Although resources were extremely limited, she tells of the enormous generosity and kindness that developed between those incarcerated within the city walls, most of whom had previously been strangers to each other.

Unbelievably, as Ivana tells her story, she laughs, full of joyful memories. She recounts tales of small groups who ventured outside the city walls, always in the dead of night, to scavenge for food and water. These men had no concern for their own safety. Capture or death were very real possibilities. Everything they foraged was shared. All worked together, caring for each other. They became *One* united community that flourished on cooperation, mutual support, kindness and a shared will to survive.

I only recently heard Ivana's story, told many years after the event. Her sense of having experienced something quite extraordinary in that disparate community is still strong and certainly, for her, quite sacred. She speaks with great warmth about every member of that 'cobbled together' community. For her, it has always been, and still is, one of the most precious times of her life. Their choice to support one another, no matter who they were, meant that everyone survived.

Ivana summed up the experience in her own words with the following: 'It was like we were *one human being*—we were not separate people'.

How would life on earth be, if we could each live by that glorious sense of *One* spirit, ONE human being, every moment of our life? We must begin with our self. We can make the choice to treat all others in the same manner that spontaneously evolved within the Dubrovnik community. They have much to teach the world about love and Oneness.

Suggested reading

Goldsmith, J.S., *God, The Substance of all Form* (1959).

CHAPTER 31

Look deeper

> Jesus said, 'No prophet is welcome in their own village. No doctor heals those who know them'.

This codex cautions against the human tendency to dismiss the most precious part of every person. We are each like an iceberg, which has approximately 90% of its mass hidden beneath the surface. The most precious and awesome part of humanity is hidden, 'visible' *only* to those who have an awareness of the Divine Self.

People with whom we share our life are often those who are most likely to dismiss our hidden treasure. Such limited appreciation can further imprison our truest and most precious self.

Jesus uses the analogy of a doctor/patient relationship to illustrate this important lesson. He states that a patient will have little confidence in the skill of a practitioner if they have previously related entirely on a personal level. A doctor, when experienced as an ordinary, fallible and inconsistent human being, will find it difficult to gain the trust and cooperation of a patient.

This lack of insight also applies, Jesus states, to prophets and those with esoteric knowledge. If we have previously known a person solely by their humanness, we are unlikely to trust their words of wisdom, even if they are, in reality, an enlightened Grand Master! We miss many blessings when we dismiss others as inconsequential and choose to ignore the possibility of something greater hidden within them.

We must remember that every person is the Divine Self having a human experience. When we really *know* that fact, we invite the very best from each person and become open to the possibility of Divine intervention for the good of all involved.

My own true story of the day I discovered the real, yet hidden, Anna

I had been using a local hairdressing salon for a number of years. It was well run by two young women, Anna and Suzie. Their warm approach to customers ensured their salon flourished.

Anna was my personal hairdresser and on the days she worked alone the salon atmosphere was calm and peaceful. Suzie, however, consistently exuded high energy, which gradually became difficult and unsettling for me. I tried to avoid the days she was at the salon but it seemed fate conspired against me. She was always present, whichever day I chose.

Over a period of several months, I began to realise Divine Intervention was forcing me to confront this issue *within myself*. The problem was mine and I was being offered opportunity after opportunity to overcome my judgement. It also occurred to me that my expectation that Suzie would irritate me, would, in fact, ensure she did just that! This clearly was all of my own making.

However, changing myself on a deep level was proving difficult. I tried every 'technique' that had previously helped with personal issues. I meditated; I asked for guidance and for cleansing; I 'tapped' to release my emotional trauma. Nothing worked. I knew, however, that this was a Divine opportunity I could not avoid. But I had no idea how to make these necessary changes within myself.

I continued to meditate, asking for help and guidance and endeavoured to trust that, somehow, my intolerance would be healed. If I avoided the issue, I knew this lesson would keep presenting itself in various forms until I resolved *my* problem.

* * *

On one particular occasion Suzie was in 'full flight', the noise and energy level extremely high. That day, however, I noticed a change in *myself*. I felt more tolerant and accepting.

Anna, in the midst of all the noise, gently started talking to me about a television programme she had recently seen. It was about a Canadian guy living in a remote part of Thailand. He had been a Buddhist monk for some 20 years, living alone and devoting his life to meditation and helping the impoverished villagers who lived nearby. His story had deeply touched Anna and she needed to talk about her experience.

Fortunately, I also had seen the programme and felt quite moved by Anna's response. We had never spoken of anything spiritual in all the years I had known her. She talked at great length about how she wanted to learn to meditate and find the peace that radiated from the monk.

For what seemed like hours we spoke quietly and openly about how she might follow this awakened yearning. Together, Anna and I experienced something out of body and out of time. We were in a different 'space'. It felt as if we were sitting with the monk, completely unaware of the noise and the energy that was around us. As I left the salon, Anna, for the first time ever, put her arms around me and held on tight. It was a very special moment, full of love and shared understanding.

The sense of Divine Intervention, for both Anna and myself, still fills me with love and gratitude. Clearly, there was much more to the Divine plan than I had realised. Needless to say, Suzie no longer troubles me!

When we choose to look, we will notice that lessons are always coming our way, each with the aim of helping our own, and possibly others', spiritual growth.

Suggested reading

Pradervand, P., *The Simple Art of Blessing* (2005).

CHAPTER 32

Seek the highest awareness within yourself

Jesus said, 'A city built and fortified on a high mountain can't fall, nor can it be hidden'.

In the original text, this codex uses the image of a city to illustrate the many facets of personality we each carry within our psyche. We are a mixture of many character traits. Some are opposing and some cooperating, some inherited, some copied; and some our natural way of being. Many of our responses in life will be habitual, without any purposeful choosing. This can result in repetitive errors of judgement and lead to unintended consequences.

My interpretation of this codex is that we must choose to develop awareness of our hidden personality traits. We are then more able to correct unhelpful beliefs and expectations.

As we grow to know ourselves in a deeper and more truthful way, we become more present to Divine inner promptings which will always guide us to act in authentic ways.

Jesus also stated that our personal 'city' should be built on high ground. In my opinion, this means we should base our life on high, strong principles. We must select a code of living founded on truth, non-judgement, compassion, cooperation and, most of all, love. Our intention must be to live a productive life, not solely for our own personal benefit, but also to contribute the best of ourselves to family, community and perhaps beyond. We must endeavour to live by our highest intentions and build our life 'upon a high hill'.

The parable also states that such a life needs fortification and protection. I believe we are always protected by higher invisible powers and that their presence needs to be acknowledged. These forces may be known as guardian angels who bring perpetual benevolence to all. It is we, ourselves, who must choose to invite the higher forces into our life to guide and protect.

'Ask and it shall be given'.

Finally, the parable states that such a life cannot be hidden from the outside. It needs to be a living example to others, without taking either pride or credit. No person is better than another, we are all on a journey towards our Divine Destiny.

Our lives, I believe, are lived not solely for our own benefit and development, but also for the shared development of the human race. We are all equal and valued parts of the Divine Story. We are asked to use the unique talents we have been given in the best way we know how, for the benefit of all.

Tilly's story

Tilly's early life-journey had not been an easy one. In the absence of a responsible adult, and being the oldest of six children, it had fallen to her to care for her siblings. Money was constantly difficult, food scarce, and evictions for non-payment of rent a regular threat.

Tilly grew into her parenting role out of necessity rather than a conscious choosing. She never questioned the hardship of her family's life. She simply did the best she could. This developed within her an inflated sense of responsibility, a commanding and uncompromising manner and a reluctance to trust anyone.

In adulthood, these traits seemed to serve her well when she gained employment within a large retail company. She gradually worked her way up the corporate ladder and, at the age of 39, she was promoted to a significant leadership position.

However, within two years she and her world began to unravel. Like a rumbling volcano, something within her was demanding to be released. She became intolerant of misdemeanours and unyielding to the mistakes of others. She had become a tyrant and a bully. The accumulated and hidden resentments from her childhood began to erupt in frequent displays of vicious anger. She was unwittingly acting in ways quite inappropriate to her position within the company.

Thankfully, Tilly was put on extended sick leave and advised to seek therapeutic help. Within six months of weekly therapeutic sessions, Tilly grew to understand herself. She realised that in her early life, family circumstances had required her to develop firm ways of coping. Whilst these had protected her young siblings, they were now totally inappropriate in an adult workplace.

Self-awareness, followed by self-understanding and finally self-forgiveness, led Tilly towards a new life that awaited her. During her months of therapy, she had attended Mindfulness classes as a way of taking better control of her emotions. Within a year Tilly had learnt to use her undoubted qualities in better, more productive ways.

She never returned to her former employment but trained as a psychotherapist. Her purpose was to help other women who constantly battled depression, anxiety and lack of self-worth. Within three years Tilly had set up a drop-in centre to provide sanctuary for vulnerable adult women. With better self-understanding and a developing compassion, she chose to put her considerable talents to more productive use.

Tilly's abilities, her strength of character and her organisational skills were no longer misused, but were expressed in the service of others. Her qualities were no longer 'hidden' and distorted by emotional baggage. They were openly and compassionately on display. She had become a living example to other women.

She had built a new life on 'high' principles. It was 'fortified' by truthful notions of self-awareness and self-acceptance. She learnt to be 'visible', sharing with others her hard-won principles of a responsible and productive life.

Suggested reading

Coelho, P., *The Supreme Gift* (2013; adapted from *The Greatest Thing in the World* by Henry Drummond).

CHAPTER 33

Let your life be a living example

Jesus said, 'What you hear with one ear, listen to with both, then proclaim from your rooftops. No one lights a lamp and puts it under a basket or in a hidden place. Rather, they put it on the stand so that everyone who comes and goes can see its light'.

Throughout history, there have been people from all traditions and walks of life who have chosen to express their highest principles and to share their truths with the larger world. We benefit from those who have revealed the highs and lows of their life-journey and have shared the many challenges that have arisen in their pursuit of a personal spirituality. Many have 'lit their lamp of awareness' and placed it for all to see and know.

Choosing to follow our Divine Path brings experiences that may greatly test us. Many provide opportunities to strengthen us. I believe it is intended that when we eventually leave this human scene, we will have deepened our personal connection to the inner Divine. We will also have shared our love, our insights and awareness with those who also seek, never imposing, but ready to share when asked. We are never depleted by giving. We are enriched by it.

'To proclaim from the rooftops', as mentioned in the translation of this codex, merely asks that we openly live our truth and be an example of the spiritual life. Authors, teachers and ordinary folk who choose to share the spiritual harvest of their lives, bring benefit to others who also seek. We are asked to refrain from hiding our light and to share the truth of our journey. Our 'Light of Truth' may light the way for others who also seek.

I have benefitted greatly from many of those inspirational characters who have shared their spiritual journey. To those, I owe a deep gratitude.

Thomas Merton

My chosen inspirational person is Thomas Merton. He became a Trappist monk in the 1940s, living within the community at the Abbey of Gethsemani, in Kentucky, US. The courage he exhibited in speaking his, sometimes controversial, truth about religion and the spiritual life has touched me greatly.

In the 1960s he spoke about the need for Western religions to seek cooperation and understanding with eastern traditions. It is my opinion that he encouraged the development of an interfaith movement to create dialogue and a mutual sharing between both western and eastern traditions. I believe Merton hoped that conversation would illustrate the notion, 'That which we share is much greater than that which divides us'.

In my personal journey, the freedom to explore Buddhism, Daoism and Hinduism has brought a deeper understanding of my personal 'version' of the Christian faith. It has enhanced my comprehension and I believe I am now more able to see tenets of spiritual beliefs from different approaches. This has enriched me with a more wholesome understanding and deepened my respect for other faiths.

Not all followers of faith have embraced this more liberal approach. There is still a long way to go as many traditionalists fear greater inclusivity. However, I believe that a literal and dogmatic approach to religion/spirituality is contrary to Truth. Flexibility need not be feared. Instead, it can deepen and enhance the sharing of spiritual values, encouraging tolerance and compassion.

It is my opinion that Thomas Merton acted from his Inner Voice, despite its often-controversial nature. He endeavoured to live by the highest principles of truth and he was not afraid to share those beliefs with the world.

By reading Merton's work, the courage and permission to fully be myself as I travelled my spiritual path, slowly grew. I learnt to give myself permission to travel the many and varied paths where my heart led.

Merton did not hide his Truth. His willingness to 'proclaim' what some in his faith may have found unacceptable, gave many of us permission to follow where our Inner Guide led.

This played a valuable role for me as I found the courage to write my interpretation of the *Gospel of Thomas*.

Suggested reading

Merton, T., *No Man is an Island* (1995).

CHAPTER 34

Choose your teacher with discernment

> Jesus said, 'If someone who's blind leads someone else who's blind, both of them fall into a pit'.

This saying draws attention to the dangers of following a self-proclaimed teacher whose spiritual awareness is limited only to their human understanding.

To teach others, I believe we must be guided by the inner Divine Presence which always brings fresh, personal and direct experience of God.

Many people have fleeting experiences of Divine Energy, which can be sudden, spontaneous and deeply moving. These 'cloud nine' experiences can be personally helpful and inspiring, but are no indicator of an ability to teach others. In my experience, they are a product of the early stages of our spiritual journey. When these brief spiritual moments mingle with our unresolved personal dramas, the experience may not be clean, clear and authentic. I believe that, although encouraging, this type of experience shows how far we still have to go in our journey.

Our life's expression is intended to be an outpouring of our Divine Nature. However, to enable this, we first must cleanse our human psyche of the many unhelpful experiences, thoughts and feelings that would distort Truth. In my opinion, it is only when we have discarded much of our personal 'baggage' that we can truly be the empty vessel capable of receiving the pure word of God. I believe authentic teaching is fresh, new, in the moment and without emotion. When Truth flows spontaneously from Soul, it is appropriate and a gift to all those present.

The world is full of books, classes and workshops that offer spiritual insights and guidance. Although many are helpful stepping stones, they are often the regurgitation of another's past experiences and perceptions. These may have been valid at the time of the original event, but empty of Presence in the retelling. A true teacher allows their soul, in the present moment, to be the mouthpiece of God. Such outpouring will be appropriate to those receiving. This form of authentic teaching can 'move mountains'. It circumvents the critical mind and seems to implant Truth within those able to receive it.

Only when we have found clarity within our own consciousness will we be led to teach others. This is a privilege that comes of its own volition. It will never be of our own choosing.

I believe that in Codex 34 Jesus wishes to alert us to the many who will claim to be a 'messenger of God'. Listen to your heart. It will always draw you and your authentic teacher together.

Addendum

Although my most spiritually significant moments have come whilst in the presence of an authentic teacher, I have also gained great benefit from many books written by people who have simply shared their spiritual experiences. They make no claim to teach or to lead, but simply express a desire to tell their story. To those people, I am grateful—very grateful! They have been precious companions along the way.

My story

In my 40s I left my safe and comfortable suburban life to find something deeper within myself. At the time this seemed an irrational and risky decision. However, my spiritual journey was my priority and I truly believed God was asking that I trust the 'unknown road' ahead and that I exchange false security for true faith.

For the first two years, I experienced many ups and downs but I rarely lost the conviction that I was safely held in the loving Divine

Embrace. At times, it was a lonely path. At times, I felt very vulnerable. At times, I experienced great loneliness.

I am sad to say that a man, who believed *himself* to be a teacher of Divine Truth, came into my life. In my vulnerability, I experienced him as eloquent, powerful and sincere. For two years I fell under his undoubted charm, believing I needed him to guide me along my Divine Path.

I need go no further with a description of this destructive and upsetting episode. Thankfully, Divine Presence gradually opened my spiritual eyes and showed me the unpalatable truth of this relationship. It was painful and humiliating to admit to myself that I was being used in a most subtle, unloving, uncaring and unspiritual manner.

With hindsight, I see this was a lesson I had needed to learn. At the time, in my vulnerability, I was quite unwilling to acknowledge the truth of the situation. I needed a sharp and painful lesson to awaken me to the reality of the relationship.

So began perhaps the most painful period of my life. I withdrew from all others and spent several months largely in quiet solitude. Gradually, a new sense of wholeness began to envelope me. As the painful memories were slowly healed, a love beyond measure began to enfold me.

I believe I had been shown an essential lesson about discerning those in whom we can trust.

In time, I was able to admit to myself that my Inner Wisdom had always known I was being used. I simply had not wanted it to be true!

Each life is full of learning and the development of self-understanding and self-belief. Our spiritual pathway is permanently present, rarely obvious, but subtly intertwined within the 'everydayness' of living. When we have the 'eyes to see', all will be revealed.

Suggested reading

Needleman, J., *Lost Christianity* (1980).

CHAPTER 35

Build a strong belief in yourself

Jesus said, 'No one can break into the house of the strong and take it by force without tying the hands of the strong. Then they can loot the house'.

In my opinion, the word 'house' in the translation of this codex refers to our consciousness; an awareness of all that we know of ourselves, our environment and of the people with whom we share our life.

Human consciousness has many levels. Being an accumulation of our life experiences, these have varying degrees of accessibility. Those close to the surface of awareness consciously inform our decisions. Those more deeply hidden can negatively and autonomously impact on our personality, our life experiences and our relationships with others.

The dark side of consciousness, known as the shadow, holds the thoughts and feelings that we have chosen to renounce as unacceptable to us. These we try to suppress. However, the bridling of difficult character traits does not eliminate them! In fact, the more effort we put into their annihilation, the more persistent and inappropriate will be their eruption. It can feel as if our 'house', our personality, has been 'looted' as we act in ways that, on reflection, are contrary to our best interests. Subsequently, we seem to lose personal authority over our life.

Our Truth is our most precious possession. We must guard it by developing mindful discernment and a strong resolve to protect it. Those people we encounter with selfish agendas may try to steal our power and inner resources. Sometimes we are required to make difficult choices about those with whom we choose to spend our time.

We are advised to build a 'house' of strength and be proactive in protecting it from 'thieves'. When we choose to 'listen' to the inner Presence, we will always be guided away from those who would harm our spiritual journey.

This saying advises us to develop the discernment and strength of character which will withstand attacks and potential looting of our inner truth. Hold strong and be firm.

* * *

One way to deny power to the weaker aspects of our personality is to face them, and even start a dialogue with them. Therapy can be helpful in facilitating this type of 'conversation'. As with all relationships, our own troublesome psyche needs to become familiar with its opposing aspects. In time, mutual understanding can pave the way for compromise and harmony, bringing order to our waring inner world. As we gain an inner sense of solidity and strength, we no longer feel threatened by external forces. Our inner strength becomes the support for outer interactions with others. This may apply to issues in our working environment, family and partner difficulties. Whatever the nature of a relationship, when we feel okay about ourselves, we can interact respectfully both with ourselves and with others.

Mary's story

As a child, Mary had been part of a large extended and seemingly happy family. Life, however, was dictated by an elderly and irascible aunt who made many unreasonable demands. Since Mary was the youngest of eight nieces and nephews, she was bullied into fulfilling many of these tiresome errands.

These seemingly trivial, but regular, occurrences created a consciousness of victimhood within Mary. The persistent subliminal lies Mary had absorbed were that she was unimportant, inferior to others and had no power of choice about following her aunt's bidding. These falsehoods were subtle and harmful and, sadly, they became Mary's truth. Her diminished sense of self persisted throughout her short adult life. Her rightful sense of personal power and value had been 'looted'.

The consequences for Mary were that she never found fulfilment in her life. She had always accepted work that was way below her capabilities. She had married a man who treated her like a servant, replicating the aunt's intimidating behaviour. Even Mary's own children mercilessly bullied her. She fulfilled the archetypal role of a victim without ever realising she could have made better choices. Unfortunately, therapy had not been an option for her.

Mary's story is a warning to check our consciousness and seek out harmful beliefs that may be hidden within us. We live out our inner belief system, even when it is false! Mary had unconsciously accepted impositions placed on her by her family, never realising that none of them was actually true. She had, in truth, been capable of achieving much more.

At the time of Mary's story, therapy was not easily available. Today, however, it is more accessible and a great asset in cleansing our 'house' from falsehoods that would 'loot' our truth. We owe it to our self and to Divine presence to clear out harmful beliefs that would diminish our sense of self. Until we are free to act on the promptings of the Inner Presence, we cannot be a true instrument of Divine Energy.

It is we, ourselves, who must make the choice as to which 'voice' we trust, believe and follow. We make this easier by building a strong belief in ourselves.

Suggested reading

Goldsmith, J.S., *Practicing the Presence* (1958).

CHAPTER 36

Be alert to trivia

Jesus said, 'Don't be anxious from morning to evening or from evening to morning about what you'll wear'.

In my opinion, this saying addresses the sense of inferiority with which many people are burdened. Although in the codex Jesus refers to concerns about our clothing and appearance, I believe he is alluding to the anxiety we experience about our standing and status within the external world.

When we look only to our humanness, we find flaws. Instead of developing authentic self-worth within ourselves, we seek recognition and approval from others. We manipulate our behaviours, our appearance, our lifestyle in the hope of gaining the love and respect we crave. Even when we find recognition and status in the outer world, this can only bring temporary relief from our lack of self-belief. We know only too well our own shortcomings. Permanent healing comes from the discovery of our Divine Centre. Here we find a wealth of infinite love, wisdom and compassion; compassion for ourselves and all others.

Undoubtedly, our childhood environment contributes greatly to the estimation we have of ourself. If we have been fortunate to develop in an affirming home, we will have less negativity to negotiate. However, until we discover something of permanent and spiritual value within ourselves, we will always feel 'lesser' and incomplete. That is because we are! Our humanity is fickle, transient and impermanent. Our Divine Self, however, is a perpetual presence of love, compassion, wisdom and joy. Our human journey, I believe, is intended to be a pilgrimage towards knowing and expressing that 'completeness' which awaits within our Soul.

Jesus teaches that our life must, ultimately, be directed by our unique expression of the One Divine Energy. When we unconsciously live by external direction, we cannot be the true expression of our God-Self. It is my belief that many lifetimes are required before we can fully live as a true Child of God.

When we are able to see beyond the hypnotic haze of human life, our soul will become the receptacle of Divine Truth, Wisdom and Love. Then we become another Living Christ.

I believe this is why we have *all* been created.

Suggested reading

Merton, T., *No Man is an Island* (1955).

CHAPTER 37

Be not afraid

His disciples said, 'When will you appear to us? When will we see you?'

Jesus said, 'When you strip naked without being ashamed, and throw your clothes on the ground and stomp on them as little children would, then [you'll] see the Son of the Living One and won't be afraid'.

The translation of this codex suggests the disciples need reassurance that they will not be abandoned by Jesus.

He speaks of the personal preparation they each must make in order to remain in contact with the inner Christhood. He states that they must remove their outer clothing, their false persona, behind which they hide. When they look beyond the outer human shell and unclothe themselves of their constructed artificial personality, they will 'see' and know the inner living Christ. They will recognise this *within all people*.

The term 'child' in the codex refers to the Child of God: the pure, innocent and unblemished essence of oneself. That which is alive and present within all people, waiting to be discovered. Only when we discard our outer façade, stripping away our constructed human identity, will we find our inner Sacredness.

We will then realise that our Divinity has never been absent and that we are already, *right at this very moment,* a beloved Child of God.

Then we will not fear.

Suggested reading

Eliot, T.S., *Four Quartets—Little Gidding* (1944).

CHAPTER 38

The illusion of emptiness

Jesus said, 'Often you've wanted to hear this message that I'm telling you, and you don't have anyone else from whom to hear it. There will be days when you'll look for me, but you won't be able to find me'.

Jesus advises that we should not be alarmed when Divine Presence would *seem* to be absent. A sense of emptiness is a common experience to all 'seekers of Truth'. This can feel disappointing and upsetting. At such times we must remember that we can *never* actually be outside of God's love and care.

In our humanness, we try to bring order to life events. We conceptualise and label thoughts and feelings generated from our experiences. As we 'travel' our life-journey, we can be faced with many bleak times of emptiness. It can be helpful to develop a tolerance for, and an understanding of, these lean times.

As we learn to be comfortable with our discomfort, we allow space to simply be open. This provides a vacuum into which something of the Eternal Message can be directly revealed to us.

When our minds are full of chatter, there is no space for God to be heard. As we practise and develop a strong and enduring trust of the perpetual Divine Presence, our confidence in 'Silence' becomes established. What has previously felt like abandonment can then be realised as Divine Stillness.

With experience, we learn to rename the sense of emptiness as the 'Divine Void' or the 'Sacred No-thingness'. These are moments filled with great meaning, to be treasured as Divine gifts.

* * *

It may take years, perhaps even lifetimes, to become sufficiently still and quiet-minded for the Voice of God to be experienced. The Divine is forever present but we are always beginners in the art of 'listening'.

The concept of 'journey's end' is false. What we seek is infinite. There is no journey's end, simply a perpetual unfoldment of Divine Energy.

Suggested reading

Catala, R., *Sufficient unto Itself is the Day* (1993).

CHAPTER 39

Beware false teachers and prophets

Jesus said, 'The Pharisees and the scholars have taken the keys of knowledge and hidden them. They haven't entered, and haven't let others enter who wanted to. So be wise as serpents and innocent as doves'.

In this codex, Jesus warns his followers about the arrogance and secrecy of the Pharisees and Elders. He states that they have 'taken' the ancient teachings which were intended for the benefit of all seekers, regardless of race, gender, status and religion. They have denied access to Truth and have 'hidden the keys' that would unlock spiritual knowledge. Those who wish to independently study the Word of God have been prevented from doing so.

For centuries the clergy have protected their status and power. Not only have they themselves been unable to understand these sacred teachings, they have chosen to withhold them from others. In my opinion, this was a serious misuse of self-imposed privilege. The precious gift of a personal relationship with the inner God has wilfully been denied to others.

Divine Truth teaches that we are all children of God. Everyone has within them the possibility of a direct and unique relationship with

Divine Source. This gift is freely available to all. We need no other to intervene on our behalf.

* * *

Jesus instructs that we must be alert to the false teachings which will undoubtedly come our way. The 'to be innocent' mentioned in the codex means to be pure and uncontaminated; able to receive Truth from within. By purposefully taking 'quiet times' on a daily basis, we cannot fail to develop the 'listening ear'. Our personal relationship with God is our surest source of spiritual knowledge.

Jesus advises his followers to be shrewd, alert and aware of the false prophets that may come into our world.

However, he also asks that we retain our innocence and avoid condemnation of those whose ignorance blinds them to Truth.

Suggested reading

Author unknown, *The Way of a Pilgrim* (1942). Foreword by Dr Andrew Walker.

CHAPTER 40

Root yourself and your life in God

Jesus said, 'A grapevine has been planted outside of the Father. Since it's malnourished, it'll be pulled up by its root and destroyed'.

My interpretation of this saying is that it teaches that a life without roots in Divine Energy is weak and vulnerable to negative influences. However, rooted in our Divine Centre, it will flourish, remaining strong and resilient. When adversity comes along, inner resources will protect, guide and lead away from danger.

It seems we are often required to remain patient and trusting as we wait for life solutions to appear. This is not punishment, nor even a test, but an opportunity to deepen our self-awareness. It may be that an opportunity is presented to develop a firm and robust trust in Divine Source. We may also later discover that the solution to our problem was not immediately available!

However, time is a human concept which we must learn to accept with confidence. It is a mechanism that allows our consciousness to unfold in stages. It offers an opportunity for the gradual integration of more wholesome ways of being. It provides space for our unique self to manifest. As a fledgling breaks free from its protective shell, so we learn to break free from the imposed constraints and mores of family and society.

We often come to know ourselves through adversity. Each time life requires more from us, we gradually learn to trust our Divine Centre. When feeling abandoned and solitary, try to remember that Divine Love and Care are truly constant companions. Aloneness is a false human concept.

When we trust in God, all our needs are provided for at the right time, in the right manner. We always have a 'guardian angel' at our side. By asking for help, we open our consciousness to receive the solution for our highest good. Sometimes the answer is immediately present, other times we must wait ... sometimes much longer than we think is acceptable! However, as is shown time and time again, the answer will, at the right time, *always* present itself.

Jill's story

Jill had consciously been journeying on her spiritual path for several years. At times her life had been difficult and trusting in Divine Presence had not always been easy. She often added to her distress by berating herself when her trust/faith seemed to have completely abandoned her.

Jill had two friends, also consciously on their spiritual journey. The three had become a considerable support for each other in the 'lean' times. During a particularly long period when the Inner Presence seemed to be absent, Jill's faith/belief began to truly waver. In addition, money had also become a serious problem. She could do nothing but meditate and seek solace from her beloved books. It was a lean and difficult time for Jill.

Several months had passed when an unexpected letter arrived. It informed Jill of a sizeable legacy bequeathed to her by a distant relative. A person, in fact, whom Jill had never actually met.

This seemed like a miracle. She could never have conceived of such a welcome gift. Her financial problems, in one stroke, had been resolved.

Her faith/trust in Divine Providence had, on many occasions, been severely tested. She had been required to wait some considerable time for the manifestation of her solution. It was a great lesson in trust, resilience and patience.

Suggested reading

Dyer, W.W., *There is a Spiritual Solution to Every Problem* (2002).

CHAPTER 41

Abundance is available to all who seek

> Jesus said, 'Whoever has something in hand will be given more, but whoever doesn't have anything will lose even what little they do have'.

In the text, this saying refers to having something extra, 'something in hand', to aid our journey. I believe this refers to knowledge of, and trust in, God's Presence, the permanent source of all our needs. Knowing this fact, and holding that awareness in consciousness, gives us access to Divine Abundance.

Those without this awareness may find it difficult to access their rightful entitlement. This is not punitive. We are *all* complete Children of God, with all our needs permanently present. To receive, however, we must choose *consciously* to accept our Divine Inheritance. Without trust in Divine Providence, we may remain unable to fulfil our part in the human story.

Without the expectation of the Divine solution, we many overlook that which is already present within us. Rendering oneself 'blind' and 'deaf' effectively denies the openness to receive.

My story

Learning to be still in the Sacred Silence gradually develops an opening, a space within us, which is of a different spiritual magnitude. For me, this has required regular daily meditation practice; twice per day, every day for many years.

As a young mother, I rose daily at 4:30 am to practise. Although there were many occasions when I resented this commitment, something within me simply refused to stop. The desire for personal comfort frequently battled with the possibility of a deepening spiritual awareness. Conflict between the contrasting aspects of myself lasted for some considerable time. This inner struggle I found profoundly difficult and seemingly at odds with the silence and peace for which I yearned.

Many find daily practice troublesome. Its purpose, I believe, is to develop the inner discipline which is essential to all spiritual paths. Wrestling with our inner demons eventually cleanses the slate on which our spiritual direction can be 'written'. Life is not intended to punish but to offer endless opportunities for an ever-deepening connection to the Divine Self.

As I reflect on past hard times, I know that without them I would not be writing this here and now. They have been my greatest opportunities for learning.

The joy I experience as I write and share my journey is beyond measure. Perseverance with our petulant and complaining human self is the *only* battle we have to win. As we slowly gain better control of our mind and emotions, the self-imposed blockages to our Divine inheritance will melt away. Then, unimaginable rewards of harmony, love and practical solutions present themselves.

Suggested reading

Merton, T., *No Man is an Island* (1955).

CHAPTER 42

Be aware of your motivation

> Jesus said, 'Become passersby'.

This saying would seem harsh and uncaring. However, I think Jesus is teaching us to be authentic in our interactions with people. If we truly care about others, we must first be sensitive to their true needs. This often includes allowing them to take some of the hard knocks of life. We must want for them whatever is in their best interest rather than what *we* think they need.

In my opinion, Jesus condones 'passing by' as a better alternative to meddling, interfering and denying someone an opportunity to find their own solutions. It is in the everyday struggles of living that we grow and come to trust in our own Divine Resources. In truth, many of us function permanently at a much lower capacity than we are capable of. When another person rushes in to 'take care' of us, an opportunity to discover our inner potency may have been thwarted and further delayed.

I believe much harm has been done in the name of Christianity. Traditional Christians have largely been encouraged to save and serve others without first having the discernment to distinguish between authentic assistance and harmful interference. With the exception of emergencies, incapacity and disasters, assistance is valid only when it helps another to help themselves. The role of 'rescuer', in normal circumstances, can be a selfish act. We must be clear about our own motivations.

Inauthentic and inappropriate help impinges on another's power, encourages dependency and stunts the inner self. Too often, 'saviours' thwart a person's opportunity to discover their inner Divine Potential. Since life constantly offers each of us scope for self-awareness and self-empowerment, we can do no better than offer another the unspoken but implicit message: 'I know you can do this. I will stand by you, while you find your way'.

An old Chinese proverb illustrates this very well: 'Give a starving man a fish from your catch, you feed him for one day. Teach that man to fish for himself, you feed him for life'.

When we give another the knowledge and opportunity to grow into an independent, proactive person, we also give them freedom to follow their own path.

Beware of 'saviours' who wish to fulfil their own personal need to be 'the good Samaritan'!

* * *

Codex 42 is perhaps one of the most controversial in this collection of teachings and yet, in my opinion, it points directly to why many people remain deeply unfulfilled. It also points to the sham of some charitable work. We need to ask who benefits, long term, from the massive resources and efforts that go into 'giving'?

This saying demands we stop 'rescuing' people. Do not become emotionally caught up in another's drama. *Pass on by*. If you wish to make a difference, then first begin by cleaning up your own life. When you no longer have a need for external confirmation of your goodness, you will refrain from interfering through false 'charitable works'. Instead, you will encourage others to pursue their own pathway to God.

At times you may be 'directed' to give guidance, encouragement, food and shelter. However, demonstrating your absolute faith in a person's ability to help themselves can change their life forever.

Suggested reading

Morgan, M., *Mutant Message Down Under* (1991).

CHAPTER 43

A product is not separate from its source

> His disciples said to him, 'Who are you to say these things to us?'
> 'You don't realize who I am from what I say to you, but you've become like those Judeans who either love the tree but hate its fruit, or love the fruit but hate the tree'.

The translation of this codex suggests the disciples may be questioning Jesus's authority to make controversial statements. He believes the disciples have not, as yet, made the connection between God and humanity. They remain ignorant that he truly is the Son of God.

Nor have they realised that this truth applies to each and every one of us: we are all an expression of Divine Energy, each with the inner potential to manifest the Divine Fruits of Truth, Love, Power and Wisdom.

* * *

Parables and symbols are often used to teach the esoteric message. In this particular saying, Jesus uses a tree to illustrate the principle that God and life are inseparable.

In reality, a tree cannot be separated from its parts and its products. God is the leaves, roots, branches, seeds and fruit. All aspects of the tree are integral to its wholeness.

Likewise, it is impossible to separate God from all life. In the same way, we are the fruit, the depiction, and the *visible expression* of God. We cannot be separate from God; and God, as our Life Force, can never be separated from us. The inner presence of God is at the centre of all life.

It is, therefore, impossible to 'love the tree and hate its fruit'. Loving and knowing God, means loving and knowing all tangible creations, including the fullness of humanity.

Suggested reading

Goldsmith, J.S., *God, the Substance of all Form* (1959).

CHAPTER 44

Judge not the manifestations of God

> Jesus said, 'Whoever blasphemes the Father will be forgiven, and whoever blasphemes the Son will be forgiven, but whoever blasphemes the Holy Spirit will not be forgiven, neither on earth nor in heaven'.

This codex teaches that God can become known to us in three distinct ways of appreciation and understanding.
These are:

- 'God as the Father': the *Source* of life
  Infinite, indestructible and eternal. Creator and provider of life.
- 'God as the Son': the *Means* of knowing God
  The myriad demonstrations by which God is expressed and made visible.
- 'God as the Holy Spirit': the *Life Force* throughout and the essence of All Creation
  Pure Spirit and Totality of God.

* * *

I believe in this codex the Holy Spirit refers to the sacred expression of God on this earthly plane. It is God made manifest, made tangible, made known to all those with the 'eyes to see'; the 'ears to hear'; the 'soul to experience'. It is, therefore, unacceptable to pass judgement on the concrete embodiment of Divine Energy. Since the visible form IS impermanent and temporal, it can be harmed and should never be condemned or judged.

* * *

We are each given a life to use as we will. As creative beings, we choose a great deal of how our life is lived.

Our task on earth, I believe, is intended for the deepening of conscious awareness. The deeper we journey into our inner being, the clearer becomes our task for which we were born. This, I believe, may take many lifetimes of experiencing and seeking before our unique soul opens sufficiently to fully blossom.

Only then can we become a pure receptacle for the outpouring of Divine Energy. Until that happens, our creativity is largely a combination of our human will together with the fleeting stimulus of our Soul. It is imperative that we have sufficient awareness within ourselves to distinguish between human demonstration and Soul-led demonstration.

Study, contemplation and meditation all lead to the preparation of a 'clean slate', upon which God's message can clearly be written. As the purpose of our Soul grows in clarity, Divine Truth can pour through us into expression.

Suggested reading

Pennington, M.B., Keating, T. and Clarke, T.E., *Finding Grace at the Center* (1978).

CHAPTER 45

We produce our own life-harvest

> Jesus said, 'Grapes aren't harvested from thorns, nor are figs gathered from thistles, because they don't produce fruit. [A person who's good] brings good things out of their treasure, and a person who's [evil] brings evil things out of their evil treasure. They say evil things because their heart is full of evil'.

In this codex, Jesus asks that we select, with caution, the expectations we choose to plant in the fertile 'soil' of our consciousness. For that which we 'sow' in our belief system, we shall surely reap. We will bring to fruition whatever we anticipate.

Therefore, we need to delve deep within our psyche and seek out unwelcome seeds of misperceptions, unhelpful expectations and inaccurate beliefs that have been 'planted' in the hidden and fertile recesses of our mind. *They* bring forth the harvest of our life.

If we anticipate goodness, we will manifest goodness. When we fill our life with seeds of loving kindness, that is what we will reap from others.

Consequently, we bear a great deal of responsibility for our life-journey. Much of what we believe has been absorbed unconsciously from external influences. This happens from the very beginning of our time on earth. Our life is the visible product of all that we have come to believe as true.

Realising this, places dominion of our life into our own hands. If you want something different, dig deep within and uncover the source, the seed-thought, of the problem. Choose to plant a different seed-thought. Whatever the cause, this saying teaches that we can change much of our life circumstances. It is within our power if we *really* wish to do so. Sadly, many revel in the powerless role of 'poor me' and have no interest in changing their personal circumstances.

The *solution* for change is simple. The *execution*, however, often requires a great deal of self-scrutiny, determination and courage! It also requires time and patience with oneself. We are always evolving; our soul is forever growing.

This saying speaks to those with an honest desire to improve themselves and their life.

* * *

It can be helpful in the self-discovery phase to have the support of a professional therapist. They are more able to identify the many ways we hoodwink ourselves as we try to deny our part in any problem. We are often programmed by society to blame others and to be a 'victim'.

Take the time and find the courage to scrutinise your consciousness. Seek out the source of your difficulties.

This is the beginning of inner healing and leads to 'planting and growing' anew. Choose wisely that which you desire and 'plant' only truth in your consciousness. The personal 'harvest' of your life will eventually develop into something productive and wholesome.

Paula's story

Paula and her older sister, Louise, had grown up in a small and isolated family unit. Due to Louise's disability, Paula received very little attention from their parents. From a very young age, Paula had unconsciously accepted that her needs were of minimal importance. The 'seed-thought' of unworthiness had taken root at a very early age.

The harvest of this self-belief would lead Paula into an adult life of low achievement. Not only did she lack confidence in her abilities, she also lacked any expectation of love and attention from others.

Consequently, Paula married an unsuitable man who frequently treated her with disdain. After six years of unhappiness, they separated and eventually divorced.

As was her pattern in life, Paula believed the break-up was her fault. She never remarried nor fulfilled her desire for children. She settled for the same diminished life that she had experienced as a child, never realising that, despite her childhood, she could have chosen something better for herself.

We can, in modern times, seek out the hidden issues that blight our lives. Many self-help books are available and therapy is now more accessible and acceptable.

Undoubtedly, it takes courage to begin the therapeutic journey. We may need to face emotionally painful places within ourselves. Paula's example, however, illustrates that choosing to avoid our inner pain does not make us happy. Instead, it leaves us stuck in the mire of the past.

Today we now have more opportunities for choice. We can make a conscious decision to seek out the weeds of limitation and give space for something new, wholesome and life-affirming to grow.

Suggested reading

Kornfield, J., *A Path with Heart* (1993).

CHAPTER 46

Be as innocent as a child

> Jesus said, 'From Adam to John the Baptizer, no one's been born who's so much greater than John the Baptizer that they shouldn't avert their eyes. But I say that whoever among you will become a little child will know the kingdom and become greater than John'.

In this codex, Jesus distinguishes between people who identify themselves simply as human, and those who identify themselves as a Child of God.

Those unaware of the Inner Christhood as the source of all life, are unconsciously held captive by a belief solely in the human outer shell. God is known only as a separate entity.

Those unable to 'see' beyond the human exterior are caught in the limitations of the human story. They believe they are 'born of a human woman' and are unable to experience the Inner Christ. They do not know that, whilst woman is the *means* by which human life is made manifest on earth, it is the Universal Christhood which actually *gives* life to all creatures.

For those still seeking Truth outside of themselves, Jesus suggests they turn to John the Baptist.

However, those who have become like a child, innocent of human limitations, are reborn as a Child of God. They have no need for an intermediary such as John the Baptist. They already know the permanence, within all life, of Divine Omnipresence.

Steve's story

Steve found the codices in the *Gospel of Thomas* hard to understand. He was a practical man who enjoyed gardening, carpentry and sport. He was comfortable with the traditional Christian teachings to which he had been exposed in childhood. He could make sense of the practical instructions regarding kindness to his fellow man, to refrain from stealing, covetousness and anger. To him, these were obvious guidelines that benefitted society.

However, to claim, for example, that woman was not the giver of life and that we each have the potential for great wisdom and power, seemed to Steve to be foolish and clearly unscientific. Over the years, as the practical necessities of life became a priority, the intrigue to investigate these esoteric teachings waned.

In middle age, however, Steve began to experience a deepening inner emptiness. His practical pursuits of endurance sport and specialist woodwork no longer held his interest. All his projects—and there had been many over the years—now did little to assuage his inner crisis.

Steve began to experience powerful and troublesome dreams. As these grew in regularity and intensity, they left him feeling anxious and unsettled. His wife urged him to seek help from their doctor. Thankfully, therapy, rather than medication, was advised. Steve was clearly seen by a doctor of great wisdom!

Steve was drawn to a Jungian therapist whose primary work focused on dreams. Following several weekly sessions, Steve became less fearful of these night-time intrusions. He learnt to accept that the dreams were a product of his own unconscious. Their purpose, he began to understand, was to draw his attention to a source of inner dissatisfaction that resided deep within himself.

He became an avid writer of a personal dream book and his fascination to explore their hidden meanings began to develop. He gradually came to understand his dreams were urging him to break free from the self-imposed prison of his own outdated opinions and limitations. His deeper self was suggesting that a new phase of his spiritual journey, one for which he was clearly ready, should begin.

* * *

Steve chose to immerse himself in Buddhist meditation practice. He gradually learnt to still his mind; to quieten his emotions and to find deep peace in the simple task of 'Being in the Silence'.

Over a period of time, an inner peace grew within Steve. He slowly discovered his past experiences of emptiness and loss had been pointers of profound importance. He grew to understand that within himself there existed a sacred space, not a barren emptiness, but one of infinite goodness. He had discovered one of the great secrets of the spiritual life. He now knew that when we seek with an open heart and an open mind, all is gradually revealed to us. As a beloved Child of God, we always have Divine Presence available to us.

We are, each one of us, embraced in the Everlasting Arms of God, even when we are unaware of this truth. At the right time, in the right way, all will discover the Divine Truth of our Being.

Suggested reading

Trine, R.W., *In Tune with the Infinite* (1965).

CHAPTER 47

Which part will you serve?

> Jesus said, 'It's not possible for anyone to mount two horses or stretch two bows, and it's not possible for a servant to follow two leaders, because they'll respect one and despise the other.
> No one drinks old wine and immediately wants to drink new wine. And new wine isn't put in old wineskins, because they'd burst. Nor is old wine put in new wineskins, because it'd spoil. A new patch of cloth isn't sewn onto an old coat, because it'd tear apart'.

This codex draws attention to our dual nature, namely our outward human self and our hidden Divinity. My interpretation of the text is that until we discover the Divine Spirit within, our humanness largely directs our life. Few people have awareness of the inner Spirit, which is our true source of wisdom and power. When we allow our human thoughts and emotions to steer our life-journey, we are led by a 'lesser' self.

We are taught to be single-minded with solidarity of purpose and clarity regarding our priorities in life. When we vacillate in our choices, we weaken our resolve to pursue our most appropriate and most enriching life-path. We are cautioned that new ways of living need personal preparation. Our consciousness needs to be cleansed of much that is false within us.

This codex states:

- We cannot pour 'new wine'—i.e. new spiritual knowledge—into 'aged wineskins', i.e. an outdated consciousness.
- Nor can we 'patch up' our new life-garment—i.e. our worldly persona—with old and redundant ways of thinking, knowing and living.
- We must allow our self to be gradually cleansed and renewed, both internally and externally, in order to contain and express a new maturing understanding of Truth.

Choosing to fulfil our Divine purpose can attract temptations and fears. These are the normal stumbling blocks that often come our way. Awareness that our resolve may be tested, is to be prepared and alert to challenges. This can come from external sources and from our own internal dialogue.

Jesus brought to humanity a different way of living. He taught the value of an authentic spiritual life. Prior to his profound revelations, devout people had slavishly followed the dictates and laws imposed by the clergy. Jesus denied these leaders their authority and power. He placed dominion within each person's hands. Effectively, he gave each one of us sovereignty over our life. This task comes with great power and the privilege of personal responsibility.

Through study, contemplation and meditation we slowly cleanse and prepare the ground of our awakening consciousness. We become receptive to new ways of being. As we endeavour to live according to authentic spiritual teachings, our psyche becomes healed of falsehoods. Our resolve to be true to our unique Divine Journey is strengthened and redundant ways of being are cleansed. Newness of thought and clarity of action begin to flourish.

When we endeavour to work faithfully with life as it comes our way, each day offers a new opportunity for inner growth and valid outer demonstration.

We must endeavour to trust that, at all times, our inner Divine Teacher is guiding and supporting us.

Howard's story

Having followed in his father's footsteps as a respected train driver, Howard was the pride of the family. He had become one of the most highly trained and respected drivers on the network.

At the age of 45, he began to experience depression. His enjoyment and motivation to continue working in his prestigious and lucrative position were at a low ebb. He had always loved his work but recently his frequent mood swings were out of character and creating tension at home and at work.

Howard eventually chose to explore his unrest in therapy. He was shocked to discover that behind his depression lay feelings of outrage. Although this revelation was deeply uncomfortable for Howard, with therapeutic support and sensitive exploration he slowly came to accept them. Only then was he able to explore and come to understand his emotional world. With the support of his therapist, Howard gradually uncovered a self-imposed and unconscious obligation that had driven his initial decision to follow in his father's footsteps.

As Howard explored his inner feelings, he realised he was experiencing a deep desire to change the course of his life. He yearned to live in a new and more creative way. He wanted to feel his heart 'sing' with joyful expression! He wanted to fully immerse himself in portrait painting. This had been an enduring hobby since his youth.

Train driving was no longer in keeping with Howard's evolving life story. His inner self was urging him to seek something new, to cautiously 'taste', but not yet fully drink, the 'new wine' of a new life-direction.

Codex 47 cautions that we cannot immediately place a new life directly into an already established life pattern. We must first be prepared and seasoned before a new direction can be 'poured' into the person we already are. As we shift from an old life, we may not at first enjoy the 'taste' of the new life. It takes time for us to adjust and become comfortable with the 'new wine' of a new life.

Howard, however, had always enjoyed his hobby of portrait painting and had become well-known in his locality. He was often asked to fulfil commissions. In addition to painting, he volunteered as a tutor for adult classes at his local college. Sharing his enthusiasm, experience and knowledge was a great joy to him.

When he received a prestigious commission, Howard knew the time had come to end his work on the railways and follow the exciting life-path that beckoned.

Anxiety often accompanies a life change. Although the adult part of Howard was ready for this, a more timid part of him was afraid. He needed time to plan, prepare and adjust to the new possibilities in his life.

When 'oughts' and 'shoulds' direct our life, we suppress our naturally maturing tendencies. Consequently, as we *depress* our rightful inner feelings, we suffer from *depression*.

We must find the courage to accept our evolving life-path. As our new self comes of age, the 'new wine', demands to be tasted. It cannot be suppressed and contained within the 'aged wineskins' of our old life. These yearnings are the signposts to the next stage of our life-journey.

Following several months of regular therapy, Howard found the courage to tell his family of his decision. In time, his father came to understand, realising we must each follow our heart.

Howard was at last prepared and ready to create a new 'life-garment'—i.e. a new persona—to experience his new life-direction.

Only when we allow and welcome this change within us will we begin to live to our full potential. Then we become the person we were always intended to be.

Suggested reading

The Bible: Psalm 23 (*The Lord is my Shepherd*).

CHAPTER 48

Healing the fragmented psyche

> Jesus said, 'If two make peace with each other in a single house, they'll say to the mountain, "Go away", and it will'.

This codex refers, I believe, to the inner fragmentation which often exists within people.

The human self, the part with which we are most familiar, lives for its own personal experience, its survival and its individual expression.

Divine Nature, the sacred life present in all living creatures, seeks to unify life. It endeavours to facilitate harmonious, cooperative and meaningful expression between living creatures. It reflects the singularity of the One Life and One Source, which is expressed in an incalculable number of seemingly individual lifeforms.

Awareness of contradictions within oneself is essential to a harmonious life-expression. Inner conflict can arise when our outer personality demands its individual, possibly selfish, expression, whilst our inner Divine Self seeks cooperation and unity. All parts of oneself are essential. It is our life task, I believe, to find ways of unifying these diverse aspects.

When we make *inner* peace, within ourselves, we become more able to live in harmonious cooperation with others. We become a 'single house', undivided, powerful and able to 'move mountains'.

Becky and Jason's story

Becky and Jason had been together for several years. For the most part, their relationship worked well. An issue arose, however, when Becky was given a career promotion which required her to move some distance away. This would mean not only moving house, but would also require Jason to seek alternative employment.

A battle of wills began, each feeling diminished in value by the other's assertion that their employment was of greater value. The argument quickly descended into childish accusations as both became driven by hidden and unresolved issues from childhood. Within weeks it was decided they could no longer live together and so Becky would take up her new position and Jason would stay put.

Thankfully, Jason talked about his sadness to an old school friend who had some skills as a befriender and counsellor. It was quickly ascertained that Jason, quite unconsciously, was feeling diminished as a person, unimportant and with little value. This added further weight to his concern that Becky would now find someone 'better'. He was quite shocked when he realised that a small part of himself was simply feeling afraid, his tantrum fuelled by unresolved insecurities from his childhood.

With this new understanding, Becky and Jason mutually decided to seek couples-counselling. It was quickly realised, by both parties, that their problem had never actually been about employment and house moves. The issue, on both sides of the argument, had activated old childhood hurts and wounds that were driving uncooperative behaviours.

In reality, the real issues for both Becky and Jason were not relevant to the current situation. They loved and respected each other and truly valued their relationship. Several sessions of individual therapy brought some healing to the 'wounded child' in each of them. From this more cooperative perspective, they were able to look differently at the issue and gradually find a suitable compromise.

We all have troublesome aspects within our psyche, some developed during our early years and some in adulthood. As these psychological wounds demand attention, our psyche becomes split and fragmented. We are unable to act as a cohesive and harmonious whole.

When we bring these needy parts to the surface of our awareness by giving them respectful attention, a healing of our psyche is facilitated. We begin to function as a more unified whole and outdated hurts and angers are no longer inappropriately projected onto current situations. From a more cooperative wholeness, we become creative, powerful and happy beings who take responsibility for our inner world and outer actions.

Through therapy, Becky and Jason had individually gained understanding and brought some resolution to their inner 'wounded child'. As their shared drama lessened in intensity, a solution to the problem unfolded. The matter was swiftly and maturely resolved when a new house, one they both loved, came to their attention. Suitably located in an accessible area for both their employment needs, an appropriate solution had presented itself.

Unsurprisingly, when their inner selves were healed, they become able and willing to look beyond their rigid and intransigent positions. Outwardly, they were able to meet each other and a workable compromise quickly came their way.

It takes courage to face and heal our inner hurts and dramas. But when we do, our outer world also is healed. Becoming more whole, we grow to be empathically powerful, creative in our solutions and able to 'move mountains'.

Suggested reading

Bradshaw, J., *Homecoming—Reclaiming & Championing Your Inner Child* (1991).

CHAPTER 49

Discover and develop your unique consciousness

> Jesus said, 'Blessed are those who are one—those who are chosen, because you'll find the kingdom. You've come from there and will return there'.

This saying teaches that those who have developed self-knowledge, self-reliance and self-understanding are 'alone' and have no dependency on another. Consequently, they have the freedom to live as God's Expression on earth. Without distractions and false obligations, they will hear more clearly the guidance of the Inner Divine Voice. All aspects of their being will act with a single purpose.

Western society is remiss, I believe, in its philosophical ideal that our life should be lived for and through others. The purpose of our life, I believe, is to communicate and demonstrate the unique Divine Life within oneself. This, of course, may include 'serving' others. Frequently, however, the 'oughts' and 'shoulds' of life are nothing more than imposed social mores that distort the ideal pathway of a developing mind and a burgeoning spirituality.

In modern times, through the development of psychology and psychiatry, we now understand the harm that can be done to a person's uniqueness and self-confidence when impositions thwart their natural life-path.

Sometimes we may be called upon to offer valid assistance to others, as in the case of emergencies, accidents and genuine need. However, when we *re*-act, we frequently interfere with another's opportunity to resolve something for themselves. We halt the possibility that the person may move toward self-sufficiency and self-reliance. As mentioned in codex 42, *Be aware of your motivation*. Often, the false rescuer is prompted not by genuine concern for another, but by their own need to be seen to be doing 'good works'.

When we act from a need for self-validation, we rob the other person of an opportunity to find their confidence, power and direction in life. Emergencies aside, it is essential that any action we undertake for another is an appropriate response to a genuine need. 'Rescuing' in an inappropriate manner can often delay the other's spiritual journey.

When we understand and trust our inner promptings, there will be no conflict within ourselves. Our outer actions will be appropriate and proportionate to the situation.

Self-knowledge and understanding of our own motivations are essential. Only by 'listening' to God do we slowly grow to become the person we are intended to be. Only then may we begin to function as the eyes, hands and heart of God.

Pamela's story

As Pamela sat alone in the coffee shop watching passers-by, she observed an encounter between a young homeless man and an elderly woman. Both were well-known characters in this small seaside town; the woman for her charitable work, the young man as a polite and helpful *Big Issue* seller.

That day, as the elderly woman talked at great length to the young man, it became evident he was becoming agitated. Eventually, he hastily grabbed his few belongings and marched off down the street. The old woman looked bemused and flustered. Finally, she too, gathered her shopping bags and walked away. Pamela had not been able to hear the conversation but clearly something was amiss. Later that morning she noticed the homeless man sitting dejectedly in the park with Peter, the café owner.

Peter was a neighbour of Pamela's and, concerned for the homeless man, she later asked about this unusual interaction. Peter explained the young man had needed to sell all his copies of the *Big Issue* before he would receive payment. That day he had no money left and badly needed those earnings. The elderly woman had so filled 'his space' with her presence and empty chatter that he had only taken a pittance. Most of his 'regulars' had simply waved and walked on by. He then had insufficient funds to pay for bed and board in the local hostel.

It seemed the young man had accurately perceived the motivation of the woman's attention. Since she rarely showed a sincere interest in his well-being, he needed to stop this regular unwanted interference. But how?! He felt diminished and powerless to stop her. He was a wise young man and recognised that her actions were motivated entirely by self-interest. Perhaps, he felt, the woman was exhibiting and flaunting her 'good works'. The young man, out of sincere kindness, felt unable to deal with her serious misjudgement. He felt disempowered and did not have the heart to ask her to move on!

This true story is not uncommon. Ego-driven 'do-gooders' can cause a great deal of harm. As I touched on in Codex 42, if we wish to help someone who has a sincere need, we must first *always* be aware of our own motivation. To 'stroke' our own ego by supposedly helping another, is most certainly not doing God's work.

Pamela had been shown the danger of assuming we know what another person may need. In observing this incident she had encountered the shameful use of another's predicament to elevate oneself. She had seen with her own eyes the truth that we can never judge where *real* kindness may lie.

In the young homeless man, who had no desire to impress others, she had seen 'God in action'. In the false Christian woman, full of hubris, she had observed a display of truly selfish behaviour.

Suggested reading

Benner, J., *The Impersonal Life* (1941).

CHAPTER 50

Owning and expressing our divine identity

> Jesus said, 'If they ask you, "Where do you come from?" tell them, "We've come from the light, the place where light came into being by itself, [established] itself, and appeared in their image"'.
>
> 'If they ask you, "Is it you?" then say, "We are its children, and we're chosen by our living Father"'.
>
> 'If they ask you, "What's the sign of your Father in you?" then say, "It's movement and rest"'.

This saying teaches that we are 'to own' and, when asked, declare our Divine Identity. Our behaviour will reveal much about who we truly are.

We must be willing to demonstrate that we are born from Divine Consciousness into the 'light' of awareness.

If asked, we are to explain that all people are children of God. However, only those with awareness of this truth are fully 'in the light' and can be identified as 'enlightened'.

Proof of our Divine Centre will be verified in the manner of our actions, our priorities and our way of being.

We shall confirm ourselves as Children of God by rendering Divine Truth visible to those with 'eyes to see'. We must be a demonstration of this teaching through the manner in which we choose to live, in our interactions with others and the example we present. Our life, made up of simple everyday actions of resting, being and doing, will be testimony to our Truth.

It is the example of our life that will reveal the Presence of the inner Divine Self, which is eternally available to all who seek.

Elaine's story

Elaine was a social animal who enjoyed fun and time spent with friends. The important aspect of her life, however, was her inner quest to discover an authentic spiritual life. Having been on many weekend retreats, sometimes Buddhist-based, sometimes Christian, meditation and contemplation had become a daily priority for her. As her inner sense of well-being increased, she became less troubled by external events. Inner peace was becoming a regular companion.

One day, an acquaintance from her workplace asked if they could take a walk together during their lunch break. Elaine was surprised by Ruth's request but happily agreed. As they walked in the spring sunshine, Ruth directly asked if she could talk to Elaine about her 'secret'. Bemused by this request, and with some trepidation, Elaine agreed, although she had no idea as to what Ruth was referring.

Ruth wasted no time in explaining that over a period of many months she had begun to experience a great calmness whenever she and Elaine had worked together on a joint project. She had noticed the type of project had no bearing on the degree of calmness she was experiencing.

As Ruth struggled to put her experiences into words, she tearfully blurted out,

> You have something that I can't identify, something special. You seem so clean and uncontaminated by life. Something comes out of you! It's like you're living a life that's similar to mine but yours is so different. What *is* your secret? I just *had* to ask!

This was the first time anyone had asked such a question of Elaine. Feeling shaken and quite vulnerable, she asked for time to consider. She was, quite rightfully, protective of her fledgling inner spiritual world. What did her Inner God want her to do? She meditated and waited until she felt sure of Divine Guidance. After several days, she suggested to Ruth that they take a walk in nature at the weekend.

Elaine cautiously and tentatively explained that meditation had become a central and essential part of her life. Through discovering a place of peace within herself, she had found a peaceful life in her external world. Perhaps, she suggested, it may be *that* that Ruth was sensing. Elaine generously invited Ruth to join her at a meditation gathering.

Without hesitation, Ruth accepted. She had been seeking something she could not give a name to, but she believed Elaine had found it!

We never know when, just by being who we are, by living truthfully to our inner guidance, we may become an example of something deep and precious. Elaine had slowly and unwittingly become a living demonstration of her growing Divine Identity. Her committed daily practice had developed into a tangible, sentient and living expression of Divine Presence. She had begun to truly live from her Divine Centre.

Ruth, perhaps because she also was seeking, had been ready and able to sense 'something' within Elaine. When we *live* our truth, we need do no more, we do not need to preach. As Elaine's story describes, those who are seeking will be drawn to us. Nothing more is asked than that we live according to our inner promptings.

Suggested reading

Kornfield, J., *After the Ecstasy, the Laundry* (2000).

CHAPTER 51

The new world is already present

> His disciples said to him, 'When will the dead have rest, and when will the new world come?'
> He said to them, 'What you're looking for has already come, but you don't know it'

In this codex, Jesus reminds his followers that worldly death is nothing more than a release from the confines of a body with its attendant thinking processes and emotionality. Death is an opportunity to let go of the limitations that, for the most part, accompany our humanness. We are released from the prison of the body into a freedom that has always been available to us.

To experience this freedom requires that we have an awareness of such. It is my belief that many lifetimes are required to develop this degree of consciousness. But until we understand the freedom that is right now already ours, we will not have the 'eyes to see'.

In the fullness of time, I believe we will all awaken from the human dream that has trapped us in a narrow and restricted version of ourselves. The eternal presence of peace, love, wisdom and freedom is already ours; it is here now. We just have to know it, claim it and learn how to live it.

Suggested reading

Tolle, E., *The Power of Now* (2001).

CHAPTER 52

Look to that which is present, here, now

> His disciples said to him, 'Twenty-four prophets have spoken in Israel, and they all spoke of you'.
> He said to them, 'You've ignored the Living One right in front of you, and you've talked about those who are dead'.

The disciples state in this codex that many prophets predicted Jesus's ministry. It would, therefore, seem strange that the Pharisees were unwilling to recognise him as the bringer of Divine Truth.

Perhaps their refusal to acknowledge him lay in his condemnation of their rigid rules and practices. Jesus's criticism would have seemed threatening, not only to their elevated position in the social order, but also to their financial security and their sense of self-worth.

By urging his followers to look deeper than 'dead prophets' and to seek the 'Living Message', Jesus was effectively denying the Pharisees their power and control.

His intention, I believe, was that people should understand him to be an example of what *all* people can be, and are intended to be. That we each have potential to become a living embodiment of Divine Energy—now.

Divine Presence, I believe, is always relevant to any situation at hand. It is alive, fresh at each moment and applicable to all people at all times.

Suggested reading

Goldsmith, J.S., *Practicing the Presence* (1991).

CHAPTER 53

Seek the truth within myths, rituals and symbols

> His disciples said to him, 'Is circumcision useful, or not?'
> He said to them, 'If it were useful, parents would have children who are born circumcised. But the true circumcision in spirit has become profitable in every way'.

My interpretation of this codex is that Jesus states that the physical act of circumcision has no value. If it were preferable for a man to have no foreskin, then Divine Intelligence would not have created it in the first place.

Over the centuries the symbolic and true meaning of circumcision has been lost. A literal interpretation has taken its place, blurring the real intention. When Jesus speaks of 'circumcision in spirit', he is referring to the opening, the release of the hidden power of Divine spirit, which is present within each and every one of us.

Our life is a journey towards the discovery of the Inner Self which awaits demonstration in our everyday lives. I believe the male phallus represents power and creation. Circumcision, then, symbolically represents the uncovering and freeing of that power in the process of human creativity.

This statement would seem to refer to maleness only. However, in my opinion, this limited perception is a reflection of the traditions operating at the time of the original writing. It is now inaccurate to have the opinion that women are without male power. Both female and male energies are present in, and available to, all human beings, albeit to the varying degrees of their personality and their choosing. This is not a gender issue. It is about owning all parts of oneself.

Masculine energy has traditionally been said to function as logic, thinking and reasoning in all people.

Feminine energy has traditionally been said to express as sensitivity, emotionality and intuition in all people.

We all have the capacity to express both energies in the combination and the manner that suit our True Self.

* * *

Symbols, fables, parables and many art forms are the means of conveying something that words alone cannot adequately express. They circumvent the literal mind, which can obscure or destroy a hidden and suggested message. Art, of all types, can portray truths the rational mind would negate. We must be willing to look deeper and develop a sensitivity to such representations. They often have much to teach us.

When we place our scientific mind on one side, we give space for our intuitive mind to 'speak'. Powerful messages incorporated into artforms may then release their communication. The logical mind needs to be 'silent' and allow our sensitive and intuitive mind to offer its valuable contribution. It is imperative we learn to be receptive to different ways of hearing, seeing, knowing and perceiving. Exploring our latent and largely unused energies can add value to our understanding of life and God.

Linda's story

In her working life, Linda had been a mathematics lecturer at a modern comprehensive school. Maths was her comfort zone. She understood numbers. They followed logical, known formulas and formats. Once the rules were understood, there was no complication. Linda had fully owned and expressed the masculine aspect of her nature. Her career was acknowledged as successful and, in her work environment, she was well respected.

In the area of personal relationships, however, her life was problematic. She married and divorced twice, each time refusing to bear any responsibility for the break-ups. In her mind, men were always the problem. For her, there needed to be 'rules of engagement' in marriage. She never doubted that she may, sometimes, be wrong in her expectations and harsh judgements. She could not, however, conceive of having a responsive and fluid relationship. Sensitivity, compassion and insightfulness had never been allowed to develop as part of her psyche. She had no understanding that these qualities were an asset to any well-rounded personality.

Needless to say, Linda grew into an elderly and irascible woman, never realising she had missed much in her life. Her excessive maleness was out of balance. She had denied herself the joys and experiences of art, story and loving relationships.

Throughout our life, we each need to grow towards a balanced personality. Whatever our gender, we need to allow our Spirit the 'circumcision of freedom' and release our life-expression in the most productive way possible.

Suggested reading

Campbell, J., *The Hero with a Thousand Faces* (2008).

CHAPTER 54

Understand true poverty

Jesus said, 'Blessed are those who are poor, for yours is the kingdom of heaven'.

This saying has sadly been misinterpreted. In my opinion, it teaches about the wealth of innocence and the poverty of judgements. It values the lack of *pre*-conceptions and *pre*-judgements. It teaches that we must be impoverished of *pre*-assessments.

When our innocence is impoverished by bias and judgements, our ability to truly know another person, in all their fullness, has been sullied. We are unlikely to see and know them as they really are.

Wholeness of Truth can be made visible to us only when we are sufficiently impoverished of all preconceptions and are sufficiently empty to receive the Fullness of Divine Wisdom, present in every person.

Emily's story

Emily had a forgiving nature. She seemed to have the ability to take others at face value, never voicing judgements. Perhaps judgement didn't even enter her mind.

When Emily's son Peter married Debbie, Emily was delighted and offered some of her savings to help with a small down-payment on a terraced house. A large amount of renovation was needed to bring it up to habitable standards. But, she felt, this would give them a start in life.

An agreement between Emily and Peter had been reached that a 'granny flat' would, in time, be added to the main building. The renovations seemed to go at a very slow pace and Emily's flat was never fully completed.

There was always an excuse. Either they were waiting for planning permission, cash was limited, or some other scheme was being considered. After three years, Peter sold the house, making a good profit. He promised his mother she would get her granny flat at the next house.

Needless to say, none of these promises were realised. This was extremely sad, especially when Emily became ill with cancer and died within the year. It seemed Peter never realised the extent of his unkindness towards his mother. She had never complained, never judged and was completely empty of harsh thoughts about her son's lack of concern for her.

Debbie, however, had observed Peter's lack of empathy towards his mother's situation. Although she felt totally powerless to make any meaningful changes for Emily, she marvelled at her mother-in-law's acceptance of her son's disingenuous behaviour. It seemed Emily recognised that complaining would have made no difference whatsoever. It would simply have created a difficult atmosphere between mother and son.

Emily had refused to judge. Perhaps she sensed her time on earth was coming to a close. In the last few days of her life, Peter broke down, asking for her forgiveness. She had had no need to point out to him the error of his ways. As so often happens, the situation itself spoke to Peter. As he held her hand, all his self-protection, his excuses, were gone. His defensive boundaries had been breached by the sincerity of a loving and non-judging mother. Their last few days together were respectful, without rancour and full of kindness.

Suggested reading

Anonymous, *Christ in You* (1910).

CHAPTER 55

Place god before all others

> Jesus said, 'Whoever doesn't hate their father and mother can't become my disciple, and whoever doesn't hate their brothers and sisters and take up their cross like I do isn't worthy of me'.

The message of this saying is that we must choose carefully which 'voice' we follow. In many households, particularly where older family members are deeply respected, tradition demands that we do as our elders have always done. In adulthood, this can result in great costs to our personal freedom, our individual life-expression, and may also inhibit our Divine Journey.

As children, we undoubtedly require parental guidance. As adults, however, we must be free to follow our own path, even when that may include making mistakes. These are often our greatest teachers. When we feel coerced into living a life that another person has chosen for us, something within us slowly begins to fade, perhaps even to die.

We are each blessed with an inner Christhood and are here, in this earthly body, to express the will of Divine Spirit. We must follow no other will. Families, partners, even friends, often try to manipulate us for their own selfish purposes. When someone truly loves us, they will harbour no selfish motive. They will want only what is best for us.

For sure, taking care of others may be an aspect of that journey. However, if we take the time to listen to our true inner voice, we will be certain of the direction in which the Divine is leading us. We will be guided in all our behaviours and our allegiances.

* * *

Breaking away from the 'oughts' and 'shoulds' of life can be a difficult period for many of us. We may need therapeutic help to separate the voice of human obligation from the Inner Pure Voice of Spirit. Be assured, the only path to true joy is the path designed for us by our Eternal Guide.

Jesus teaches that we place our Divine Journey above all others. We are on earth to discover and express our God-Self and this must, forever, be our priority.

Suggested reading

Dyer, W.W., *There is a Spiritual Solution to Every Problem* (2002).

CHAPTER 56

Look deeper, beyond the human façade

Jesus said, 'Whoever has known the world has found a corpse. Whoever has found a corpse, of them the world isn't worthy'.

In this codex, Jesus claims that the conventional world in which we live appears to be devoid of Divine Presence. If we seek only with our five senses, we will come to know nothing but humanness. We will remain ignorant of the true and hidden life which waits within each and every one of us.

An egg illustrates the point! Although the outer shell initially serves a purpose, it has no lasting function. When the contained creature has hatched, the shell is empty and discarded. Equally, our body and perhaps even our personality, are merely shell-like containers for the real and true life that exists deep within us. Without the discovery and release of that contained Inner Spirit, our life will have limited purpose and value.

Our task in life is to discover our Spiritual Identity. It waits for us to break through the shell of superficiality into a living consciousness which waits within our soul. As our earthly existence becomes transformed by the freeing of the Spirit, we learn to look beyond our human limitations. We seek that which is deeper, permanent and of eternal value.

Fred's story

Fred was just an average guy who enjoyed sport, friendships and trekking. When he received a debilitating injury to his hips, his life changed forever.

For many months he grieved for the past life that would never return. With the support of counselling, Fred slowly came to accept his situation and to seek something different, something suited to the life he was now forced to live.

Help came in the form of a physiotherapist named Dawn. For several months Dawn treated Fred at his home. On a physical level, she was able to help with mobility and some rehabilitation. However, when she introduced mindfulness techniques and meditation, she brought a slow but effective healing to Fred's overall sense of well-being.

Fred slowly began to understand that, even with limited mobility, he was still Fred! In fact, his daily hour-long meditation practice became his most valued occupation. He came to realise that, although he had lost some of his physical ability, he had actually gained something of the greatest value. He had found his inner Divine Self, the source of wisdom, peace and love.

Persistent and committed meditation practice had developed his Sacred Muscle to such a degree that his sense of inner wholeness became well-established. Although Fred's experiences were profound and life-changing, he had discovered something within himself of eternal value.

A year later, Fred was surprised to be invited to train for a charitable placement which mentored teenagers with life-altering issues. After much consideration, and encouragement from Dawn, he began a year of professional Emotional Therapy training.

Fred thoroughly enjoyed this new direction. He quickly grew to be a treasured member of the team that supported the young people in their care.

In time, he and Dawn were able to introduce mindfulness classes and meditation practice to some of these young people. Although still with limited physical mobility, Fred felt his life now had real purpose.

He came to believe his accident and change of circumstances had brought benefit to others. He was the most fulfilled he had ever been.

Finding deep personal satisfaction in this new life, Fred had discovered a 'worthy life beyond the carcass'!

Suggested reading

Hanh, T.N., *Being Peace* (1992).

CHAPTER 57

Blessings of our harvest

> Jesus said, 'My Father's kingdom can be compared to someone who had [good] seed. Their enemy came by night and sowed weeds among the good seed. The person didn't let anyone pull out the weeds, "so that you don't pull out the wheat along with the weeds", they said to them. "On the day of the harvest, the weeds will be obvious. Then they'll be pulled out and burned"'.

My interpretation of this teaching is that it explains that Divine Presence within us supplies all our needs according to our expectations. The 'good seeds' produce not only our daily practical necessities, but also the wisdom, power and love which direct our human journey. However, we are all contaminated with worldly ideas, thoughts and emotions. These are identified as the 'weeds' which, at the correct time, should be eliminated.

Our consciousness is the soil into which 'seeds' are planted. The seeds grow and manifest as our life. That which we anticipate, that which we believe to be true, becomes our life. We possess far more control of our life-journey than most of us realise.

Many people focus on news of disaster, violence, poverty and illness. Some have an addiction to victimhood and prefer to identify with those less fortunate. This can be the result of inadequate parenting, which leaves a child unsure of its own true worth.

Children are highly sensitive and easily intuit adult behaviours and feelings. They know when a parent has little interest in them. Believing in the invincibility of their parent, children unconsciously blame themselves for any lack of attention and love. The result is that harmful beliefs are 'planted' in a child's unconscious mind. We 'grow' our life from those seeds planted within our psyche.

* * *

Jesus states that seeking 'the weeds' of self-destructive beliefs can best be achieved by observing one's life. As 'the weeds' grow and become apparent, they can then be eliminated. We must have the desire to root out and destroy the harmful tendencies that lurk in the recesses of our mind. The process of seeking and eliminating, although emotionally painful, eventually brings the highest rewards.

The analogy of a field filled with a mixture of crops and weeds illustrates the task in which we each must participate. With stones and weeds removed, the harvest of our life will be good, true and wholesome.

Sandy's story

Sandy was a mature woman who chose to focus only on the difficult aspects of her life. Even though she had little to complain about as an adult, she would dwell on negativity.

Following her husband's death, she no longer had someone to bring balance to her depressive emotional state. As her victimhood deepened, her family began to lose patience. They found her tiresome and draining and chose to spend less and less time with her. She was creating her own drama of loneliness.

Sandy focused increasingly on friends who were of a similar negative mind-set. She remained blind and deaf to the few brave souls who offered her interesting and joyful friendships. As a result of an oppressive upbringing, she was recreating the same miserable environment in which she had been raised. Her comfort zone existed in the dark mode of being the victim.

The translation of this codex suggests our life will 'make visible' the weeds which we can, *if we so choose*, eliminate from our life. We must, however, first have the desire to change. We must want something better for ourselves. Sandy, sadly, was not able or willing to 'seek out the weeds' that distorted her personality and her life.

Many things we can change. Some, however, we cannot. Those issues that we must learn to live with, often become our greatest teachers.

Suggested reading

de Mello, A., *Sadhana: A Way to God* (1984).

CHAPTER 58

Work diligently to discover the truth of life

> Jesus said, 'Blessed is the person who's gone to a lot of trouble. They've found life'.

To find life means, I believe, to find the fullness and completeness of life. To discover and grow in understanding of our Divine Centre, and learn to live that Truth.

Through our outer life-expression, it is intended that we harness spiritual truth and bring it into human demonstration. We each have, I believe, a personal journey which no other can undertake. When we discover our inner Christhood, we express our own version of Oneness. I believe to recognise and live that, is the purpose of life.

* * *

We are familiar with the theory of DNA, the genetic coding held in our cells. Each person's genetic code is unique. The difference between people may be minuscule but a uniqueness nevertheless exists.

At the same time, we are each an outpouring, a manifestation, a tangible representation of the One Infinite Divine Energy which gives expression to all life in the universe.

Endeavouring to express our uniqueness requires commitment and courage. At times we can be guided by others, but no one can actually lead us into the sanctum of our own Being. This is the solitary and sacred aspect of our journey.

People's accounts of their search for truth can be helpful and encouraging. Immersing ourselves in the spiritual atmosphere of study literature, sacred texts and personal stories, can offer valuable support and encouragement during spiritually 'lean' times.

Study helps to develop discernment for what is false and what is true. Although the choice of study literature is vast, listening to our inner promptings may be the most reliable method of selection. Many people report that books literally fall off the bookshelf and into their hands when they seek in earnest! The 'right' books will come to us when we have a joyful expectation.

Ultimately, though, we must find our own unique path. Regular daily practice of 'Being in the Silence' opens a space into which our individual understanding of Truth may present itself.

Your reward will be the discovery of true 'life'—your life!

Charlie's dream

For several months Charlie had been meditating with a small group of people. They met three times a week and sat in silence for one hour each session. They were truly committed to their spiritual journey.

As Charlie's busy mind grew more still and more centred, he began to have vivid dreams. These, he believed, were guiding messages from his Higher Self. One of the dreams, however, he felt sure was a communication for the whole group. He willingly shared it with the other members.

The dream itself

Charlie was standing looking at a great and beautiful mountain. It was covered in swathes of colourful vegetation. Many paths, perhaps billions, led up to the summit. Some meandered gradually up the mountain; some routes covered difficult rocky terrain; many twisted and turned, seemingly with little clear direction. A few paths took a direct route straight up to the summit.

People sat at the foot of the mountain, relaxing and perhaps contemplating their particular approach. Lots, however, were already making their way up. Some took designated paths. Some were creating their own. Some were hurrying, some taking their time; some were resting and chatting with fellow travellers.

A small number had reached the summit.

* * *

Charlie shared his understanding with his fellow meditators:

- The mountain represents the earthly journey.
- The summit represents the 'place' where we discover and unite with our unique Divine Self.
- The multitude of paths represent the infinite number of ways we can each take to reach our personal summit.
- Each climber is having their own unique experience on their way to the summit.
- Many gather at the base, unsure and uncertain, waiting for guidance.
- The atmosphere of the scene is one of calm, relaxed peace.

* * *

Charlie believed he had been shown an overview of humanity and the great variety of life-journeys we undertake. He valued this confirmation that eventually all paths will reach the summit, where we will each become united with our Sacred Christhood.

Suggested reading

Laird, M., *An Ocean of Light* (2019).

CHAPTER 59

Seek your truth in this life

> Jesus said, 'Look for the Living One while you're still alive. If you die and then try to look for him, you won't be able to'.

In this saying, Jesus teaches that we must seek the Living, the Divine part of ourselves, whilst on this human plane. Life offers endless opportunities to know our Divine Self. Everywhere, in every situation, in every creature, God is present as the One True Life. It is our choice to accept and acknowledge this at every opportunity—every day, in each moment.

Codex 59 states that whilst on the earth-plane and in bodily form, we must seek our Divine Centre. Heaven is right here, right now, within us. If we do not discover our Divine Centre whilst in human form, what certainty do we have that we will find it after death?

To be fully present in the moment, with an open and expectant mind, offers infinite opportunities for Truth to be revealed to us.

Seek, be open and you will find.

Gerry's story

Gerry was raised in a deeply Christian family. When he was a young boy Sundays had always consisted of church attendance both morning and evening. He was a choir boy and no excuse for avoidance was allowed. When Gerry became a teenager he finally rebelled. Nothing, he claimed, would force him back into the narrow confines of church life. And so began his personal search for meaning through reading, seeking and studying.

Gerry's growing search led him to walk the Camino Way. There he met many free-spirited people from various walks of life, each with their own particular reason for 'walking'. He spent interesting times with other 'rebellious seekers' who were also forging their individual and independent approach to spirituality. Although he did not need approval, he seemed to gain sanction, succour and encouragement from these fellow travellers.

* * *

Many people no longer need buildings, teachers and a Creed to follow. We, as the human race, are growing in confidence to discover and live out our own particular and unique Divinity. As a result, external preachers and formalised worship are becoming unnecessary. The flourishing of our self-reliance and self-belief encourages us to seek our own particular pathway to our Divine Centre. We are discovering our power and confidence to break free from rhetoric and truly live with Divine Awareness in our own individual way. Those who are 'alive to Truth' are discovering the 'living one' whilst still on the earthly plane of existence.

NOW is the time to seek.

Suggested reading

Tolle, E., *The Power of Now* (1997).

CHAPTER 60

Stay conscious and awake

> They saw a Samaritan carrying a lamb to Judea. He said to his disciples, 'What do you think he's going to do with that lamb?'
> They said to him, 'He's going to kill it and eat it'.
> He said to them, 'While it's living, he won't eat it, but only after he kills it and it becomes a corpse'.
> They said, 'He can't do it any other way'.
> He said to them, 'You, too, look for a resting place, so that you won't become a corpse and be eaten'.

In the interpretation of this codex, Jesus uses the example of the lamb that, whilst it is alive, cannot be eaten/devoured. However, when not alive, it will certainly be eaten and destroyed.

Likewise, when we are alive and awake to the permanence of God within ourselves, we are fully conscious of Divine Presence and cannot be consumed by human cares and negativity.

Until we discover the True Life within ourselves, we are susceptible to human emotions, which can spread unseen like a contagion. Fears of disease, loss and evil easily render us powerless. In turbulent times we can become consumed by mass anxiety, even mass hysteria.

In this technological era, with the invasive and perpetual presence of social media, our peace of mind is becoming ever more vulnerable. Conscious awareness of these powerful intrusions is our protection.

Being alive and vigilant to the vulnerability of our spiritual connection to Truth is our personal task. Our spirit will never die but our conscious connection to that precious aspect of our Self, is vulnerable. Stay conscious, stay awake and stay alert. Do not give negative influences any opportunity to inhibit your inner Divine peace of mind. Remain conscious and alert to that which is forever present.

Luke's story

Luke was an ordinary guy who enjoyed cycling, running and outdoor bowls. When his wife demanded a divorce, he was shocked to learn she had been unhappy for quite some time. How had he not noticed?

So began Luke's therapeutic journey. Within a matter of weeks, he realised he had been 'sleep-walking' through the last five years of his life. His day-to-day routines had become robotic to such a degree that he had slipped into an emotional disconnect, not only from his wife but also from life itself.

The counselling arrangement of one session per week lasted several months. During that time Luke grew to understand himself in ways he had not previously considered. He found the courage to face issues that in the past he had chosen to ignore. Signs of inner discontent, he came to realise, cannot be ignored. They must be addressed with sensitivity and a willingness to discuss and compromise, by both sides of the relationship.

In the past, Luke had chosen to be 'dead' to problems. This, together with his lack of emotional sensitivity, had killed the marriage. He and his marriage had become a 'carcass' that could no longer be saved.

My interpretation of this codex is that it teaches us that we must become aware of both our inner emotional self and our outer relating self. Without conscious awareness, we can easily be consumed by negativity, despair and despondency.

Staying alert is to stay alive to life.
Staying awake is to remain powerful and proactive.
Staying conscious is to be attuned to our intuition and sensitivities.

Suggested reading

Thorne, B., *The Mystical Power of Person-Centred Therapy: Hope Beyond Despair* (2002).

CHAPTER 61

Become whole, become enlightened

>   Jesus said, 'Two will rest on a couch. One will die, the other will live'.
>   Salome said, 'Who are you, Sir, to climb onto my couch and eat off my table as if you're from someone?'
>   Jesus said to her, 'I'm the one who exists in equality. Some of what belongs to my Father was given to me'.
>   'I'm your disciple'.
>   'So I'm telling you, if someone is /equal\, [sic] they'll be full of light; but if they're divided, they'll be full of darkness'.

This saying relates to our dual nature, which can function in conflicting ways. We are familiar with human nature and its self-centred demands. Orthodox religions have tried to tame those egocentric urges by teaching the value of service, kindness and charity. Some have offered the 'lure' of a special place in heaven for those deemed 'good enough' to enter. These guidelines have done little to curb the natural selfish human tendencies with which we all battle. Just as animals strive for their own survival above others, we too have an unconscious and natural drive for survival.

Our Divine Nature, however, is life itself. It is pure and infinite goodness. Although we are all born with a capacity to express this, we must first become conscious of its presence. As we learn to *be whole*, we become complete and have access to the fullness of Truth. This must be worked and struggled for. Through regular study and committed contemplation, we will create the right conditions for our inner growth.

My interpretation of the original codex is that this teaching points to the fact humanity has gained little from the religious dogma laid down over the centuries. Sincerity of wholeness cannot be forced upon us by laws and creeds. It must develop from within oneself.

Jenny and Peter's story

Peter and Jenny were regular attendees at the local parish church. They had been on several Bible study courses and began to offer regular classes in the village hall on a monthly basis. Their confidence and apparent knowledge seemed to have given Peter and Jenny a revered status within their community.

All seemed well until an issue arose about a conflict of dates in the run-up to Christmas. The community choir needed the village hall for a one-off carol practice on the same evening that the Bible group had their fixed arrangement. Jenny and Peter were assertive about the need to retain the regularity of their classes. Equally, the choir master felt that Christmas came only once a year and carols should have priority.

A most unchristian row erupted as both groups defended the status they believed they held within the village. Neither was willing to back down and compromise. Their selfish demands highlighted a lack of spiritual wholeness within the people involved. Their inner darkness would not allow for the healing light of compromise.

When we function from an understanding of The One Life, expressing as all living beings, we cease to act in self-centred ways. We endeavour to heal disputes by taking responsibility for our actions. We seek to eliminate from ourselves anything which could cause disharmony.

Sadly, on this occasion, it became necessary for the Vicar to resolve the issue. As individual egos rose in justification, he could find no willingness for mutual compromise. There was no 'light' to remove the darkness of the self-centred egos.

In the event, the Vicar felt he had no option but to deny all use of the hall on that problematic date!

Suggested reading

Merton, T., *The Power and Meaning of Love* (1976).

CHAPTER 62

Protect divine mystery

Jesus said, 'I tell my mysteries to [those who are worthy of my] mysteries. Don't let your left hand know what your right hand is doing'.

My interpretation of this codex is that we will understand the Mystery Teachings only when we have developed an ability to discern them. This requires that the capacity for intuitive experience has developed within us. Esoteric truths do not speak the language of logic.

Only when our consciousness has become adequately attuned will the fullness of these enigmatic teachings become accessible. Then, all will be revealed and nothing will remain hidden.

We are advised to keep Divine Truths secret and close to our heart. Many people, without the benefit of sacred knowledge, may fear them. They may deny them and attempt to destroy them.

Those who seek with respect and sincerity, however, will protect them. Stay alert. Keep this wisdom hidden, sacred and close to your heart.

Amelia's story

Amelia had received several years of Jungian Therapy. Whilst she had found it challenging, this type of self-exploration suited her character. She engaged easily with the use of images through the medium of her dreams and responded cooperatively to the analysis of her unconscious. She had grown to be skilful at discerning meaning conveyed by symbols, fairy tales, fables and imagery. These were written in a language that truly 'in'-spired her!

The therapy had prepared Amelia well for her later quest to understand the *Gospel of Thomas*. The 114 codices can seem uncompromisingly obscure and inaccessible. The style of language and writing forces us to work hard to discern their hidden meanings. It is, however, the very nature of their concealment that makes them not only challenging, but also hypnotic in their attraction.

Amelia was able to engage with the symbolic language. She found the depth of the commentary enthralling. To bring these teachings into the light of awareness became her passion.

An avenue of expression opened when she was asked to share her personal understanding with a group of women. They previously had approached the *Gospel of Thomas* through the avenue of logic and literal interpretation. As Amelia guided this small bunch of pioneers, they quickly became aware that a new manner of seeing and reading was called for. They were being required to open the 'eyes of the Soul'.

Unsurprisingly, several of the members fell away from the group but the three most intuitive and sensitive remained. And so began a sacred and precious journey for the surviving women. Their commitment to the teachings, and to each other, was of paramount importance. Such a journey cannot be forced, but it can be nourished and encouraged. The *real* teacher would be *their* inner soul guide. The support and great value of a shared experience would come from each other.

The true spiritual journey cannot be exhausted. Truth is infinite. At times it seemed beyond their capacity and futile to make sense of seemingly senseless and contradictory statements in the translations. Only with hindsight in later years would the women reflect with awe on the gentle development of their sacred understanding. They recognised there were many times when 'something' had led and held them. They had each experienced great wonder at the sense of sacred guidance which had led their regular meetings.

Embarked on such a journey, through sharing and supporting each other, they had grown to understand the hidden mysteries. They realised their spiritual journey was infinite. There is no end, no finale to reach. It is eternal.

Suggested reading

Vaughan-Lee, L., *The Return of the Feminine and the World Soul* (2009).

CHAPTER 63

Live fully in the moment

> Jesus said, 'There was a rich man who had much money. He said, "I'll use my money to sow, reap, plant, and fill my barns with fruit, so that I won't need anything". That's what he was thinking to himself, but he died that very night. Anyone who has ears to hear should hear!'

This saying asks that we be aware of our priorities in life and avoid time-wasting on irrelevancies and trivia. Our ultimate purpose is to discover and live according to our particular unique Divine Calling.

Although we are each fashioned from the One Wholeness, we are intended to be solitary in its expression. Only *we* can express our individual part. Since no other can fulfil our particular purpose, it is our prerogative to wisely invest our time and effort for the benefit of the whole. Do not undervalue life—your life!

Every person's Divine story has sacred meaning and, as such, is a vital piece of the Whole Earthly Picture. *Perhaps* it is intended that one day the human story will be complete, with every individually awakened piece in its rightful place.

Julie's story

Julie had been a village shop keeper for many years. Her shop was a treasure trove of everything that anyone could ever need. At the heart of a rural and vibrant community, Julie's shop provided the communal space where villagers met to exchange news, gossip and maintain friendships. Without any conscious intention, Julie offered a shared place of friendship for the whole village.

Now in her early 50s, Julie was beginning to question the purpose and meaning of her life. She had inherited the shop from her grandmother some 20 years before. There had been many changes to the village as families moved away and newcomers renovated old derelict properties. She began to question her motives for staying and felt it was time to do something different with her life.

Ideas came and went, but nothing held her interest for long. One day she noticed an announcement in the county circular. A seven-day silent retreat was to be held at a Spiritual Centre just 50 miles along the coast. The sense of rightness about this retreat filled Julie with feelings which she later found impossible to describe. Although she had no experience of retreats, she had little hesitation in booking her place immediately. Only in the days leading up to it would she question her hasty decision.

Friends had arranged a working rota to keep the shop running whilst Julie was away. Finally, the day of the retreat arrived. With her car packed and ready, there was no backing out now. As Julie approached the gateway to the retreat house, her nervousness increased. She had no idea what to expect from the coming days.

As she drove up the long winding track, she absorbed the wildness and beauty of the surrounding gardens. The place seemed lush with life, un-manicured and natural. A calmness enveloped her. Perhaps, she felt, this could turn out okay!

As she entered the spacious hallway she received a warm, easy welcome and an invitation to tea and cakes in the large adjoining room. Julie felt safe.

The first two days were spent in silent and solitary exploration of the gardens and her thoughts. The retreatants were allowed to roam, sit and just 'be' with wild nature, wherever they chose. Gradually, Julie's busy mind began to quieten. With nothing demanding her attention, she relaxed into the serene rhythm of this extraordinary place. She had time to sit within the bosom of nature, to think and to consider herself and her needs.

The retreat house also provided a sanctuary where retreatants could explore their troubles. Nervously, Julie asked for a 45-minute session with one of the counsellors. She had not previously considered professional assistance to explore her future options but perhaps now was the time to do so.

The counsellor listened and asked Julie pertinent and practical questions. None of which she had an answer to. Perhaps, the counsellor suggested, Julie could find a still and private spot in the retreat garden and simply ask Mother Nature for guidance.

Julie was very sceptical this would help but felt she should at least give it a try. On the third day of asking, she physically sensed an aura of love and peace descending and enveloping her. It was a most extraordinary experience. It happened again the following day and, for a final time, on the third day.

No tangible solution about the future came to her but she no longer felt alone in the world, no longer 'left behind', no longer 'good old Julie behind the shop counter'. She felt that Mother Nature, by acknowledging her and respecting her anxiety, had lovingly bestowed upon her an equality, a value, that she had not previously realised was missing.

Although there was no miracle solution to her predicament, this was the turning point for Julie. She made a promise to herself that she would seek counselling on her return home. Julie stuck to her commitment.

The outcome of this self-attention and growing self-respect was that Julie began to sincerely value herself. She felt if the awesome power of Mother Nature was willing to listen and help her, then her personal and intrinsic value must be equal to all others, including the wealthy newcomers in the village.

On her return home, villagers were keen to hear about her experience. Julie, however, chose to say very little. How could she describe and explain such 'other-worldly' experiences?

Thankfully, she chose to protect her 'spiritual investment' and rarely made any comments about it to others. She believed Mother Nature had given her a gift beyond measure and this she would protect.

In the next few months, Julie made no adjustments to her working life. However, by changing her attitude to one of sincere self-appreciation, she began *noticing* the tangible support she was receiving for her ever-growing business. She *consciously* noted that she alone was responsible for the increased trade from the addition of the bakery, the delicatessen, the wine cellar and the weekly door-to-door deliveries.

She now realised she had rarely given herself the credit she deserved. The intervention of a wise counsellor within a peaceful sanctuary had allowed Julie the time and space to 'reset' her self-judgement button.

She vowed to return to the Spiritual Centre in the near future. Learning to appreciate herself, exactly as she is, had allowed her to let go of negative self-judgements and to enjoy all she was achieving. Life felt good, right here, right now.

Be awake, be aware and be open-hearted to what is already around and within you. Appreciate yourself as you are, *here and now*!

Suggested reading

Goldsmith, J.S., *Living Between Two Worlds* (1975).

CHAPTER 64

The banquet is already prepared

Jesus said, 'Someone was planning on having guests. When dinner was ready, they sent their servant to call the visitors. The servant went to the first and said, "My master invites you". They said, "Some merchants owe me money. They're coming tonight. I need to go and give them instructions. Excuse me from the dinner"'.

'The servant went to another one and said, "My master invites you". They said, "I've just bought a house and am needed for the day. I won't have time". The servant went to another one and said, "My master invites you". They said, "My friend is getting married and I'm going to make dinner. I can't come. Excuse me from the dinner"'.

'The servant went to another one and said, "My master invites you". They said, "I've just bought a farm and am going to collect the rent. I can't come. Excuse me"'.

'The servant went back and told the master, "The ones you've invited to the dinner have excused themselves". The master said to their servant, "Go out to the roads and bring whomever you find so that they can have dinner". Buyers and merchants won't [enter] the places of my Father'.

This scenario in this codex illustrates that many people prioritise and value money, possessions and worldly honours above all else.

My interpretation of this codex is that the 'prepared dinner' relates to food for the Soul rather than food for the belly. A feast of Divine Wisdom, Infinite Potency and Authentic Love awaits those with spiritual hunger.

The banquet has already been prepared for each and every one of us. No more can be done. We ourselves are responsible for attending the 'banquet' and consuming the 'spiritual food'. The desire to know and internalise Truth will not be forced upon us. We have free will.

The part we must each play in our spiritual journey is to acknowledge and use the feast of great wisdom that is already prepared. All are welcome to partake in this abundance but few understand the greatness of that which is offered. They turn away, ignoring the magnitude that awaits their acceptance.

It is entirely our prerogative to ingest the 'feast'.

Only we, ourselves, can choose to allow the fathomless depths of wisdom, love and potency to fill our Being.

Suggested reading

Laird, M., *An Ocean of Light* (2019).

CHAPTER 65

Do not kill the messenger

He said, 'A [creditor] owned a vineyard. He leased it out to some sharecroppers to work it so he could collect its fruit. He sent his servant so that the sharecroppers could give him the fruit of the vineyard. They seized his servant, beat him, and nearly killed him.

The servant went back and told his master. His master said, "Maybe he just didn't know them". He sent another servant, but the tenants beat that one too. Then the master sent his son, thinking, "Maybe they'll show some respect to my son". Because they knew that he was the heir of the vineyard, the sharecroppers seized and killed him. Anyone who has ears to hear should hear!'

This saying asks that we be awake and alert to Divine Truth, which may come from almost any source. Even those who would *seem* to be far from the path to God may bring lessons for us. Shun no one. Abuse no one. Treat all with the respect they deserve as a Child of God. Each encounter is yet another opportunity to deepen our awareness of Divine Omnipresence; these encounters may bring spiritual lessons of great value.

I interpret this codex as: when we 'see' only the flawed human being, we 'kill' the internal Son of God. All experiences offer valuable scope for both personal and spiritual growth.

God is life itself: *all life*. Until we truly know and acknowledge that, we crucify the expression of Christ, both within others and in ourselves.

Suggested reading

Fromm, E., *The Art of Being* (1993).

CHAPTER 66

Find the cornerstone of your life

Jesus said, 'Show me the stone the builders rejected; that's the cornerstone'.

In this saying, the original codex speaks of a 'building', which I believe represents our individual consciousness: that which has been developing throughout our lifetime from experiences and our life-journey. We accumulate knowledge about ourselves, the world in which we live and our place within that world.

Our personality may be constructed of inaccuracies passed on to us by others. Our self-knowledge may also be distorted. Consequently, we build a false persona from which we navigate and explore the external world. We base our actions and reactions on that which we have come to believe is true, *even when it may actually be false.*

The cornerstone of any building gives essential stability to its overall structure. Here it symbolises the Infinite and Eternal Self, which gives our life enduring, permanent grounding in Divine Truth, Power, Love and Wisdom.

This saying teaches that we seek authenticity about ourselves and about life itself. Without the conscious awareness of God as the cornerstone of our life, we may construct a life on shaky ground. Until we know the truth of our Being, we remain vulnerable. To be indestructible, our life must rest on sound foundations of Divine Awareness, which is forever at the core of our Being.

Knowing and seeking to live that Truth is the purpose of our life.

Suggested reading

Goldsmith, J.S., *The Infinite Way* (1995).

CHAPTER 67

Know yourself

> Jesus said, 'Whoever knows everything, but is personally lacking, lacks everything'.

Jesus states that those who have worldly knowledge but lack self-knowledge have missed the purpose of life. Their knowledge is of little value.

An awareness and understanding of Eternal Oneness as the source and centre of *all* life, is fundamental to knowing Truth. Without that, we have missed the rudimentary task of life: to know deeply, within one's soul, that the Divine Wellspring creates, sustains and maintains all seemingly separate beings, from the minutest particles to the, as yet unknown, galaxies.

To discover and live according to this truth is, I believe, the mission of this particular period in the history and evolution of humankind.

Suggested reading

Catala, R., *Mysticism of Now: The Art of Being Alive* (1998).

CHAPTER 68

Loved and blessed beyond measure

> Jesus said, 'Blessed are you when you're hated and persecuted, and no place will be found where you've been persecuted'.

The translation of this codex comforts and reassures us that we are forever held in God's love and protection. Should we encounter opposition as we journey our chosen path, we must hold to the truth that we are never alone.

At times, being true to oneself can feel difficult and uncomfortable. Others may feel threatened by those who seem spontaneous and unconcerned about artificial conventions and customs. Living in accord with one's inner guide is, I believe, the purpose of our life. Should we encounter hostility, this saying asks that we recognise the indestructibility of our Inner Self. Our innermost Being can never actually be harmed.

Dawn's story

Dawn had raised her two sons largely on her own. Husband Johnny, and father to their children, worked on the oil rigs. Consequently, Dawn spent much of her time both running her small fashion business and caring for their two sons.

Dawn recognised the lack of fatherly attention in her sons' lives and endeavoured to fulfil the almost impossible dual task of being both mother and father. In later life, she conceded there were many mistakes she had made in her sons' upbringing but knew she could have done no better under the circumstances.

The two boys grew into fine young men with successful careers, married wonderful women and produced two young sons apiece. All was well until Dawn, at the age of 59, finally divorced Johnny and married Sean. On a superficial level, her new husband was accepted by her sons. Johnny, however, now retired and fully integrated with his sons, jealously guarded his fatherly status.

Dawn began to find herself in a difficult position. Although she and Sean were included in family gatherings, the seething jealousy that Johnny emitted could barely be contained. Dawn knew from past experience that it would take very little for the dam to one day burst. For her, family gatherings became unhappy tense affairs. Her sons, for their own reasons, were unwilling to occasionally exclude their father. Taking Johnny's alcoholism into account, Dawn made the choice to refuse most, though not all, family invitations.

To Dawn's deep distress, her sons showed little understanding of her predicament and the relationship with her sons became fractured, inconsistent and, for her, deeply painful. The family dynamic had been fractured.

It broke Dawn's heart to let her sons go forward into their chosen lives knowing they now believed the worst of their mother.

Aware that she felt 'hated and persecuted', she turned to the *Gospel of Thomas* (Codex 68) for succour, understanding and support. She gradually realised and began to experience that, in her deepest self, she was truly known and valued without judgement; that her intentions were full of integrity and would eventually be seen as honourable; that she would always be divinely loved beyond measure.

Perhaps one day, she felt, her sons would become sufficiently mature to recognise the love and support she had given them in their younger years.

Suggested reading

Goldsmith, J.S., *The Gift of Love* (1975).

CHAPTER 69

Have the courage to be true to yourself

Jesus said, 'Blessed are those who've been persecuted in their own hearts. They've truly known the Father. Blessed are those who are hungry, so that their stomachs may be filled'.

This saying offers encouragement for those times when we may be challenged about, perhaps even judged for, our seemingly unscientific and possibly unorthodox beliefs. However, should we encounter hostility, this codex states we will bear little hurt. In the fullness of time, it will pass, leaving no lasting harm. We are all deeply loved and protected by the Divine All-Embracing Presence.

Holding strong to what is true for oneself can sometimes be painful as relationships become difficult. We may be tested when our path to God seems to cause difficulties with those we love and care for. Jesus forewarns of this. However, in this codex he states that we will experience many blessings when we have absolute trust in the guidance and enduring support from our Divine Centre. When we have discovered our interconnectedness with our God, we have discovered Sanctuary. Our 'hunger' for truth and comfort will be fulfilled.

Knowing the inner Presence in all people, we 'invite' a response from their True Self. This may facilitate extraordinary encounters for all those involved. Often, people seeking and hungry for Truth are drawn into our life, perhaps drawn to us in order to 'fill their stomach' with spiritual nourishment.

Adam's story

Adam was 16 when he began to question the Christian faith in which he had been raised. His maternal grandmother, Sadie, had cared for him since he was six. She had a kind heart, but life had also given her an uncompromising personality. When Adam became a permanent addition to her household the responsibility and an extra mouth to feed often tested her patience.

As a practising and life-long Christian, Sadie prayed every night to a God 'somewhere' in the clouds. She had always insisted Adam say his prayers at bedtime. However, as he developed into a happy outgoing teenager, this bedtime ritual had become almost unbearable for him.

On several occasions, Adam had secretly visited the local Hindu Temple with his best friend Nishant. He was hungry for 'something' spiritual in his life but traditional Christianity was leaving him unfulfilled. He told none of this to his grandmother. He felt it would be too controversial for her to hear.

However, Divine Power, whether we identify it as Christian, Hindu, Muslim, or Buddhist, to name but four, works in miraculous ways.

One day, to Adam's great surprise, Sadie calmly asked about his visits to the Temple! She explained that her friend and owner of the local corner shop had recently asked to speak with her regarding a 'difficult matter'. He needed her discretion and also her advice. He cautiously explained that, as a Hindu, he regularly visited and prayed at the local temple. On three occasions he had noticed Adam peering through the open door and reading the notices. Perhaps, he wondered, was this out of idle curiosity or was Adam 'hungry' for spiritual sustenance; perhaps he was searching for something that offered an approach that was different to Christianity?

He needed Sadie's guidance. If she felt it was appropriate, he was willing to take Adam to the Temple. Neither of them knew what Adam was seeking, but both wanted to help without interfering. Sadie trusted that a way of bringing this 'into the light' would eventually present itself.

Sadie was a wise old soul and asked 'her' God for guidance on how best to approach this difficult issue. She carried on with life as before, anticipating that the correct solution would come to her at the right time and in the right way.

Several weeks passed before the opportunity presented itself. Over breakfast one day, Adam rather nervously mentioned he was thinking of attending a local festival with Nishant and his family. Sadie was sure this was connected to the Hindu Temple. Here, she felt, was the opportunity to bring the 'secret' into the light. And so began a deeply respectful and honest discussion between Grandmother and Grandson.

Sadie explained she was aware Adam may have been seeking *his* spiritual path, one perhaps that differed from her own. With an open heart, she said she welcomed his exploration. She actually rejoiced in his quest to find *his* truth and was proud of his courage to 'seek until he found'. Sadie further explained that she had freely chosen her way of worshipping herself, to suit her background, her experiences and her personality. She wisely wanted Adam to be offered the same freedom to follow his path and to find spiritual nourishment in a way that suited him. Sadie showed great wisdom and compassion in a situation that many others, of whatever faith, may have found difficult to accept.

Tears of joy and hugs of relief were shared. Sadie's God had spoken to her and through her.

Suggested reading

Jung, C.G., *Modern Man in Search of a Soul* (2001).

CHAPTER 70

Be authentic

> Jesus said, 'If you give birth to what's within you, what you have within you will save you. If you don't have that within [you], what you don't have within you [will] kill you'.

This saying refers to that which is permanently present within each and every one of us. My interpretation of the codex is that our task is to come to know that inner Self, to express it and to 'bring it forth' as our unique life story. We must seek to be authentic in all we do in life.

If we are unwilling to express our truth, in time it will eventually destroy us. We may experience a deep sense of discontent and distress as stagnation affects our mind, our body and our spirit. I believe our task in life is to *be* our unique truth to the best of our ability. Sometimes this demands courage and perseverance. It is, however, the Divine purpose of our life.

The true pathway is solitary in its demonstration but shared by all at its Divine source. We risk wasting our soul energy when we seek confirmation from others about our chosen path. Given time, we learn to be comfortable—perhaps even comforted—by living our unique ideas. We grow to be at ease with the many contrasting opinions we encounter, no longer feeling the urge to 'convert' others to our way of thinking.

The Divine permission to be true to oneself is the gift we have each been given. It is also the gift *we* must offer to all others.

This saying states that, as we find the strength and courage to live out our particular truth, we are protected by the Inner Christ. As we *be*, *live* and *express* this, we become impervious to external pressures to be otherwise.

It is only when we shrink from being true (authentic) to our inner self that we risk losing the point and focus of our life.

Joanna's story

Joanna had been raised in a family dominated by her father. Joanna's mother, Patty, was gentle and quiet. She never raised her voice. Nor did she comment on her husband's bullying ways. It was only when Joanna left home at the age of 18 that the full understanding came to her of the strain her father was placing on the whole family.

Joanna tried on several occasions to gently address this issue with her mother, unfortunately, to no avail. She would not even consider that her husband was treating her badly. Their way of relating had become deeply embedded within their relationship. Eventually, Joanna was left with no choice but to accept this long-standing situation.

Joanna visited her parents once a month. Each time she noticed the increasingly subtle changes in her mother's demeanour and appearance. Patty gradually became indifferent to Joanna's presence. She took less care of herself. It seemed she rarely left the house to visit friends and neighbours. Most worryingly, other family members had ceased to call.

For Joanna, returning home became ever more depressing and deeply worrisome. She felt as if she was witnessing the slow death of her mother's desire to live. Having tried to help in the past, Joanna realised with painful sadness that she could do no more. She took counsel and decided she must take care of her own well-being and protect herself from what seemed like a subtle extermination of her mother's will and power.

* * *

When we cannot find the courage to fully live our life, we inadvertently play a role in the death of our true self. We have each been given a life to be expressed to the best of our ability. When we are compliant with the selfish wishes of others, we have participated in the diminishing of the life given to us. We have allowed our Divine Gift to be used for another's selfish purposes.

This type of relationship was not uncommon in the past. In current times, thankfully, this seems to be on the decline. The change has been slow in coming. It may take generations for all people to recognise their own power and to live fully in a good and productive way for the benefit of themselves and others.

Suggested reading

Pradervand, P., *The Gentle Art of Blessing* (2005).

CHAPTER 71

Only truth is eternal

> Jesus said, 'I'll destroy [this] house, and no one will be able to build it ...'

Jesus taught that human consciousness, with all its limitations, will eventually cease and the human story as we know it will end.

Only Divine Spirit, the fullness of which is beyond the capacity of human understanding, is indestructible. Its presence within each and every one of us is everlasting.

Suggested reading

Eliot, T.S., *The Four Quartets—Little Gidding* (1979).

CHAPTER 72

The fulfilment of your needs is within you

> [Someone said to him], 'Tell my brothers to divide our inheritance with me'.
> He said to him, 'Who made me a divider?' He turned to his disciples and said to them, 'Am I really a divider?'

The translation of this codex states that in response to a request for the sharing of possessions and a division of resources, Jesus says he does not divide nor separate. There is no need to do so.

He teaches that we each have access to the fullness of God—not a portion, not a share. It is only human belief that puts a limitation on what we are able to receive. We acquire according to our understanding and our expectations.

The human desire to accumulate 'stuff', 'things', 'possessions', has blinded us to the Infinity of true wealth that awaits us. Our values have become misplaced and misguided. As a result, the more material belongings we accumulate, the less we are satisfied. The emptiness we experience is, in reality, the spiritual emptiness within our soul.

Soul is, I believe, intended to be a conduit for Divine Source. When its value and purpose goes unrecognised, we inwardly hurt. We try to quell that painful sense of emptiness with superficial distractions which, in reality, offer no true easement. Society has become embroiled in a propaganda machine that promises happiness from possessions. This is a lie.

As we spiritually mature, we begin to notice the emptiness that often follows the acquisition of new 'trinkets'. Instead of buying yet more 'stuff', it would be beneficial to seek the source of authentic joy, gratitude and loving kindness.

As our spiritual understanding deepens, we begin to value love, friendship, wisdom and courage above possessions. Autonomy, resolve and authentic expression also become priorities. We each have within us an abundance of all these qualities and much, much more! To discover that fact and to gradually develop and incorporate these qualities into the expression of our everyday life, is the part *we* are required to play in this earthly journey we share.

The manner in which we choose to live life is our own responsibility. No other can fulfil our journey for us.

Suggested reading

Hay, L., *The Power is Within You* (1991).

CHAPTER 73

Harvest the spiritual crop

> Jesus said, 'The harvest really is plentiful, but the workers are few. So pray that the Lord will send workers to the harvest'.

This codex speaks of the Divine Harvest, which is of the greatest magnitude. An abundant 'crop' of love, wisdom, power and resources is readily available to everyone. The seeds of such spiritual awareness have already been 'planted' in human consciousness.

As worldwide communication has increased, spiritual knowledge from a diversity of faiths is becoming familiar to all who seek. Watered by the growth in meditation practice and an increasing attendance at retreats, the interest in a diversity of spiritual practices has developed. Many more people now recognise the great variety of ways to access the Inner Divine Truth.

The yield—the spiritual rewards—from the advance in human consciousness has prepared the 'Divine harvest' for people of many nations and faiths. More people who seek a spiritually enriched life have greater access to Divine Resources.

One Intelligence and Power connects *all* life. A better understanding of this is bringing a greater freedom to choose our own particular spiritual harvest. The abundant diversity of spiritual resources is becoming available for the benefit of many. This 'harvest' has long been prepared for the whole of humanity. In most parts of the western world, there is no discrimination; many are free to access their particular Divine Calling.

However, to gather the spiritual bounty we must first become conscious of its availability. As in nature, a farmer can harvest his crop *only* when he is aware of its existence! Without that conscious awareness, the produce goes to waste.

Similarly, the Divine Harvest awaits with ultimate patience for our realisation of this truth. It is our prerogative to seek and to gather our unique 'crop' of Spiritual Wisdom. No other can do this for us, it must come of our own volition and our own seeking.

Ivy's story

Ivy had experienced a loving but turbulent upbringing. Although her single mother, Mary, had struggled with limited resources, she had taken Ivy to Sunday school each week. Although Mary had little time for religion, she appreciated the kindness and support those teachers gave to all the young children. Ivy loved attending. With cakes, biscuits and fizzy drinks always available, it seemed like a party every week!

Each Sunday the children listened to the simple Christian stories about Jesus. From the age of 3 until 14, this was a regular and comforting feature of Ivy's turbulent life. She grew to believe she would always have a friend in Jesus. Sadly, when the church closed its doors, Ivy drifted away from religion. However, the gentle teachings were forever planted in her psyche, never fully leaving her. These were to give her essential support when, in her 30s, times became difficult.

Ivy's life changed when she knew for certain that her husband 'visited' a string of women on his deliveries around the Midlands. The day she discovered a young pregnant woman sitting on her doorstep, demanding to see Fred, Ivy made a bold choice.

She would no longer turn a 'blind eye' to the squandered wage packets, the absence from kiddies' birthdays, the stolen cash from her precious safety reserves, the holiday fund squandered on weekend binges with his mates. It was time for her and her four young children to leave.

With very little family support and limited social benefit, life was difficult. Ivy fought and won several custody battles for her children. She struggled with social services over child maintenance issues. She was rehoused time and again, going from one shabby flat to another. For several years she endured serious hardship. This had been a harsh and poor environment in which to raise four vulnerable children. But she did it.

Because of Ivy's inner belief in a Divine Power, she had 'something' to hang on to. She believed 'her' God would keep her and her young family together. Several years later Ivy was able to recognise the spiritual harvest that provided for her and her four children.

Within eight years Ivy had found a new husband who adored both her and her delightful family. She had also worked her way into a managerial position at the local Spar shop. She and her children were truly flourishing.

Sometime later, when asked how she had found the strength and courage to keep going through so much hardship, her answer was simple:

> I prayed every night to God. I trusted He would help me to help my children. When I needed courage, I asked and it seemed to come to me. When I needed support, it was always provided. When I was desperate for money, it came my way. But most of all, when I needed love, my children gave it to me in great abundance. I was afraid many times, but nothing bad actually happened. Because I prayed and asked for help, something, someone always came to my aid.

Ivy had learnt to harvest the seeds of trust in Divine support. During her time at Sunday School her beliefs had been nourished by those kind, committed women. In adulthood, Ivy's regular prayers had watered and tended her seeds. The crop was ready to harvest during the difficult years. She had the awareness, the confidence and the ability to reap her own harvest of a good and resourceful life.

Suggested reading

Merton, T., *New Seeds of Contemplation* (1972).

CHAPTER 74

Seek within yourself

> He said, 'Lord, many are gathered around the well, but there's nothing to drink'.

The 'emptiness of the well' mentioned in the translation of this codex refers to the false places where seekers endeavour to access God. As before, in Codex 39, Jesus warns against following empty teachings and false prophets, where nothing of value is available; where the thirst of the seeker remains unquenched.

This codex advises us to develop the discernment to seek rightfully where the eternal fountain of Truth is readily accessible, ever Omnipotent and Omniscient, never diminishing. This is the Eternal Fountain of Life present within each and every one of us. This source is alive, abundant and awaiting our realisation. When we seek Truth outside ourselves, we seek amiss.

During periods of meditation practice, we may catch glimpses of an inner Wellspring of Love. Although it is permanently present, we experience it as fleeting and ephemeral and we revert to our familiar human habits. This happens on many, many occasions until we begin to trust that the Divine Presence is always here, right now, in every moment.

In our search to 'quench our thirst', this codex warns we may travel false paths and pursue false prophets. However, each of these spurious trails will contribute to a developing discernment within us to choose our Rightful Path. There is no such thing as time in the spiritual world. We have eternity on our side!

As our yearning for Truth grows, so does a strong and intuitive wisdom. This will support us as we delve ever deeper into our inner well of Wisdom and Love. Our prepared path is forever present, forever available and will never desert us.

That which we seek is already within us.

Oliver's story

Oliver had lived a hard, fast and reckless life. He was drawn to the dangerous sport of high-altitude skiing. On more than one occasion he had needed to be rescued. Deep within himself, Oliver knew his luck must be running out. In an attempt to shore up his diminishing reserves of courage, he had begun to self-medicate with addictive drugs. These further compromised his ability to make sound judgements.

The day came when, skiing alone, he lost his bearings. A sudden and prolonged snow storm obliterated all indictors of the way back down the mountain. He had taken few provisions and no extra clothing. No one knew his location. As his phone signal began to fail and night fell, he knew he was in serious trouble. Oliver's rising panic further compromised his judgement.

As darkness closed in, Oliver continued to struggle through the ever-deepening snow. With no visible stars by which to orient himself, he realised at first light that he had trekked in a large circle. Hopelessness overwhelmed him. At that moment of utter despair, he lost his remaining powers of concentration and tumbled into a deep craggy gully. He does not know how long he lay there unconscious, but on opening his eyes he was immediately aware of an intense pain in his lower right leg. He had sustained a severe break close to the knee.

Now he felt all was lost. Even if he had known which direction to take, he simply could not walk. He had not eaten for some time and melted snow was the only sustenance he was taking. For the first time in his life, he became conscious that death was a possibility.

As so often happens in such extreme situations, a deep calm descended upon Oliver. When the Inner Divine Voice is no longer crowded out by mundane thoughts and feelings, a different impetus often begins to unfold.

Although Oliver had never tolerated anything of a spiritual nature, now, in this seemingly impossible situation, he became aware of 'something'. He would later describe this as being held and comforted in a warm deeply loving embrace. He felt cocooned, safe and totally at peace.

How long Oliver lay in this surreal and semi-conscious state is uncertain. However, when he regained consciousness in hospital, love and appreciation for life itself filled ever part of his being.

* * *

Oliver had been lost in the mountains for four days. He was discovered in a remote area by two skiers and eventually rescued by an emergency helicopter. Frostbite had claimed both his legs below the knee.

He had, however, begun a different journey! The road to clean and conscious living. He vowed he would never return to substance abuse.

Oliver was filled with a great sense of gratitude for his survival and also for this experience, which he felt had 'reset' his life. He believed he now had personal knowledge of something within himself that was beyond ordinary understanding. Whilst he never publicly identified this in spiritual terms, privately he knew he had encountered a Presence that was deeply loving, all-embracing and without worldly reference; something which can *only* be experienced.

* * *

When physically recovered, Oliver decided to train as a youth counsellor. He believed sharing his experiences may encourage disadvantaged teenagers to seek something good and fulfilling for themselves. Although he rarely spoke of his 'other-worldly experience', he hoped to show, rather than teach, that there is within us so much more than our outer form and persona. He wanted to broaden young minds and hearts to the opportunities that are all around and for them to realise these chances and choices are there for each one of us, *including them.*

Oliver went on to mentor, teach and encourage many young people to experience life in all its fullness; to understand and reject the 'empty well' of drug and alcohol abuse and to believe in their own inner resources ... however, those resources are identified and labelled.

Suggested reading

Eliot, T.S., *Little Gidding—Four Quartets* (1979).

CHAPTER 75

Becoming one, becoming whole

> Jesus said, 'Many are waiting at the door but those who are one will enter the bridal chamber'.

This codex, I believe, refers to the state of becoming a unique individual, whole and complete within oneself. My interpretation is that as we break from the traditional obligations and mores of society, we are no longer dependent on external dictates. We have become complete and whole within ourselves, able to act entirely from our inner promptings. We are free to follow the leadership of Divine guidance.

The reference to 'enter the wedding chamber' symbolises the uniting with God into a Divine Oneness of Being. As we become unified in mind, body and soul, we find the courage to live the life that was predestined for us.

Then we have truly become another living expression of Christ. This, I believe, is the purpose intended for each one of us, whatever faith or creed we follow.

Suggested readings

Jung, C.G., *Modern Man in Search of a Soul* (2001).
The *New Jerusalem Bible*: John 14:12.

CHAPTER 76

Protect that which has eternal value

> Jesus said, 'The Father's kingdom can be compared to a merchant with merchandise who found a pearl. The merchant was wise; they sold their merchandise and bought that single pearl for themselves.
>
> You, too, look for the treasure that doesn't perish but endures, where no moths come to eat and no worms destroy'.

Parables, fables and symbols convey deep meaning using an economy of words. In the parable of the pearl, Jesus uses this image to represent our soul, our personal and priceless source of Divine wisdom. This is everlasting, indestructible and incorruptible.

In earthly terms, a natural pearl takes a great deal of time to grow, mature and come to completion. It develops in a concealed environment within the protective shell of the oyster, preserved and unseen in the depths of the sea. It is a product of grit and sand which have caused irritation to its host. The end product is a pearl of great beauty and value. It is universally recognised and sought after. For the pearl to become known, an oyster fisherman must courageously dive to great depths and bring it to the surface.

Likewise, a developed soul is the product of the grittiness of life from which it has slowly emerged. The human journey, with all its difficulties, facilitates a developmental process which we all must undertake. The dramas, the highs and lows and the disappointments of life are essential aspects of the human journey. Problems are the irritations and difficulties which cause the Soul, like the pearl, to slowly mature and evolve.

For the Soul's value to be realised, it must be brought to the surface of consciousness into the light of everyday life. As our Soul gradually develops, it becomes a 'pearl of great price', valuable to both ourselves and all others with whom we share our life.

Jan's story

Jan had always sought the baubles and trinkets of life. Her two failed marriages, both based on what the husband would provide, had stood little chance of succeeding. At the age of 49 and with her beauty fading, she became depressed. Her doctor recommended 'talking therapy'.

After much deliberation and resistance, Jan finally settled into a regular routine of fortnightly appointments with the therapist. Her limited finances also forced a decision between therapy and the trinkets and trivia of life. Jan's conscious choice of renewal and healing heralded a new start. She was at last realising baubles did nothing to soothe her inner pain and emptiness.

As Jan's historical trauma slowly revealed itself, she uncovered her hidden 'wounded child'. She became aware of her younger self who had frequently been ignored by a fragile and troubled mother. Often disappearing for days, the mother left Jan in the care of an elderly neighbour. The guilt-ridden mother would return several days later with gifts of cheap toys and trinkets. Jan's young life was peppered with these traumatising absences and the 'gifts' that became a symbol to Jan of her mother's love.

After several weeks of regular therapy Jan's emotional state became more stabilised. She learnt to trust her therapist and slowly found the courage to face her inner pain and deep hurt. In time she began to further explore her underlying lack of self-worth. She was shocked to discover her need for baubles and trinkets had been driven by a deep need for affirmation, love and kind attention.

Jan spent two years in regular therapy. She courageously faced the deep hurts she had carried for many years. As painful memories began to heal, other memories, some of the truly happy times spent with her mother, gradually rose to the surface of awareness.

Emotional pain, until it is exorcised, can hold captive our memories, even the happy ones. We are often afraid to let go of familiarity, even when it is painful. We get 'stuck' in habitual thinking. Without professional support, it can be difficult to let go of past hurts in order to find the bigger and more complete picture.

As the pearl must be released from its shell for its value to be known, so the soul must be brought to the surface of consciousness. Only then can our 'pearl of great price' become known.

* * *

Many spiritual treasures are prepared for us. We must play our part by allowing these to come to the surface of consciousness and to pour into, and through, our life.

With the healing power of time, we can learn to bless and value all people, including ourselves.

Suggested reading

Pradervand, P., *The Gentle Art of Blessing* (2005).

CHAPTER 77

Finding divine presence in all situations

> Jesus said, 'I'm the light that's over all. I am the All. The All has come from me and unfolds toward me. Split a log; I'm there. Lift the stone, and you'll find me there'.

In this codex, Jesus refers to the 'I' at the centre of all life and the essence of all creation. There is only one 'I'. It is known by many names according to religion and culture. Terms such as God, Allah, Shiva, The Dao, Oneness, Omnipresence, Source, all refer to Divine Energy, the creator and maintainer of life.

This can be a difficult concept for many to accept. Tragedies and problems are often cited as hard evidence for the absence of any form of God. A Divine All-Loving Presence, some say, could never allow His creation to suffer. To understand the teaching in Codex 77, and to reap the benefit, requires that we learn to experience life in a different way.

We begin by realising we each have a great deal of control over how we feel. It is we, ourselves, who select the emotions we experience. Much of this is habitual and the repetition of learnt behavioural patterns. At any given moment, however, we are responsible for the emotional response we experience. We can focus our attention on what is difficult OR we can focus on what is okay.

Unhelpfully, we exist in a culture of blame and victimhood. This encourages the mistaken belief that bad things 'happen' to us, without any participation of our own.

Consequently, we remain ignorant of Divine Omnipresence when, in truth, there is no situation which is devoid of God. Knowing this truth is identified as 'Being in the Light'.

It refers to a perspective on life where the darkness of negativity has no reality; where there is no tangible substance called darkness. It disappears when we switch on the light! It also disappears when we recognise that we are forever in 'The Light' of God.

My story

In the early days of my spiritual journey, I found this a difficult concept to accept. My birth family were prone to blaming others and I unwittingly learnt to react in the same way. I resisted any suggestion that my feelings were my responsibility. It was habitual for me to see myself as the victim of circumstances. This removed any obligation on my part to change my perspective on life, events and circumstances. My flawed way of being changed when I read Edie Eger's astonishing book *The Choice*.

Edie relates the true story of herself as a young teenager incarcerated in Auschwitz. She was one of a limited number of people who witnessed and also survived the terrible cruelties meted out on a regular basis. Having read other similar harrowing accounts, it seems a common thread of perspective often stands out amongst those who survived their ordeal.

Some people discovered an ability within themselves to decide where they placed their attention. When, for example, they chose to focus on minute acts of kindness that sometimes passed between fellow prisoners, this brought small rays of hope into their terrible world. It kept alive a belief that humanity may still possess qualities of decency and love. Choosing to share one's daily ration of 'potato water' with a very sick person would bring a brief sense of deep companionship. Such small acts of loving kindness were present, if one chose to look for them.

It seems we have far more power over our perceptions, our thinking and our feelings, than many of us realise. The Light and Truth of God is *always* present, whatever the circumstances. As Jesus states in this codex: if we look, even in the darkest of places, God is there. How do we know that?

Because God *is* life, *all life*.

Where there is life, *there* is God.

Life teaches us that survival in terrible and traumatic situations often depends on an ability to control our darkest emotions and thoughts. To develop a capacity for hope, even the tiniest ray of hope, keeps a precious awareness of God alive.

Reading Edie's story, for me, upheld that belief. We each make moment-by-moment choices about how we feel, about where we elect to place our attention, whether we choose to notice the good or the bad.

I vowed I would endeavour to never again see myself as a victim.

Suggested readings

Eger, E.E., *The Choice* (2017).
Frankl, V.E., *Man's Search for Meaning* (2008).

CHAPTER 78

Seek truth where it rests

> Jesus said, 'What did you go out into the desert to see? A reed shaken by the wind? A [person] wearing fancy clothes, [like your] rulers and powerful people? They [wear] fancy [clothes], but can't know the truth'.

In this codex, Jesus asks, 'For what reason do they come? What do they seek?'

He challenges the mistaken confidence in church elders, rulers and the so-called powerful ones. He states that those people with no substantial knowledge or experience are weak. Their outer persona, their 'clothing', reveals the shallowness of their consciousness. They have nothing solid, robust or powerful to teach. They have no true awareness of eternal values.

* * *

This codex is similar to Codex 59 in that the translation advises us to seek our own personal experience of God. We can do this through meditation and contemplation. No one can give us meaningful and eternal knowledge. Some may be able to lead us to it, but only *we* can discover it for ourselves. The potential to truly 'know' God resides, I believe, within all people. It waits for our readiness and commitment to seek. Until then, it will remain hidden within us, not outside of our self.

It is our prerogative to seek. Only then will we find.

Suggested reading

de Mello, A., *Sadhana: A Way to God* (1984).

CHAPTER 79

Blessed are those who have discovered the truth

> A woman in the crowd said to him, 'Blessed is the womb that bore you, and the breasts that nourished you'. He said to [her], 'Blessed are those who have listened to the message of the Father and kept it, because there will be days when you'll say, "Blessed is the womb that didn't conceive and the breasts that haven't given milk"'.

Jesus states that the truly blessed are those who have truly understood his teachings and have learnt to live by those truths.

Sacred understanding is freely available to all.

This Divine Gift is not restricted to the select few but waits for each one of us to begin our search for meaning. An invitation has been offered and awaits our choice for its participation in our lives.

Suggested reading

Benner, J., *The Impersonal Life* (2015).

CHAPTER 80

The relatedness of all life

> Jesus said, 'Whoever has known the world has found the body; but whoever has found the body, of them the world isn't worthy'.

Jesus states that those who focus entirely on earthly life, its inhabitants and all its lifeforms, have explored *only* the physicality of life. Although this knowledge is of value and vital to our consciousness, it is limited to the world of time and space where Divine Presence remains largely unknown.

Those who have discovered the *Truth* of physical matter, recognise its value as limited and transient. At best, it is a temporary channel of corporeal existence. Although it provides us with the means of exploring our human self, its merits remain limited to mortal existence.

Those with knowledge of Truth have realised the immortality and boundlessness of Divine Life within the body.

Sharon's story

Sharon had flourished in her career as an independent and prominent journalist and had travelled to many far-flung places in pursuit of the 'story'. She had seen and experienced different cultures and ways of 'being'. Although she had never married, she had not been without suitors. Personal freedom, however, had always been her priority.

As the middle years approached, an inner dissatisfaction grew. New prospects, new horizons, new stories did little to ease her increasing despondency. She began to question her life choices. Perhaps she should have settled for a life of greater stability; perhaps sought a committed relationship and raised a family.

As her depression became more acute, a close friend suggested a retreat on a remote island off the coast of Thailand. Sharon had her doubts. The financial cost was not an issue but this was contrary to her normal way of coping with depression. The idea, however, lingered and niggled until, finally, she acquiesced. After all, what or who else could she spend her money on? She had nothing to lose!

On her arrival at the idyllic island, she discovered the days could be filled with a choice of body therapies, mind therapies, group therapies or simply relaxation. 'Encouraged' by the kindly intervention of a personal mentor, she decided to make use of all that was available. She even attended daily Tai Chi classes and yoga sessions.

Art therapy, supervised by a trained therapist, was also available each afternoon. With just four other participants engaged in creating artwork, the group easily and quickly bonded. The artistic expression soon became a means of self-exploration, with open and honest communication adding to the shared experience. Sharon felt not only free to explore her inner distress through painting, but also safe to do so. The small group of five became a great source of support and encouragement to each other.

From 5 pm each day, the entire community became silent. It remained so until 8 am the following morning. The evenings initially proved very difficult for Sharon. However, for the first time in her life she slowly began to experience calmness and serenity. She now treasured the preciousness of birdsong, the soothing power of waves lapping on the white sand, and the awesome beauty of a sunset. For the first time in her life, she became conscious of peace. Sharon's troubled and aching soul slowly opened and revealed its trauma.

She began to understand that, although her life had been filled with many wonderful experiences, these could no longer satisfy her new inner yearning. It was time her life focused on something completely different. After six weeks on the island, she was ready to return home.

Sharon chose to end her lucrative career in journalism and began training as an art therapist. She continued with Tai Chi classes and diligently meditated every morning and every evening.

Sharon's plan to return to the beautiful island never transpired. Instead, she discovered within her locality a small community of fellow meditators and therapists, all of whom welcomed her in sharing their bi-weekly gatherings.

At times, on her return home, Sharon found her new regime challenging. Slowly, however, the 'old self' began to release its hold on her, becoming little more than a memory. Over a period of time a hidden, peaceful—yet powerful—Light deep within her began to glow. She was slowly 'meeting' *her* inner peace and becoming the woman she was always meant to be.

Following three years of training and much personal therapy, Sharon qualified as a psychotherapist. She chose to use her accumulated wealth to help troubled youngsters in her locality. She gathered together therapists, helpers and volunteers to turn her fledgling project into a practical and functioning reality. Undoubtedly, each day brought its own problems and issues, from traumatised teenagers to deeply troubled families.

Sharon, however, had never been happier nor more fulfilled. Her early career in journalism had helped her develop courage, resilience and great vigour. All of which were now needed in abundance. Over the coming years, many young people greatly benefitted from Sharon's personal and practical resources.

On reflection, years later, she wondered if there had been some Divine guiding purpose to her life-journey. Her accumulated wealth, her powerful confidence, and her strength of character had all contributed to an ability to make her worthy project not only a long-term possibility, but also a great resource for many young people.

She wondered if her whole life had been 'directed' towards creating this project. Was it possible the 'plan' had been prepared by 'higher forces' even before her life had begun?!

Suggested reading

Catala, R., *Mysticism of Now: The Art of Being Alive* (1998).

CHAPTER 81

The secret meanings of wealth and power

> Jesus said, 'Whoever has become rich should become a ruler, and whoever has power should renounce it'.

The worldly sense of wealth refers to the financial value of a person's assets. This definition is subjective.

Each person's sense of wealth is individual to them, based on their life experiences, social environment and personal attitudes.

Much of the world would seem to value financial wealth above all else. Our sense of self-worth and personal power are often linked to the level of our bank balance. Without a certain level of assets, many believe they are a 'nobody'. A lack of self-worth can drive some to seek more material possessions in the false hope that they will be better loved and more valued.

* * *

True wealth, referred to us by Jesus, means an inner source of Divine Wealth which has developed through a lifetime of study, spiritual exploration and contemplation. True spiritual knowledge and understanding is not easily acquired. It takes commitment and a dedicated yearning to discover and, at times, experience Divine Presence. We all possess the potential to achieve this, it is denied to no one. However, our will and tenacity to seek this can be weakened by external and erroneous influences.

Life's challenges are always appropriate to our particular journey. They come to us as Divine opportunities for personal growth. Sometimes we encounter difficulties that may require an attitude of acceptance on our part; sometimes an unexpected challenge can shake our comfortable but stagnant life; sometimes we encounter an ordeal whose purpose is to facilitate the development of resilience and tenacity within us. Always, though, challenges are gifts to enable our inner growth. Working through human problems develops our character, wisdom and compassion for others.

We are each on a journey of discovery and are learning how to express our personal and unique destiny. This, I believe, may take many lifetimes. Although we may try to avoid difficult personal issues, there is no permanent escape from them. They repeat themselves in differing forms and different scenarios until we are willing to 'hear their wisdom'. In the fullness of time, we will acknowledge these as Divine gifts of learning.

We have within us an infinite capacity for Divine wisdom, power and courage. We must learn to be open to this Presence, *which is always accessible*, and to embrace our Divine birthright. Rightful power, however, must be expressed with love and caution. It is intended to be used in a helpful and altruistic manner rather than as power over another.

Alan's story

As a sensitive teenager, Alan found his father's extrovert personality terrifying and overwhelming. His younger sister, Mary, was full of confidence and constantly overshadowed this withdrawn young man. He misunderstood the families' many attempts to draw him into family life. In his growing paranoia, Alan became reclusive and began to study the world of motivational psychology. He was intelligent and developed a deep understanding of the human weakness for wealth and power. Alan easily identified with this theory.

He discovered he could use this particular human vulnerability to legitimately coerce people into parting with their finances. By using their greed, their insecurity and their need to feel valued, he grew wealthy on the weaknesses of his 'customers'.

Lacking any conscience, Alan had developed the ability to control and manipulate needy people. His own need for power dominated his life. The more wealth he accumulated, the greater his need for power became.

Sadly, never able to trust others, he became a lonely recluse. He never discovered the Divine Gifts of True Wealth or True Power within himself. At a young age, he died a very wealthy man.

Throughout his short life, Alan battled with a sense of powerlessness. He experienced the world as humiliating and his lack of self-worth required him to build a barrier of protection around himself. The more successful he became financially, the more he unconsciously disliked himself.

His deep fear of people meant he shunned any love or appreciation the outside world may have offered. He took the only route that seemed available to him, to 'even things out', as he saw it. Each time his wealth increased at the expense of another's loss, his self-esteem briefly soared. Power, he felt, was rightfully restored to him. These highs brought only temporary relief from his ever-deepening emotional crisis.

Sadly, although Alan understood peoples' compulsion for wealth and power, he had no knowledge of the love and joy that makes life truly worth living.

Divine Abundance is present in each one of us and fulfils our every need in the most appropriate, loving and wholesome way. We need no other power. A great wealth of wisdom, courage, strength and love resides permanently within each one of us. It is forever within our capacity to discover and to live from that place of abundant Divinity. This is the true place of joyful peace.

Suggested reading

Fromm, E., *The Art of Being* (1993).

CHAPTER 82

Spiritual fire

> Jesus said, 'Whoever is near me is near the fire, and whoever is far from me is far from the kingdom'.

The translation of this codex uses the term 'fire' as a metaphor for the cleansing and regenerating power of Divine Energy. Jesus states that when we live in harmony with the wisdom of his teachings, erroneous and false ideas will 'burn away' and be destroyed; new and accurate truths will become manifest and spiritual discernment will flourish. In the fullness of time, humankind will reap the fruit of a more enlightened, just and respectful society.

A new way of living will become possible.

Daisy's story

Daisy claimed she had been searching for the 'Hidden Truth of God' all her adult life. Each January she would state that this would be the year all her past woes would be gone; she would be able to live a life free of problems.

Over a period of years, she had sought spiritual guidance from various Christian groups. She had approached mystical teachers of diverse faiths. She had engaged in esoteric practices. Neither her life, nor Daisy herself, changed. Each year the same patterns of behaviour and ways of thinking produced the same disappointing life issues. She habitually placed blame outside of herself, refusing to recognise that changes would need to begin within herself. She remained unable to face and address her chaotic inner world.

We are each the 'gardener' of our life. Our thoughts, emotions and expectations are the metaphorical seeds that we 'choose' to plant in our consciousness. There is no punishment in the resulting consequences. It is simply a function of the impersonal laws of spirituality. Consequently, if we want to 'grow' different outcomes, we must consciously strive to 'plant' more wholesome ways of Being. We are never 'done to', other than by our own habitual choosing.

Courage is undoubtedly required when we decide to face our self-made dramas. However, taking responsibility is the key to making lasting changes.

This codex states that, as we live our life in conscious connection with Divine Source, we allow our erroneous ways to be 'set on fire'. New wholesome ways of Being can then grow and become established. Nourished by perpetual Divine Presence, these will become actualised as the essence of our life.

Suggested reading

Coelho, P., *The Supreme Gift* (1991; adapted from *The Greatest Thing in the World* by Henry Drummond).

CHAPTER 83

Spiritual light

Jesus said, 'Images are revealed to people, but the light within them is hidden in the image of the Father's light. He'll be revealed, but his image will be hidden by his light'.

This codex teaches that an image is a depiction of something rather than the actuality of the thing itself. Our five senses produce tangible knowledge of physical and temporal representations. We *hear* the birdsong; we *smell* the rose; we *taste* the coffee; we *feel* the sunshine; we *see* the landscape.

We also have a sixth sense, commonly known as intuition. This is the faculty of knowing beyond the five physical attributes. Some people are highly attuned to this type of awareness. Most, however, have limited use of this attribute.

In our current scientific era, the value of intuition is largely dismissed as unreliable and its development almost discouraged. Sadly, I think few people are conscious of its great potential. It largely remains under-used and under-valued.

Intuition, I believe, registers our innermost response to external events. It should undoubtedly be used with caution—it is easy to believe we are intuiting something about another person, when in fact we are actually projecting something of ourselves onto them.

In more recent times the power of our inner world has gained scientific recognition through the disciplines of psychiatry and psychology. Since these focus largely on the negative impact intuition can inflict on the personality, it is rare for the sixth sense to be considered an asset.

However, in the spiritual world of Divine Energy, our sixth sense can be considered of great benefit when used 'cleanly' and wisely.

In my opinion, this translation of codex 83 makes clear that the physical observation of Divine Spirit is not possible. An image is a mere representation, not the thing itself. Religious practices have encouraged followers to revere icons, statues and depictions of God. I think this is an unhelpful and long-outdated practice. It denies our natural and inherent ability to experience the direct presence of God within ourselves. A conscious soul, I believe, is the receptacle of Divine knowledge. Through the committed daily practice of three disciplines—meditation, contemplation and study—our soul begins to blossom.

It is often likened to the blossoming of the exquisite lotus flower. The lotus plant sits with its roots firmly established in the dark muddiness of silted water. These conditions seem to be less than ideal for this beautiful flower. However, when the time is right and its development is almost complete, the exquisite flower rises to the surface, blooms and becomes a joy for all to experience.

The soul develops through a comparable process. Our 'roots' are held in the dark potential and 'messiness' of human life. These circumstances offer experiences and challenges which slowly awaken our consciousness. As the soul blossoms it becomes a receptacle of Divine Impulse.

Conscious development of our Soul, through committed contemplation and meditation, will, at the right time, bring direct and personal experience of Infinite Presence. It is we who must commit to the dedicated daily practice of stillness, in both mind and body. In my experience, this takes time and commitment. Presence is always within us and all around us. However, until our soul opens and blossoms, tangible *experience* of God largely remains out of reach. It is we who must 'seek until we find' the spiritual light.

* * *

Authentic 'inner-tuition' is an attribute of the Soul. Its task is to lead us to a uniquely personal and direct relationship with our Innermost Divine Self. I believe it is within many peoples' capacity to seek and develop this faculty. Our conscious will, however, must be present. Nothing is ever withheld from us when our commitment is sincere.

Knowledge passed onto us by another is 'second-hand' and something of its original, deeper essence will inevitably be lost. Wisdom, however, that comes directly from the depths of our own unique Soul cannot be lost or misunderstood. When our attunement is honed and perfected through regular daily meditation and committed periods of stillness, we gain personal access to an infinite source of wisdom, guidance and strength.

It is possible, in my opinion, that much of scientific discovery has been led by the intuition of the Soul. Some scientists have openly identified with those moments of great inspiration when new avenues of exploration have led to the discovery of something previously unknown. When science and intuition consciously walk hand-in-hand from a position of mutual respect, I believe the greatest wisdom will flow into human consciousness.

Some of humanity's most moving stories have come from difficult human experiences. It has been illustrated, time and again, that when life seems utterly hopeless and our five human senses finally just 'give up', a place deep within oneself opens. In the most hopeless of situations, many people describe an experience of being lifted to a place of 'in-spiration', abundant with love, wisdom and power. If we took the time to reflect, many of us would be able to identify with this statement.

Divine Presence is *forever* upholding, guiding and supporting. Stop, listen, feel and come to know the Voice of the Soul within yourself. You may discover that the Divine Voice frequently 'speaks' but often goes unheard.

Scientists

The biographies of some of our greatest scientists frequently introduce the notion of 'intelligence beyond the norm'. Their ponderings and experiments have opened avenues of wisdom previously unknown to science. It is not uncommon to read of experiences where ideas suddenly emerge, 'out of the blue', unexpectedly providing accurate and vital instruction.

We will never see God. We will never touch Divine Essence. We can, however, experience Presence. We can consciously choose to be open to 'in-spiration' and 'in-tuition' through the awakening Soul.

Suggested reading

Vaughan-Lee, L., *The Return of the Feminine and the World Soul* (2009).

CHAPTER 84

Discover the fullness of being

> Jesus said, 'When you see your likeness, you rejoice. But when you see your images that came into being before you did—which don't die, and aren't revealed—how much you'll have to bear!'

This saying teaches that we live a diminished and distorted version of the life intended for us.

We limit ourselves with narrow false images about who we are and are content to live trivial, shallow and self-centred lives.

Always and forever, a powerfully wise and immensely compassionate inner Self awaits our acceptance and integration into our life-expression, right now! I believe it is our responsibility to consciously accept its assimilation into the fullness of our Being. Only we can give the necessary consent. It is never imposed upon us.

This Truth may be difficult for many to accept. Understanding that we each possess depths of wisdom, love and potency that remain largely dormant, can be difficult to appreciate. However, realising this truth whilst in human form is greatly beneficial, not solely for oneself but also for the expansion of human consciousness.

Each one of us must play our part in the discovery of the Divine Truth. We are each a vital piece of the Sacred Story. Until all pieces are fully and consciously awake to the Truth, the Divine Message is incomplete and its message largely remains untold and unknown.

Suggested reading

Laird, M., *An Ocean of Light* (2019).

CHAPTER 85

The truth of life and death

> Jesus said, 'Adam came into being from a great power and great wealth, but he didn't become worthy of you. If he had been worthy, [he wouldn't have tasted] death'.

Adam represents humanity.
    We all carry within us great power, wealth and wisdom. Most people are not conscious of these facts.
    We are each a Child of God and possess eternal life. Eventually, the flesh will deteriorate and decompose. The Inner Sacred Self *never* dies.
    Only when we *know* these truths will we realise death does not exist and we will no longer fear transition from one sphere of existence to another.

My story

My beautiful mother left her human body at the age of 80. She had no fear of death. She knew she was merely exiting a sick body that had run its course. It was time for her to engage with another level of existence. She was totally at peace. As her life gradually faded away, we shared the precious sense of an extraordinary Presence around us. We both knew she was held and guided by a great powerful love.

During her final hours, I only left her side for brief spells. As I held her hand, she began to drift in and out of consciousness. I was overwhelmed by the presence and sense of an immensely Pure Love that embraced us.

As she released her final breath and her body gave up its human life, I seemed to soar with her into an indescribable peace and then, suddenly, she was gone.

I feel greatly privileged to have shared with my mother the moment of her transition.

I *know* there is nothing to fear.

I *know* that death does not exist.

Suggested reading

Anonymous, *Christ in You* (1910).

I give grateful thanks to Watkins Bookshop of London for keeping this precious book in print since 1910.

CHAPTER 86

True identity

> Jesus said, '[The foxes have dens] and the birds have nests, but the Son of Humanity has nowhere to lay his head and rest'.

When we identify ourselves solely as human beings, we deny our exalted position as a Child of God. We experience a sense of separation from our Divine inheritance and consequently ignore our full entitlement to wisdom, power, resources and boundless love. This treasure is our birthright, but to receive it we must *consciously accept it*.

Failure to do that means we live fearful lives, isolated from our rightful Divine Treasure of Wisdom, Love, Power and resources.

Suggested readings

The Bible: Psalm 23 (*The Lord is my Shepherd*).
Morgan, M., *Mutant Message Down Under* (1991).

CHAPTER 87

Soul

> Jesus said, 'How miserable is the body that depends on a body, and how miserable is the soul that depends on both'.

My understanding of this codex is that the person who believes only in the physicality of life will live a shallow and limited existence. Such a person/body, lacking fulfilment and purpose, lives a 'miserable' life.

When the Soul remains largely hidden and unrecognised, it suffers, thwarted from its full expression. It is intended as an avenue of Divine demonstration within the human world. Denied its authentic purpose, the stagnant soul can bring depression, illness and misery.

Suggested reading

The New Testament: John 14:12–18.

CHAPTER 88

Insights and opportunities

> Jesus said, 'The angels and the prophets will come to you and give you what belongs to you. You'll give them what you have and ask yourselves, "When will they come and take what is theirs?"'

Our life is given to us so we may discover and learn to express our particular and unique Truth. We are supported by unseen forces as we seek that which is hidden within us. During the progress of our life, we may not recognise the potential lessons of those who may be our greatest teachers.

This is the case when they seem to bring nothing but difficulty! The challenges they provoke may offer insight into unrecognised yet troublesome characteristics within ourselves. When we approach difficult situations with openness, our problematic traits are given the opportunity to become known to us. However, change is impossible whilst we remain in ignorance.

In my opinion, it is wise to consider each encounter with others as an opportunity to experience the Divine Centre present within all life. Such valuable opportunities rarely 'travel' in one direction. They offer a two-way exchange of lessons and insights. Even those totally unaware of Presence may gain some benefit from our unspoken acknowledgement of God within them. We are all each other's teacher.

Suzy's story

Suzy's father had been her greatest challenge. Not only did she witness his maltreatment of her subservient mother, but she herself had been at the mercy of his violent temper and, as a result, grew to have little self-respect.

She was unconsciously drawn to men who were bullies. Her life bounced from one unhappy encounter to another as she unwittingly repeated the violent experiences of her childhood. Each new relationship seemed to promise a better outcome, only to deteriorate into yet another disaster.

Until the age of 48 Suzy had never allowed herself to experience kindness and sensitivity from a man. She shunned advances from gentler men, labelling them as 'not her type'. Each new violent relationship played its role in further pushing Suzy to a point where she realised she did want something better. The final straw came when she was badly beaten by a man who had promised to care for her. Thankfully, she was at last willing to seek professional help.

On the recommendation of her doctor, she began attending a bi-weekly therapy group for women in abusive relationships. She also used a small inheritance to pay for extra private counselling. Over a period of several months, as Suzy faced the truth about her choice of men, she grew in self-understanding and confidence. She realised she had never felt valued by her parents and, consequently, had no value for herself.

As Suzy worked deeply on this issue, she slowly came to understand the sad consequences of her violent childhood. She also realised she need no longer repeat these destructive patterns. Before we can expect others to value us, we must first find respect and love for ourselves. This is an essential foundation for all successful relationships.

Sadly, it had taken the experience of serious violence for Suzy to face her past. Gradually, significant changes began to happen both within herself and in her life. She grew to understand she had the power to choose only that which was consciously acceptable to her. She now knew she was entitled to kindness, appreciation and goodness.

Eventually, Suzy was able to welcome a good and kind man when he came into her life. She felt able to accept his gift of love, recognising it as something precious to be shared. Slowly, her confidence blossomed and eventually her life grew to be one of fun, kindness and love, for the benefit of both her and her partner.

Sadly, Suzy's story is not an uncommon one. Many people accept abusive relationships because they know no better. Our situation often has to become really tough before we are ready to make significant adjustments.

However, all experiences, especially the difficult ones, are opportunities to choose something better for ourselves. These can bring great blessings and healing if we are open to the possibilities they offer.

Gradually, through her insights, Suzy was able to welcome the 'messenger/prophet' who brought goodness and joy that was rightfully hers!

Suggested reading

Pennington, M.B., Keating, T. and Clarke, T.E., *Finding Grace at the Center* (1978).

CHAPTER 89

Discovering oneness

> Jesus said, 'Why do you wash the outside of the cup? Don't you know that whoever created the inside created the outside too?'

This codex draws attention to the Oneness of our being. We have a discernible body and mind, with which we function in the external world. When we die, we shed those tangible parts. The Inner invisible Life Spirit, however, is eternal. Its presence, participation and contribution to our expression is permanent, with or without a physical body.

The external human self is a projection of our inner Life Spirit in the same way that our human form projects its shadow on a sunny day. All are one undivided Divine Expression.

This is true of the billions of seemingly separate selves on planet earth.

Every life is a unique projection from the One Divine Whole; each a unique demonstration with its own particular purpose.

We are One Divine Intention, expressed in billions of ways.

An example of unity in nature

Science has taught us that a tree is one unit, made from a multitude of interconnecting and cooperating parts. Each part contributes an essential service to the whole. If any part of the tree is unable to fulfil its particular function, the tree will, to some degree, experience loss. The sustainability of the whole largely depends on each part fulfilling its particular task.

In the same manner, as the tree, the human race is one unit. Every being brings their own particular purpose and contribution to the well-being of the whole. Each person is made of the same Divine Energy, but 'arranged' in their own particular and unique way. All visible 'parts', although appearing different, are identical in essence.

Suggested readings/study

Catala, R., *Sufficient unto Itself is the Day* (1989).
Wohlleben, P. (DVD) *Intelligent Trees* (2016).

CHAPTER 90

Our divine resources

> Jesus said, 'Come to me, because my yoke is easy and my requirements are light. You'll be refreshed'.

This codex suggests we seek help and consolation from our Divine Source in times of difficulty. Problems are an inevitable part of life and, indeed, are highly valuable to our growth.

It is my belief there resides a 'real self' at the centre of each person. A centre which is Divine in essence, unique in its truest expression, and the Holy Grail of our own life. It is the place where we find true rest from the earthly world.

* * *

Understanding the notion of the 'real self' begins with an awareness of how personality develops. Young children have an enormous capacity for absorbing information, both true and false. They act like natural sponges, soaking up experiences, observations, sensations and perceptions. In the early stages of development, they collect not only information from their own personal experiences but also from imitating those around them. They have, as yet, no capacity for discernment and may absorb many untruths.

Our accumulated belief system about ourselves, the external world and our place in it, often becomes the raw 'material' for therapy in later years! The purpose of therapy is to help us become fully conscious of our personal belief system and to develop a capacity for discernment of what is true and what is false. Therapy aids in the development of that discernment.

Human life is a place of education, an experimental laboratory to discover who, as an individual, we actually are. However, since I believe the Real Self is eternal and infinite, perhaps that search will never end. We are each an ever-unfolding 'story', in which the earthly world is our experimental playground.

As we discover and learn to live authentically from our real self, our identity as a Child of God is gradually revealed and we grow in harmony with an ever-deepening sense of Divine care, love and protection. We become enriched with infinite love, wisdom and power.

Tina's story

Tina was an only child in a tightly controlled family unit. Throughout her early years, she experienced acute loneliness and a painful sense of isolation from the outside world. Home was a highly disciplined and tense environment from which her only release were the days she attended school. Although introverted and painfully shy, Tina loved school. There, she felt safe and affirmed by her kind teachers. How grateful Tina was to realise in later life that her early school years had been sufficiently nurturing to keep some part of her inner self alive and within reach.

Tina's family were totally unaware of the consequences of their harsh judgements on her during her formative years. For the first 40 years of her life Tina lived as if those judgements were true.

She came to accept that she was inferior and a disappointment to the family.

The situation remained unchallenged until Tina was forced, due to severe depression, to undertake therapy in her later years. Professional psychological help was advised and so began a three-year journey to discover the truth about herself and the reasons for her anxiety and self-loathing. The 'deep cleanse' of therapy eventually bore rich fruit.

Slowly and painfully, a more confident and less anxious Tina began to emerge.

Years later, Tina would liken her therapeutic journey to the emergence of a beautiful butterfly from its cocoon. She slowly discovered a person within herself whom she now loved, respected and eventually admired for her capacity to have survived those difficult years. The personal judgements with which she had been burdened eventually began to crumble. Largely, but not completely, they faded into the nothingness they really were.

With her new-found freedom, Tina's life took on a new and interesting trajectory. As she sought her personal truth, she found she had a natural love for children and experienced deep joy in their companionship. Life, the world and its myriad of people grew to be interesting rather than terrifying.

With continuing professional and spiritual support, Tina not only found forgiveness for her now-deceased parents, she felt she was at last becoming the person God had always intended her to be. Her new life became complete when she began to work with disadvantaged children.

In following the Still Small Voice of God, 'whose yoke is easy and mastery is gentle', Tina found her Divine Resources. She was largely healed and found 'rest' for herself.

* * *

Sadly, this is not unusual. Many people are greatly burdened by harsh judgements made against them in their early years. Tina's story shows that with courage and commitment we can choose to leave much of our past behind. Unseen forces, perhaps guardian angels, support our quest to become our real self and to know the loving Divine Presence, which is forever a place of 'rest'.

Suggested reading

HH The Dalai Lama and Cutler, H.C., *The Art of Happiness* (1999).

CHAPTER 91

Learn how to seek

> They said to him, 'Tell us who you are so that we may trust you'.
> He said to them, 'You read the face of the sky and the earth, but you don't know the one right in front of you, and you don't know how to read the present moment'.

My interpretation of this codex is that people are searching for the truth regarding Jesus. They need proof of his identity and are seeking reassurance. He challenges their superficiality and urges them to seek within themselves for answers. He has taught that God is within each and every one of us. However, people seem unable to understand that *All* life is a depiction, a visible manifestation of Divine Energy. We must, however, have spiritual awareness and the 'eyes' to see this.

No other person can take us into our Divine Centre. Some people may lead us along our rightful path, but it is we ourselves who must make the commitment to 'enter' our inner sacred space. When we seek Truth with sincerity, all will eventually be revealed. Our 'spiritual eyes' will be opened.

Simon's story

Simon was in his mid-30s when he developed an interest in positive thinking. He had read many self-help books and hoped to find a way of easing his turbulent life. He joined a small self-support therapy group and regularly attended their monthly meetings. His search for a deeper meaning to life was sincere.

Simon had grasped the concept that we create much of our own drama. He had grown to know himself well and was able to identify many of his false assumptions and preconceptions about life. He learnt to recognise the ways he unwittingly compromised situations and relationships. Although his self-understanding was helpful, he found difficulty in sustaining lasting changes within himself. At this point in his journey, he turned to professional therapy.

Gradually, with the support of a therapist, he no longer dismissed new openings, both in his work and personal life. In the past, he had often rejected new opportunities. Slowly, he began to feel more confident in his ability to explore new avenues. He began to experience inner wellness. As old inhibitions were gradually released, a new sense of freedom developed. He began to live from his real self.

During any new stage of life, we can experience uncertainty and fear. This may present itself in a myriad of forms. However, situations that are 'tailor-made' to assist our spiritual growth will be drawn to us. It is helpful to value these seeming difficulties as the Divine gifts they really are.

At this crucial point in his life, Simon saw a television documentary titled *The Big Silence*. The programme featured five ordinary people who had volunteered to live for several days in silence with Christian monks in their isolated monastery. As Simon watched the series, a deep desire to participate in something of this nature took hold.

Within a matter of weeks, he was accepted onto an eight-day silent retreat at the very same monastery. This opportunity offered lay men and women the chance to 'opt out' of everyday life and to experience prolonged silence in a safe spiritual setting.

Simon's experience during those eight days was profound and life-changing. He shifted the focus of his attention from introspection and self-analysis to 'something' beyond the personal. He found a greater depth within himself. In that rarefied atmosphere, devoid of distractions, he was drawn into the inner Wellspring of Divine Wisdom, Love and Power which resides within all people.

At that time Simon was unaware of the magnitude of the shift that had taken place within himself. However, returning home he felt compelled to simplify his life. He gave up a busy job, moved to a small simple cottage in a quiet location and chose to make a living from his beloved hobby of nature photography.

Simon was no longer controlled by his internal drama. At the monastery, he had learnt to be still and to wait in confidence for direction from 'the still small voice of God'. This gentle and loving guidance had always been present within him, as it is for all of us. But until we learn to engage with our inner stillness and silence, the voice of God remains unheard; present but ignored.

Suggested reading

Laird, M., *Into the Silent Land* (2006).

CHAPTER 92

Persist in your search for truth

> Jesus said, 'Look and you'll find. I didn't answer your questions before. Now I want to give you answers, but you aren't looking for them'.

As with many of the codices, this saying also emphasises the need to seek—to seek repeatedly, with determination and perseverance.

It is unclear why Jesus previously refused to impart his knowledge. Perhaps he himself was not ready to convey these sacred truths. Or perhaps he was guided to test the questioner's sincerity and commitment to Divine Understanding.

Ella's story

Ella had dipped in and out of many spiritual groups. She found it difficult to sustain the resolve and determination our spiritual journey demands. Although she had some sense of the inner Divine Presence, she lacked the tenacity that deep spiritual unfoldment requires. For most seekers it may take many years, perhaps many lifetimes, of contemplation and study before the sacred 'opening' becomes consciously real.

Almost unnoticed, Ella's persistent commitment to her sacred journey slowly prepared the way for the 'veil' to be parted. It had happened almost outside of her awareness. The changes, however, were apparent in the new life priorities she chose. She had a new tolerance for viewpoints which differed from her own. She felt a generosity and love towards all life, regardless of any difference. She began to experience compassion towards those whom she would have previously felt judgement. In time, she was able to recognise that something within her had, indeed, changed.

We do not know the time or place of the unfolding of our conscious awareness. We must place complete trust in Divine Wisdom and Power to direct our journey. As I have mentioned before, all is revealed at the right time, at the right place, in the right way.

* * *

We can never judge another's path. Each of us has our own unique and individual journey to take. Since time has no relevance in the spiritual kingdom, we can take as long as we need, we can take as many detours as are necessary, we can respond to all opportunities until we discover the doorway to our unique and inner Sacred Centre. Then, we grow to become an instrument of Divine Purpose.

Suggested readings/study

Dyer, W.W., *You'll See It When You Believe It* (2005).
Dyer, W.W. (DVD) *The Shift* (2009).

CHAPTER 93

Protect that which is revealed to you

> 'Don't give what's holy to the dogs, or else it might be thrown on the manure pile. Don't throw pearls to the pigs, or else they might ...'

This saying speaks of the preciousness of spiritual truth and the personal vulnerability we may experience regarding our Truth. We begin our spiritual journey as fledglings, easy prey to challenge, criticism and ridicule.

Our 'apprenticeship' as spiritual seekers often requires the support of teachings and, perhaps, a teacher. An authentic and enlightened teacher knows when to gently guide and when to allow the student to seek and struggle alone. No one can be spared the difficulties often involved in the spiritual journey. We may need to face many challenges that strengthen and assist our development.

* * *

Traditionally, in many faiths, it was believed only the clergy/leaders could interpret meaning and offer guidance to a 'seeker'. Thankfully, this is no longer the case. It is my belief that only we ourselves can truly discover the Divine Presence hidden within our being.

Retreats offer space and stillness for reflection and contemplation. Meditation groups can provide regular silent times in which the busy external world can slip into the background of a busy life. As our daily practice becomes established, we grow attuned to our inner Divine Voice, which has always been present but unheard. We each have our own internal Guide and Teacher. Regular daily practice 'opens' the door to silence where a sense of 'Presence' is forever with us.

Light-touch guidance and perceptive external support can be helpful. Psychotherapy is also a great asset in helping to shift intrusive emotional baggage and turbulent thoughts. Our task is to discern the Divine inner voice and develop the ability and courage to express its wisdom. Much of the 'noise' that fills our mind has accumulated throughout our lifetime. A great deal of this stored information may not only be false but potentially harmful to our well-being. Learning to distinguish the voice of wisdom from false 'chatter' is an essential aspect of our spiritual journey.

My interpretation of this codex is that the desire to know God is present within each one of us. It waits for the 'Seed of Yearning' to germinate and flourish. When the time is right, our soul journey becomes conscious and we begin to live the life which God has always intended for us.

Our uniqueness is of the greatest value. No other can express and live our particular Divine Story. The early stage of our journey is a time of vulnerability which needs conscious protection. It must be nurtured and shared *only* with those of maturity and the ability to perceive the preciousness of the unfolding spirit. We risk condemnation when we reveal our truths to those who are, as yet, unable to understand them. We are like tender saplings, prone to damage from external elements.

Place trust in the guidance of Divine Spirit and disclose precious insights only to those with spiritual maturity. Do not cast 'pearls before swine'.

My story

I learnt this particular lesson the hard way. Early in my journey, communicating with others of a like mind was important to me. I yearned for the joy of sharing experiences and hard-won insights.

During a small gathering of meditators, also consciously on a spiritual path, I spoke about a dream that had touched me greatly. It carried great significance and meaning for me. Even now, some 24 years later, its clarity and beauty can still move me. It was extremely precious.

At discussion time, in my naïvety, I shared my dream with the group. I described its contents, explained its meaning and the valuable instruction it had brought to me.

Almost immediately two members of the group began to attack my insight and to criticise the profoundness of the dream's meaning. The two seemed to 'feed off' each other in an attempt to destroy the beauty of its message. I was shocked and deeply hurt by their insensitivity. I felt demeaned and extremely foolish.

For some time following the verbal attack, the dream lost all its beauty and meaning. It became a symbol of humiliation. However, with therapeutic help, I was able to understand that my dream had exposed a deep rawness in my detractors. I had unwittingly stepped into their painful emotional world and unleashed their unresolved pain and anger. With this deeper understanding, the value of the dream slowly returned to me.

From that painful experience, I decided I would never again share my precious insights until I was sufficiently strong to withstand any harsh judgements that may unexpectedly come my way. We never know the hurts that are hidden within another's psyche. Our Divine Truths are far too tender and valuable to be revealed to those unable to appreciate their blessedness.

I believe this saying cautions us to reveal 'pearls of wisdom' only to those with the power of discernment and maturity of spirit to appreciate them.

Suggested reading

Dobisz, J., *One Hundred Days of Solitude* (2008).

CHAPTER 94

Truth is freely revealed to all who seek

> Jesus [said], 'Whoever looks will find, [and whoever knocks], it will be opened for them'.

This saying is also about seeking. It offers assurance that a sincere desire to find our Divine Centre will always be fulfilled. When we seek with commitment and an attitude of openness, the ever-present Soul will be revealed in the most helpful and fruitful manner.

For some people, Divine Truth is made known suddenly and quite unexpectedly. For most, however, it may be a slow unfoldment which only becomes apparent over a period of years, perhaps over several lifetimes.

As we are led towards the doorway of our unique Truth, we are supported and nurtured throughout the entirety of our spiritual journey.

Suggested reading

Hanh, T.N., *Being Peace* (1992).

CHAPTER 95

Freely share that which you have

>[Jesus said], 'If you have money, don't lend it at interest. Instead, give [it to] someone from whom you won't get it back'.

This saying asks that we be generous and share whatever we have. In giving, do not seek reward or recompense.

We must freely give in the same manner that God freely gives to us. The fulfilment of our needs is permanently present, ready for our taking. It is we who do not realise this truth and, therefore, do not gather that which is already ours.

Jesus asks that when we give to others, we look neither for gratitude nor profit but share unconditionally.

Nature's story

Nature expresses this truth beautifully.

Unless subjected to interference by humankind, she indiscriminately gives her produce to all creatures alike. She simply does what she does, freely and unconditionally, providing support to all lifeforms. The list of nature's gifts is almost endless.

We are asked to do likewise without discrimination, seeking neither recompense nor reward.

This saying can be difficult to comprehend in our modern consumer-driven world. Money has become the means of exchange for goods and services. Whilst most of us believe in fair exchange, modern society has 'conditioned' us to believe that the more we can get in return for our endeavours, the better/the cleverer/the wiser we are. In my opinion, the correct attitude of giving has all but disappeared in this consumer age.

I believe it is not so much *what* we contribute to life on this planet that matters, as the *manner* in which we give. The saying in this codex counsels that we give graciously whatever we are able. It may be a simple smile offered to a lonely neighbour or a kindly gesture of acknowledgement to a grieving acquaintance. Often it is the fact that we have bothered, that we have noticed, that can make the day a lot brighter for another.

None of these simple suggestions costs money, they need only an attitude of 'bothering', of 'noticing', of 'caring'—simply the generosity of spirit to pay attention to another.

Suggested reading

Morgan, M., *Mutant Message Down Under* (1991).

CHAPTER 96

Value hidden talents

> Jesus [said], 'The Father's kingdom can be compared to a woman who took a little yeast and [hid] it in flour. She made it into large loaves of bread. Anyone who has ears to hear should hear!'

This saying asks that we value and utilise our attributes, however insignificant they may seem to us. It teaches the worthiness of the simple tasks we each perform on a daily basis. It is the intention with which these are done that often carries the greatest meaning.

The activity of baking has been performed for thousands of years. Yeast is the essential ingredient which activates the transformative process of turning inedible dough into nutritious bread. Without yeast, this essential part of everyday life, for many civilisations, would be missing.

I believe this saying is asking us to discover the 'yeast' within ourselves. To seek that which gives our life purpose and which nourishes ourselves and others. When we discover and appreciate the God-given qualities we have been given, they will grow and become useful in everyday life. As the humble yeast innocently provides an essential service without discrimination, so we also are asked to discover our inner 'yeast'.

This saying teaches that we may easily discount and devalue our attributes—we rarely look within and 'see' our own worth. We are asked to honour and appreciate all that which has been secreted within us. It may add something of great value that renders a more 'palatable and nutritious' aspect to our own and others' lives.

Each of us carries a form of 'yeast'. It is our purpose to discover, develop and freely give our 'yeast' for the betterment of ourselves and others. Choosing false modesty, rather than valuing one's talents, demeans God's gifts.

Containing the ever-present human ego

To avoid the dangers of self-aggrandisement we can choose to bestow equal value on all people and all attributes, even though our fickle human ego strives for superiority over others. We must recognise the worth of *all* life and *all* expressions of that life. Each must be assigned equal value, whether it be the road sweeper who keeps our streets clean and safe or the surgeon who restores sight. Every piece of the human jigsaw is essential to the whole.

We live in a society that demands study, practice and the accumulation of qualifications before we believe our worth can have value. Even undertaking the simplest of tasks seems to require instruction. This subtly denies the quality of our 'inner yeast'.

We are each born with abilities and talents. Everyone has something to offer society, should they choose to do so. Study and instruction may develop and enhance our abilities but I believe we should also find merit in the talents we already possess.

Sir Captain Tom's story

Sir Captain Tom More, during the UK Coronavirus Pandemic in 2020, through his totally selfless actions, taught with great humility that we can all contribute to life.

He showed appreciation for the UK National Health Service and its enormous workforce. In seeking to express his thanks, he illustrated to the world how to value each other for the gifts we each bring to society on a daily basis. He discovered and appreciated the 'yeast' in himself and everyone.

We can all do likewise by appreciating what others do for us. To judge tasks and talents by placing them in a man-made order of merit is to demean the Divine Life that is expressed through all people.

Suggested reading

Merton, T., *No Man is an Island* (1997).

CHAPTER 97

Stay conscious and alert

> Jesus said, 'The Father's kingdom can be compared to a woman carrying a jar of flour. While she was walking down [a] long road, the jar's handle broke and the flour spilled out behind her on the road. She didn't know it, and didn't realize there was a problem until she got home, put down the jar and found it empty'.

This saying asks that we stay mindful and vigilant as we journey through life. We have each been given all the resources we need and must remain conscious of the fullness of our Divine Inheritance. Access is ours to power, courage, wisdom and love. When we treasure these, we will use them wisely.

The translation of this saying asks that we take heed of the woman's plight which shows how, through ignorance, she wasted all she had been given.

We must be watchful and alert to carelessness. It is our responsibility to seek out productive ways in which to make use of our gifts.

This saying seems to work in tandem with Codex 96. It says that to squander/spill our Divine Treasure is to devalue God-given talents and opportunities.

Stay alert. Remain vigilant.

We each have differing talents and attributes. *All* of which are equal. Choose to live with diligence and rigour. Follow *only* your inner Divine Voice.

Suggested reading

Kornfield, J., *A Path with Heart* (1993).

CHAPTER 98

Know the powerful shadow

> Jesus said, 'The Father's kingdom can be compared to a man who wanted to kill someone powerful. He drew his sword in his house and drove it into the wall to figure out whether his hand was strong enough. Then he killed the powerful one'.

We each have a shadow. Not only a physical outline projected by the sun's rays, but also a psychological shadow. This is largely an unconscious yet active aspect of our psyche. Until it becomes known to us, usually through the means of therapy, it can exert enormous power over our lives. It prompts actions and responses from us without our conscious consent, often in a problematic way. My interpretation of the translation of this codex is that *the shadow is the 'Powerful One'*.

* * *

The psychological shadow contains aspects of our persona that we believe are unacceptable. It gathers opinions and judgements throughout our life. It also contains parts of ourselves that we have been unable, perhaps due to lack of confidence, to bring into conscious expression.

Young children are sensitive to the disapproval of adults. They quickly learn to hide aspects of themselves that attract adult displeasure. This creates inner tension, conflict and fear of the natural tendencies within themselves. Rather than learning to address unacceptable impulses, children often suppress these and a powerful and uncontrolled shadow is created. As problematic emotions are further added to the internal baggage, the shadow's size and power grows.

Undoubtedly, children must be helped to find a way of living within society's laws and mores. They need loving guidance in order to integrate their individuality into the collective norms of society. This does, however, come at some cost to their sense of freedom and spontaneity. Thankfully, we have progressed from the Victorian rigour of 'children should be seen and not heard'. Too much carer control can lead to an inhibited and suppressed adult. Too little can lead to a life as a social misfit.

* * *

Throughout our life, our powerful shadow continues to exist, poised to express its contents, usually at the most inappropriate moment. We all have experience of those 'slips of the tongue' or outbursts that leak out as our shadow tries to release its tension. In such scenarios, we re-experience the original feelings of shame, frustration and resentment. Sadly, these difficult feelings accumulate, creating uncertainty about our acceptability and 'loveable-ness'. In adulthood, it is unlikely we will understand the original cause of our social discomfort and inhibitions. This is the purpose and great value of therapy.

The powerful shadow is also in action when we feel inexplicable rage towards another person. This is often caused by unconsciously observing a characteristic in another that we have come to believe is unacceptable in ourselves. Such strong inappropriate reactions can take us by surprise, evoking a need to justify our behaviour. The shadow's power is robust and undisciplined. It is capable of creating dysfunctional lives and disruptive behaviours.

My interpretation of the translation of this codex is that it makes clear it is our responsibility to seek out and kill the 'powerful one' within our psyche ('kill', in this respect, meaning to bring it to conscious awareness and work through the issues it raises). In modern times, this usually requires professional help in the form of therapy, benefiting our life and our relationships.

Vera's story

Vera was born into a wealthy farming family. As an only child, she carried the family's expectations regarding the continuation of the farm. It was this unspoken assumption that was at the centre of Vera's deepening depression and the cause of her increasing outbursts of rage.

In therapy, she came to realise the extent of her inner trauma. She was an exceptional artist who had wanted nothing more than to devote her life to the exploration of her art. For several years, unable to face the disappointment of her parents, she had continued to expand the farm. She 'knuckled' down, believing no other choice was available to her.

The more imprisoned Vera felt, the more her resentment and distress grew into a great bundle of fury that became uncontrollable. Her powerful shadow began to express itself with increasing ferocity. She lost all reason and grew to believe that her only way out of this very painful dilemma was to end her life. Thankfully, a serious attempt at suicide failed. Professional therapy was found for Vera.

After six months of weekly appointments, Vera grew to understand herself and her rage. She became conscious of her shadow and the hidden yearnings of her soul. With continuing and regular therapeutic support, Vera grew to accept that her life had been given to *her*, not to her parents.

She realised she must find the courage to be honest and she must also learn to live in the manner of her own choosing. Only then would her shadow release its great power to disrupt her life.

Telling her father of her decision to leave the farm, and her intention to attend art college in Italy, was the most difficult thing she had done. Vera's awakening soul came to her aid in the form of an inner power that had previously remained out of sight. Her unique life-expression was gradually finding freedom from its prison.

That which had seemed impossible became possible through facing and vanquishing her powerful shadow, and releasing her Soul Energy.

Suggested reading

Levine, P.A., with Frederick, A., *Waking the Tiger: Healing Trauma* (1997).

CHAPTER 99

Recognise your true kinfolk

> The disciples said to him, 'Your brothers and mother are standing outside'.
> He said to them, 'The people here who do the will of my Father are my brothers and mother; they're the ones who will enter my Father's kingdom'.

Jesus teaches that our spiritual family is of greater significance than our birth family. Although our birth family provides the means for the exploration of our humanness, our spiritual family provides Divine support for the journey of our soul.

Our spiritual family consists, I believe, of souls with whom we may have journeyed over many lifetimes. There is a belief that souls unite and establish groupings to give support as we endeavour to *live* our spiritual truth.

We may also experience soul connection when we feel an affinity towards someone with whom we would seem to have no conscious relationship. In my opinion, we are given as many lives as we need in seeking our true self.

As our life-journey progresses towards an ever-deepening awareness of the 'Father's Kingdom', we are always assisted and supported by forces both known and unknown to us.

Suggested reading

Kharitidi, O., *Entering the Circle* (1997).

CHAPTER 100

Three facets of a conscious life

> They showed Jesus a gold coin and said to him, 'Those who belong to Caesar demand tribute from us'.
> He said to them, 'Give to Caesar what belongs to Caesar, give to God what belongs to God, and give to me what belongs to me'.

This codex, in my opinion, brings to our attention the different aspects of consciousness. It requires a willingness to understand and value each of the three seemingly different ways of perceiving and valuing life-expression.

Give to Caesar that which is Caesar's

In my opinion, this asks that acknowledgement and recognition is given to Caesar for the creation and maintenance of running an organised society. One that offers a place in which people live and can express the life given to them.

Give to God the things that are God's

Accurately accredit the source of life itself, in all its forms. Recognise God as the provider and the wellspring of all our physical needs and experiences. We are asked, I believe, to give God the credit and the praise for ourselves and our lives.

Give me what is mine (give to Christ that which is Christ's)

Jesus (Christ) brought us Divine teachings. These bestowed spiritual recognition and awareness of the Divinity within all people. This gave each person sovereignty over their life.

The inner Christ

It is my belief that the Inner Christ, present within all beings, constantly receives the Divine Impulse. We have the choice to respond to, or ignore, that Impulse. In responding, we become a channel for Divine Expression, giving and serving as the 'Hands, Eyes and Voice of God'.

As we do so, we offer recognition of the inner Divinity present in all.

My story

I spent many years searching for authentic meaning in my life. At the right time and in the best possible way, my teacher was drawn to me.

I believe I had 'paid my dues' by preparing the ground of awareness. I was conscious and able to recognise the Divine Gift that was placed before me. My Inner Christ was open to the Divine Message for which I yearned.

* * *

My spiritual teacher, Rafael, came into my life through an elderly friend. She 'happened' to read about a forthcoming spiritual class to be held in the UK. It detailed a five-day residential class for approximately 15 people. Anyone could apply. The class would be led by Rafael, a resident of the US, where he taught small groups of committed seekers of Spiritual Truth.

I was 1 of the 15 fortunate people who met for the first five-day class in the UK. Rafael was a tough teacher in his demands for personal honesty and a sincere commitment to our spiritual journey. Our small group focused on self-understanding and the nature of Divine Truth. In total, Rafael came to the UK on six occasions over the course of the next four years. During each one of those five-day classes, I was deeply challenged. It seemed as if a tornado held me in its grip, shaking every cell in my body and my mind, challenging deeply hidden hypocrisy and falseness.

This emotionally challenging process continued for approximately four years. It was a difficult and painful time and, without doubt, the most intense period of my life.

One day the spiritual tornado simply stopped. A peace, like no other I had ever experienced, enveloped me. What remained was the gift of a conscious and perpetual sense of Divine Presence.

* * *

During the four years that Rafael came to the UK to teach our small group, he was a guest in my family home. Following what was to be his final UK class, Rafael had four days remaining with us. Instead of sightseeing, he insisted my son and I study the *Gospel of Thomas* under his guidance. I had never before seen or heard of this precious manuscript, nor did I realise it would eventually change my life.

On those final days, Rafael demanded that we 'dig deep' within ourselves to discover the Truths contained in the ancient texts. The codices made little sense to us and the exercise seemed quite futile. By the time Rafael left for the US, we were utterly exhausted and shaken by the intense experience. At that time it seemed an extraordinary and unnecessary ordeal. I could see no purpose to what we had both endured.

Over the next few years, I occasionally revisited the *Gospel of Thomas*. Always to no avail. It was quite beyond my understanding. If fact, I began to feel deeply challenged by its presence on my bookshelf. I could make no sense as to why this seemingly inaccessible book had come my way—and yet would not let me go.

That is, until some 18 years later ...

In 2016, sitting in my conservatory on a miserable January day, I was reflecting on the seeming barrenness of my life when my eyes were drawn, yet again, to my original copy of the *Gospel of Thomas*. As I randomly opened the book that morning, the words seemed alive!

Something within me had changed. I felt utterly compelled to deeply explore and record *my* meaning/understanding of each 1 of the

114 codices. Instead of feeling challenged and irritated by the seemingly inaccessible language, I felt energised; the words spoke to me. I was deeply moved by the rich and beautiful teaching. To work with these precious sayings became pure joy, their meaning an awesome puzzle of discovery. Most importantly, though, I understood that their oblique nature was intentional! It demanded that we each search deeply for *our own* meaning contained in these sacred passages.

If there are 7.8 billion people on earth, then I believe there are 7.8 billion ways to make sense of these precious teachings.

This book is *my* very personal journey into the *Gospel of Thomas*. That, I believe, is the meaning of 'Give me what is mine'. It asks that I bring into human consciousness that which has been placed within me by God. As I live out my Truth, I believe I am 'giving back to God' that which has been given to me.

I believe the purpose of *all* human life is the discovery of our own unique story, our authentic and entirely individual life story, which has been placed within us. This, I believe, may require many lifetimes of seeking.

Suggested readings

Krishnamurti, J., *Freedom from the Known* (1969, 2010).
Tolstoy, L., *The Kingdom of God is Within You* (Chapter 3; 2010).

CHAPTER 101

Know the true giver of life

> 'Whoever doesn't hate their [father] and mother as I do can't become my [disciple], and whoever [doesn't] love their [father] and mother as I do can't become my [disciple]. For my mother ... but [my] true [Mother] gave me Life'.

This saying teaches us to distinguish between earthly existence, which consists of billions of seemingly separate lives; and Soul existence, which expresses Sacred Oneness.

In Truth, I believe all life is a depiction of One Omnipresent Energy.

Science has brought to our awareness the magnificence, the awesome complexity and interrelatedness of all lifeforms, from the tiniest earth-bound microbe to the farthest reaches of the known universe. We have become familiar with the concept of an interrelatedness between countless billions of diverse species.

* * *

Earthly parentage, including many lifeforms, requires both a male and a female contribution.

Divine parentage also requires two seemingly different aspects: God as the *Source* of Life, and Soul as the *Receptacle* of that Source.

The term 'God', I believe, represents Divine Idea, the initiating force of all life-expression. The term 'Soul' represents the means by which that Divine Idea is invested with form into a knowable creation.

Divine Idea (Father) and Divine Demonstration (Mother), express jointly as creation. The clearest example of this is the awesome and precious creation of a new baby.

* * *

Jesus asks that we remove all falsehoods and recognise God as our true parentage. We are asked to know God as *both*:

- True Father, the initiator of life; and
- True Mother, the manifesting force of that life.

I believe this saying teaches that earthly parents are the *means*, not the creators, of life. They should be loved and valued accurately, for the part they have played in our life demonstration.

Suggested reading

Goldsmith, J.S., *A Parenthesis in Eternity* (1986).

CHAPTER 102

Remain vigilant to those who would inhibit your journey

> Jesus said, 'How awful for the Pharisees who are like a dog sleeping in a feeding trough for cattle, because the dog doesn't eat, and [doesn't let] the cattle eat either'.

This saying is critical of the Pharisees, implying they are ignorant and metaphorically asleep. Not only do they lack awareness of their own spiritual needs, they are also ignorant of the needs of their 'flock'. In their foolishness, they deny the enrichment of God's Grace and Wisdom to all who seek.

In the Western world, our more enlightened times offer freedom to those who seek Truth. We are fortunate in our liberty to pursue any tradition or path that 'calls' us. It is important to give ourselves time to 'listen' and to consciously wait until we are sure of God's direction for us, even when this may seem unreasonably protracted. Often, delays are an aspect of learning. Patience teaches trust. When we do this, at the right time and in the right way, that which we seek will come to us and 'all shall be well'.

Freedom to follow our inner sacred prompting is, perhaps, one of the most precious gifts we can have. In my opinion, this should be recognised, valued and used wisely. History testifies that many lives have been sacrificed in the pursuit of the freedom that many of us now enjoy.

* * *

I believe freedom must come with the caveat that personal responsibility is a requirement of liberation. Each of us is responsible for our own actions. However, whilst we have a duty to consider the impact we may have on others, our own spiritual journey can never be sacrificed to another's self-centred drama.

When we allow our inner Divinity to guide us, we can be sure its promptings will never lead us to harm another.

Suggested reading

Tolstoy, L., *The Kingdom of God is Within You* (Chapter 3; 2010).

CHAPTER 103

Know thy self

> Jesus said, 'Blessed is the one who knows where the bandits are going to enter. [They can] get up to assemble their defenses [sic] and be prepared to defend themselves before they arrive'.

My interpretation of this saying is that it teaches us that our task is to grow in self-awareness and come to know all parts of our Self. It is our personal responsibility to understand our idiosyncrasies, weaknesses, intolerances, judgements and also our talents and our strengths. It demands that we befriend all those parts of ourselves that we may try to deny, and those parts which we lack the courage to express. It also teaches acceptance, with loving forgiveness, for those parts of ourselves of which we are ashamed. These are the parts that sap our energy and try to steal our rightful spiritual inheritance.

Jesus states that we are blessed when we become conscious of the intrusions that lurk within ourselves yet outside of our awareness. We must prepare against their onslaught by becoming acquainted with these 'robbers'. To be on our guard against them demands resolve, courage and tenacity to stand firm. Our Divine Destiny is sacred and of the highest value.

Of equal importance is the tenacity and courage to 'follow our dream'. Many are afraid to follow their rightful life-path in the belief that it may cause disruption to close relationships. We must never let others deliberately, or unconsciously, influence our journey. Our life-path is our responsibility, on which no other person has a rightful claim ... even though some may believe otherwise!

* * *

To discover, understand and value all parts of one's self, is to 'bring together our estate and arm oneself' against that which would rob us of our precious truth.

Through the means of reflection, study and personal therapy, we become informed. We learn to identify who we really are and find the courage to *be* that person. Making informed life choices, we ignore *all* opposing opinions. This is the way to 'arm' oneself against attack. This task is our personal responsibility.

Freedom comes with knowing our inner and outer 'opposers'.

Suggested reading

Merton, T., *No Man is an Island* (1955).

CHAPTER 104

The awakened Soul

> They said to [Jesus], 'Come, let's pray and fast today'. Jesus said, 'What have I done wrong? Have I failed? Rather, when the groom leaves the bridal chamber, then people should fast and pray'.

Jesus would seem to be dismayed that the disciples wish to pray and fast whilst he is with them. He states that they can do this when he is no longer physically in their midst.

He identifies himself as the 'bridegroom' who is the initiator of soul awakening. Soul, I suggest, refers to the creative and expressive feminine energy present in *all* people. Although present in all, it can be limited in its creative and visible expression.

As a bridegroom sexually awakens his bride to the fullness of her fertility, the Divinely awakened Soul awakens to its uniquely creative purpose. It becomes the conduit for the expression of Sacred Truth, Love, Wisdom and Power.

Interpreting symbolic representations

- 'Marriage' represents eternal conscious union with God.
- 'Bride' represents all people seeking conscious Divine Union.
- 'Bridegroom' represents the initiating power of Spirit, which awakens Soul into its Divine Expression.

Jesus teaches that when the 'bridegroom' seems to be absent, *that* is the time to withdraw into meditation/prayer in order to consciously reconnect with Inner Divinity. We are never outside of Divine Presence. It is our awareness of that fact that needs constant renewal through the practice of Mindfulness. As worldly affairs demand our time and attention, it is a constant challenge for each of us to remain awake to Presence and Inner Light.

Suggested reading

Krishnamurti, J., *This Light in Oneself: True Meditation* (1999).

CHAPTER 105

Do not compromise divine creation

> Jesus said, 'Whoever knows their father and mother will be called a bastard'.

In my opinion, God as True Father is the initiating Divine Source of all creation. All life-expression, whether human, animal, plant, mineral, etc. emanates from One Idea. Holy Spirit, as True Mother, actualises and manifests that Idea into tangible and multiple forms.

Human parentage offers Soul the opportunity to manifest Sacred Energy as human life. When we credit earthly parents with giving us life, we compromise Truth and our Inner Divinity remains unrecognised and unacknowledged. The sacredness and value of our life—in fact, all life—is diminished by this lack of awareness.

In the same way that a 'whore' sells her body for money, we must not 'sell'—compromise—our soul to meaningless and false ideas. All life is sacred and Divine.

What we do with the life given to us, is our choice. The part we each play in the human story is intended to be unique. We must learn through study, contemplation and meditation to use our precious freedom well and to choose wisely.

Suggested reading

Merton, T., *New Seeds of Contemplation* (1972).

CHAPTER 106

Know and express the wholeness of being

> Jesus said, 'When you make the two into one, you'll become Children of Humanity, and if you say "Mountain, go away!", it'll go'.

This saying teaches of our Divine purpose, which seeks expression through our humanness. When the inner Christ and our outer human self collaborate and become one, our hidden Divinity is revealed. We become able to 'move mountains'.

Jesus achieved the joining of the two identities and was, therefore, able to perform what became known as miracles. It seems he believed this was possible for all who understood these Truths. He taught that we are each an avenue for the expression of Divine Grace and, as such, are capable of 'Moving Mountains'. This applies to all people.

In my opinion, it is our unbelief, our self-doubt, which inhibits our life. When our Soul has awakened and we are conscious of the inner Divine Power, we become capable of all things, through God.

Suggested reading

Catala, R., *Mysticism of Now: The Art of Being Alive* (1998).

CHAPTER 107

Return to God's embrace

> Jesus said, 'The kingdom can be compared to a shepherd who had a hundred sheep. The largest one strayed. He left the ninety-nine and looked for that one until he found it. Having gone through the trouble, he said to the sheep: "I love you more than the ninety-nine"'.

The translation of this saying teaches that even when we choose to walk away from our Divine Path, we are still loved and valued by God. We are free, and indeed encouraged, to explore life and all its possibilities. Never dejected, Divine Love patiently waits until we return to the Divine Embrace.

It suggests, I believe, that those who have the courage to explore life's possibilities, perhaps seemingly rejecting God's love, are valued above all others. They have lived a fuller life, uninhibited by fear. Through the process of being and living, they have come to know life and themselves.

We have been given the power to choose how we express our life energy. Whatever path we take and however many lifetimes we deviate from the sacred ideal, we are supported by Divine Grace. Every one of us is known, treasured and loved by God. When we understand that we draw to ourselves whatever comes into our life, we gradually learn to make better choices. Every life-path is an opportunity to learn. God is never absent. We are always loved without judgement.

When we understand this Truth, we become capable of expressing great love and wisdom.

Suggested reading

The Bible: Luke 15:17–24 (*The Prodigal Son*).

CHAPTER 108

Be the inner Christ

> Jesus said, 'Whoever drinks from my mouth will become like me, and I myself will become like them; then, what's hidden will be revealed to them'.

This teaching asks, I believe, that we acknowledge Jesus as an example of what we may all become. It states that when we understand, absorb and internalise his teachings, we will become like him. We will express the truths that he taught, through our life and in our interactions with the external world.

When we understand that we are *all* potentially Christ in human form, we become open to the Divine Impulse which is present within each and every one of us. As our attunement develops, our inner 'still small voice' becomes clearer and more pronounced. We more easily sense its promptings and guidance. This Divine Gift has always been present within each of us. It is the *awareness* of this presence that we lack.

As we develop spiritually through study, contemplation and meditation, we grow exponentially and our capacity to express Divine love and wisdom becomes possible. In the fullness of time, we will each bring our own particular contribution to the wholeness of the human story. As each seemingly separate life contributes its Divine uniqueness, Sacred Wholeness becomes ever more visible and known. The seemingly 'hidden things' are revealed.

Suggested reading

Eliot, T.S., *Four Quartets—Little Gidding* (1944).

CHAPTER 109

Discover the legacy within

> Jesus said, 'The kingdom can be compared to someone who had a treasure [hidden] in their field. [They] didn't know about it. After they died, they left it to their son. The son didn't know it either. He took the field and sold it. The buyer plowed [sic] the field, [found] the treasure, and began to loan money at interest to whomever they wanted'.

This saying asks that we recognise the 'treasure' which is concealed within our very Being. It states that we each possess great spiritual wealth. Trusting in this permanent source will ensure we grow to understand and reap the rewards of our great gift.

Do not ignore, waste or squander the Divine Wisdom and Power that is our birthright. This Truth is omnipresent and available to *all* people. However, it remains—for each one of us—our personal prerogative to seek its discovery. As we 'plough' deep within ourselves through contemplation and study, we begin to discover the fertile 'field' of Divine Presence, the place of abundant spiritual wealth which furnishes our lives with Love, Wisdom and Power.

We are never alone on our spiritual journey. Our trust in Divine Supply, however, is often tested. We are encouraged to look deeply within ourselves and to seek out the doubts with which we must battle. We each have a 'doubting Thomas' within us. It is a part of ourselves that we must challenge, wrestle with, and overcome.

Suggested reading

Trine, R.W., *In Tune with the Infinite* (1965).

CHAPTER 110

Understand true wealth

> Jesus said, 'Whoever has found the world and become rich should renounce the world'.

This saying teaches us to seek the truth about earthly life and the real meaning of wealth. It asks that we renounce shallow values held by much of the world and replace them with authentic understanding of abundance.

The appreciation for creativity, generous friendships, mutual trust, love of life and respect for each other, brings a different sense of worth. It bestows upon us feelings of satisfaction and deep gratitude for that which we already have, *right now*!

When we understand that the permanent inner presence of Divine Energy is the rightful source of *all* our needs, we gain access to that which brings joy, peace, and yes, prosperity! As we commit ourselves to discovering the life divinely designed for us, our priorities adjust to a more wholesome reality. We become attuned to the awesome bounty of Divine gifts *already present*.

Financial wealth is undoubtedly a valid requirement for this life and, I believe, it is not intended that we live permanently without it. However, for some, financial problems can be a difficult and all-consuming aspect of their spiritual journey. The more we worry about it, the further its resolution seems to drift. In my opinion, and also my personal experience, it is our *attitude* to money that needs an adjustment.

When we renounce the world's value system and reassess our personal priorities, life begins to feel abundant with the high-value experiences of wonderment, joy, love and peace.

As we adjust our perceptions to appreciate *all* the gifts that have already come into our life, our attitude becomes positive. We recognise the gifts that we have, *right now*. We become a 'half full' person rather than a 'half empty' person. This strengthens a channel of positivity, drawing endless blessings to us.

Seek Truth and renounce the world's false understanding of wealth.

Suggested readings

Dyer, W.W., *There is a Spiritual Solution to Every Problem* (2001).
Price, J.R., *The Abundance Book* (1987).

CHAPTER 111

Trust the living presence within

> Jesus said, 'The heavens and the earth will roll up in front of you and whoever lives from the Living One won't see death'.
> Doesn't Jesus say, 'Whoever finds themselves, of them the world isn't worthy'?

My translation of this saying is that it recognises God as the One Source of all that is 'seen' and 'unseen'. An infinity of creation perpetually pours from the invisible into the visible and knowable. When we understand this, heaven and earth will 'roll up' and be recognised as One Manifestation. We will know that there is no separation. Whoever has attained this awareness will not experience the artificial separation of death.

Jesus also states that the world is an unworthy place for the person who has discovered Truth about themselves and earthly life. One's values and priorities change when we know the spiritual reality of *all* life. As the baubles and trinkets of earthly life begin to lose their appeal, our primary concerns begin to adjust to a more authentic reality.

We also grow in awareness of our own actions and the subsequent consequences to others. We learn that even our thoughts can impact on the lives of ourselves and other people. As we become more considerate in relationships, we recognise that, as children of the One Divine Energy, we are truly all spiritual brothers and sisters.

Suggested reading

Morgan, M., *Mutant Message Down Under* (1991).

CHAPTER 112

Choose well whom you will serve

> Jesus said, 'How awful for the flesh that depends on the soul. How awful for the soul that depends on the flesh'.

This saying urges us to have an accurate understanding of the true purpose of soul and body.

In my opinion, both body and soul are intended to function in the service of God: the soul as the vessel of Divine wisdom, power and guidance; the body as the visible and concrete manifestation of that Divine Impulse.

As the capacities of the soul develop through meditation, contemplation and study, we grow in attunement to the will of Divine Power. Our spirituality can be likened to the opening of the lotus flower, which has long been associated with the awakening soul.

As the fleshy body and the conscious soul begin to cooperate, they no longer function solely in the service of the ego. We gradually grow to be the hands, eyes and voice of God.

Humanity, I believe, is intended to convey and live from Divine Inspiration and to be the expression of God on earth.

Suggested reading

Needleman, J., *Time and the Soul* (2008).

CHAPTER 113

The Kingdom of God is before you

> His disciples said to him, 'When will the kingdom come?'
> 'It won't come by looking for it. They won't say, "Look over here!" or "Look over there!" Rather, the Father's kingdom is already spread out over the earth, and people don't see it'.

This saying confirms God is ever-present, in every moment, in every minute particle, in all space, always has been and always will be. The Kingdom of God is all around us and in every one of us. It is we who are 'blind' to the Perpetual Presence. Only by seeking the Divinity within ourselves, through silent meditation, contemplation of Truth and the study of great 'seers', do I believe we will come to discover our Truth.

Although we are always supported and guided, it is we who must make a conscious effort to discover that which calls each one of us. Reflecting on my life-journey, I can now recognise the invisible, but tangible, force that had indeed been gently and lovingly guiding my journey.

This discovery of our inner Truth is possible for *all* who desire to know and understand.

* * *

At the beginning of our process towards the Divine Embrace, people are rarely able to explain it. For some, it has felt like an inexplicable compulsion to discover; for many others, simply a gentle encouragement to pursue a more fulfilling life.

For me, my spiritual journey has seemed a beautiful and natural process which began of its own volition. It quickly took precedence in my life when all commitments to others had ceased. I was able to give myself wholeheartedly to this new and intense journey that took my life in a wholly (or perhaps, holy!) different direction. How deeply blessed I feel!

Through meditation, contemplation and study, our awareness of the intangible immediacy of God develops. Total trust in the Presence, both within and around us, becomes a beautiful and perpetual gift. We see the 'Father's Kingdom spread out upon the earth'. Our search for the experience of God in every moment has become conscious.

Divine beauty, symmetry and wisdom is present all around us. It is there for all to know and experience.

- Trust, listen to the Wisdom of Silence.
- Remove the 'goggles of limitation'.
- Seek the awesome fullness of Divine Expression which is already laid out before us on Earth.
- Look with unhindered vision.

Suggested reading

Goldsmith, J.S., *Practicing the Presence* (1958).

CHAPTER 114

Wholeness of Soul

> Simon Peter said to them, 'Mary should leave us, because women aren't worthy of life'.
>
> Jesus said, 'Look, am I to make her a man? So that she may become a living spirit too, she's equal to you men, because every woman who makes herself manly will enter the kingdom of heaven'.

We are living through an era of great change. On a human level, we are witnessing, and also participating in, a re-evaluation of humankind. We are learning to give equal value to all nations, all ethnic groups and to all variations of gender. The human race is slowly developing into a community which is appreciative of diversity and difference; where each individual being is attributed with equal worth.

I believe the translation of this codex, with its outdated and unacceptable language, can now be reconsidered in the light of this present-day wisdom. It is my belief that the original language is not only inappropriate, it is also disingenuous. Consequently, the message conveyed in this highly significant and most precious of codices has largely been ignored.

The true meaning of Codex 114 is of profound importance and has no connection, whatsoever, to gender. The classifications of 'male' and 'female' refer, I believe, to types of energy. The misleading identification with gender has, I believe, distorted the Great Truth held in this teaching.

Types of energy

So-called male energy has traditionally been identified with the expression of thinking, reasoning, judgement, logic and deductive rationality.

So-called female energy has traditionally been identified with feelings, instinct, intuition and empathy.

These polarised energies describe the manner in which we function, not only the way in which we perceive, experience and make sense of the world around us, but also how we choose to evaluate and respond to that.

Both energies are present in *all* humans. One quality may be overtly expressed in life, with its opposite almost dormant. Most people, however, express a variable degree of both.

In current times we are experiencing a period of evolution where these energies are seeking equality, both in recognition and in action— where they are free from censor and discrimination and where they mutually find value in each other's demonstration; where all aspects of personality are respected and have equal rights of expression.

As we grow towards a united wholeness within ourselves, we offer the same respect to the great diversity of energy expressed by all others. Inner balance and non-judgemental appreciation is becoming established.

As predicted in Codex 114, we are becoming a 'living spirit'; enlightened by the conscious awareness of Divine Presence deep within each one of us.

Soul has become alive and consenting to its Divine Purpose.

Suggested reading

Needleman, J., *Lost Christianity* (1980).

CONCLUSION

It may be worth reflecting on the timing of this great find in Nag Hammadi.

These Christian writings, possibly among the earliest ever discovered, remained concealed for almost 2000 years. So why was their unearthing in 1945? Why then?

The timing of their discovery followed a period of prolonged and unprecedented worldwide mass murder, carnage and destruction. In my opinion, this cannot be a coincidence.

The central message of the *Gospel of Thomas* is one of personal responsibility and accountability. Perhaps the Sacred Energy from which these powerful teachings have emerged has silently waited until humanity had run its selfish and destructive course.

Science seems to confirm we are now at that point.

The choice is ours: whether we wake up to our personal responsibilities towards each other, to the animal and plant kingdoms and to Planet Earth itself, or whether we continue on our course of mutual destruction.

BIBLIOGRAPHY OF SUGGESTED READINGS/STUDY

The *Gospel of Thomas* can be accessed at: www.biblicalarchaeology.org.

Mark M. Mattison's translations are also freely available on www.gospels.net (NB the 's' after gospel).

Anonymous, *Christ in You* (London: Watkins Bookshop, 1910), 9781397874184.
Anonymous, *The Way of a Pilgrim* (London: SPCK, 1942), 9780060630171.
Alexander, E., *Proof of Heaven* (US: Simon & Schuster, 2012), 9780749958794.
Benner, J., *The Impersonal Life* (US: DeVorss & Co, 2015), 9780875163017.
Berne, E., *Games People Play* (New York: Grove Press, 1964), 0345410033.
Bible: John 14:12.
Bible: Psalm 23 (*The Lord is my Shepherd*).
Bradshaw, J., *Homecoming—Reclaiming & Championing Your Inner Child* (GB: Piatkus Books, 1991), 0749910542.
Campbell, J., *The Hero with a Thousand Faces* (US: Pantheon Books, 1949) 9781577315933.
Campbell, J., *Thou Art That* (California: New World Library, 2001), 1577312023.
Catala, R., *Mysticism of Now: The Art of Being Alive* (US: Acropolis Books, 1998), 1889051195.
Catala, R., *Sufficient unto Itself is the Day* (Washington: Ventura One, 1989), 0962251704.

Coelho, P., *The Supreme Gift* (Barcelona: Sant Jordi Asociados, 1991), 9781519006462; Adapted from *The Greatest Thing in the World* by Henry Drummond.

H.H. The Dalai Lama and Cutler, H.C., *The Art of Happiness* (GB: Hodder & Stoughton, 1998), 9780340750155.

de Mello, A., *Sadhana: A Way to God* (New York: Doubleday Dell, 1984), 0385196148.

Dobisz, J., *One Hundred Days of Solitude* (US: Wisdom Publications, 2008), 0861715381.

Dyer, W.W. (DVD) *The Shift* (US: Hay House, 2009), 9781401926342.

Dyer, W.W., *There is a Spiritual Solution to Every Problem* (London: Thorsons, 2002), 9780007131471.

Dyer, W.W., *You'll See It When You Believe It* (London: Arrow Books, 1990), 9780099474296.

Eger, E.E., *The Choice:* (London: Penguin Random House, 2017), 9781846045127.

Eliot, T.S., *Four Quartets—Little Gidding* (London: Faber and Faber, 1979), 0571176526.

Eckhart, T., *The Power of Now* (GB: Hodder & Stoughton, 2001), 9780340733509.

Frankl, V.E., *Man's Search for Meaning* (US: Rider, 2008), 9780807014271.

Freke, T., *Rumi Wisdom—Daily Teachings* from the Great Sufi (GB: Godsfield Press, 2000), 184181024X.

Fromm, E., *The Art of Being* (GB: Constable & Co, 1993), 0094720908.

Gibran, K., *The Prophet* (London: Mandarin Paperbacks, 1991), 0749307382.

Goldsmith, J.S., *A Parenthesis in Eternity* (New York: HarperCollins, 1986), 9781939542656.

Goldsmith, J.S., *God, the Substance of all Form* (London: L.N. Fowler, 1959), 7981889051307.

Goldsmith, J.S., *Living Between Two Worlds* (UK: L.N. Fowler, 1975), 9781889051819.

Goldsmith, J.S., *Living the Infinite Way* (London: George Allen & Unwin, 1954), 1889051799.

Goldsmith, J.S., *Practicing the Presence* (US: Atlantic Books, 1991), 9780062503992.

Goldsmith, J.S., *The Gift of Love* (US: I-Level Publications, 1975), 1889051101.

Goldsmith, J.S., *The Infinite Way* (US: DeVorss & Co, 1995), 0875163092.

Hanh, T.N., *Being Peace* (GB: Rider, Random House, 1992), 0712654127.

Hay, L., *The Power is Within You* (US: Hay House, 1991), 9781561700233.

Johnston, W., *The Still Point* (New York: Fordham Press, 1970), 0823208613.

Jung, C.G., *Modern Man in Search of a Soul* (Oxon: Routledge, 2001), 9780415255448.

Kharitidi, O., *Entering the Circle* (London: HarperCollins, 1996), 0062514156.

Kornfield, J., *A Path with Heart* (US: Bantam Books, 1993), 0712657800.
Kornfield, J., *After the Ecstasy, the Laundry* (London: Bantam Books, 2000), 0712606580.
Krishnamurti, J., *Freedom from the Known* (London: Gollancz Paperbacks, 1991), 0575032642.
Krishnamurti, J., *This Light in Oneself: True Meditation* (Colorado: Shambala, 1999), 9781569571583.
Laird, M., *An Ocean of Light* (US: Oxford University Press, 2019), 9780199379941.
Laird, M., *Into the Silent Land* (US: Oxford University Press, 2006), 9780195307603.
Levine, P.A., with Frederick, A., *Waking the Tiger: Healing Trauma* (US: North Atlantic Books, 1997), 155643233X.
Lindeblad, B.N., *I May Be Wrong* (London: Bloomsbury, 2020), 9781526644824.
Martin, J. SJ, *Becoming Who You Are* (US: Hidden Spring, 2006), 158768036X.
Merton T. *New Seeds of Contemplation* (Canada: Penguin Books Ltd, 1972), 081120099X.
Merton, T., *No Man is an Island* (GB: Burns & Oates, 1955), 086012004X.
Merton, T., *The Power and Meaning of Love* (GB: Sheldon Press, 1976), 9780281063284.
Morgan, M., *Mutant Message Down Under* (US: M M Co., 1991), 1883473004.
Needleman, J., *Lost Christianity* (New York: Doubleday, 1980), 1585422533.
Needleman, J., *Time and the Soul* (US: Berrett-Koehler, 2003), 1576752518.
Pennington, M.B., Keating, T. and Clarke, T.E., *Finding Grace at the Center* (St Bede Publications, 1978), 9781594731822.
Pradervand, P., *The Gentle Art of Blessing*, (GB: Cygnus Books, 2005), 9780954932640.
Price, J.R., *The Abundance Book* (US: Hay House, 1996), 9781561703470.
The United Nations Handbook on Restorative Justice Programmes www.restorativejustice.org.uk.
Thorne, B., *The Mystical Power of Person-Centred Therapy: Hope Beyond Despair* (London: Whurr Publishers, 2002), 1861563280.
Tolle, E., *The Power of Now* (Canada: Namaste Publishing, 1997), 9780340733509.
Tolstoy, L., *The Kingdom of God is Within You* (Chapter 3; US: Pacific Publishing, 2010), 1453640703.
Trine, R.W., *In Tune with the Infinite* (London: G. Bell & Son, 1965; Registered at Stationers' Hall, London), 9781543129090.
Vaughan-Lee, L., *The Return of the Feminine and the World Soul* (US: Golden Sufi Center, 2009), 9781890350147.
Wohlleben, P. (DVD) *Intelligent Trees* (Dorcon Film, 2016).

INDEX

Adam, 277
aloneness, 146
analogy of doctor/patient relationship, 117
animal instincts, 19–20, 21–22
artificial and cloned persona, 76
authentic
    assistance and harmful interference, 149–150
    being, 231–233
    compassion, 171–173
    'inner-tuition', 273
    in interactions with people, 149
    living, 163–166
    self, 165–166
    service, 171–172
    teacher, 130
    teaching, 129–130
authenticity
    awareness of oneself, 32
    and caution on spiritual path, 45–46
    and completion, 75–78
    and Divine Essence, 139–140
    and divine support, 57–60
    embracing authentic path, 43
    journey from conformity to, 315
    and journey of self-discovery, 17–18
    in life, 221–222
    overcoming resistance to, 76–77
    path of, 231–232
    power of, 175–177
    pretense to, 16
    renewal and, 31–32
authentic support, power of, 149–150
awakened
    consciousness, 28, 29–30
    Soul, 42, 329–330
awakening
    to abundance of spiritual wisdom, 239–240
    childlike, 159–160
    to Divine Awareness, 203–205
    to divine oneness, 113–115
    to Divine Within, 293–295
    empathy, 105–108
    fire within, 269–270

from ignorance, 325–326
from illusion, 75–76
inner child, 159–161
inner Christ, 61–63
to inner guidance, 171–172
journey of redemption and inner, 244–245
lessons in spiritual, 130–131
to oneness, 84
to our true identity, 279
path of, 160–161
sacred self, 275–276
seeker within, 28–29
self, 214–216
to wholeness of divine equality, 207–208
awakening soul, 4
divine purpose, 281
intuition and divine connection, 271–274
awareness
of contradictions within oneself, 167
within yourself, 121–123

barrenness to blooming, 32–35
becoming Christ, 337–338
becoming enlightened, 207–208
becoming one, 247
becoming whole, 207–208
being authentic, 231–233
being conscious and alert, 311–312
being inner Christ, 337–338
'Being in the Light', 254
being true to oneself, 225, 227–229, 232
being unique, 57, 75–76
Buddhism, 33

call of change, 163–166
childlike awakening, 159–160
Children of God, 175–176
children's individuality, 314
Choice, The, 254
'chosen', 83
Christ
becoming, 337–338
Identity, 67

Christianity, 47
hypocrisy within, 43
Lost Christianity, 34
reimagining, 20
circumcision, 183
of freedom, 183–185
in spirit, 183
cloned persona, 76
co-creators, becoming, 11–12
codex, xix
collective
unconscious, 84
world view, 77
communion with God, direct, 42
conflict, resolving, 167–169
conscious
beliefs, 155–156
connection, 269–270
growth with professional support, 156
soul, 272
union, 86–87, 329–330
conscious awareness, 203–205
blasphemy, divine expressions, and soul's journey towards, 153–154
Divine Harvest, 239–241
conscious life facets, 319–322
acknowledging God's provision in our lives, 320
embracing Divine Teachings, 320
Inner Christ, 320
recognizing role of society in our lives, 319
consciousness, 71–74, 77, 133, 164, 203–205
aspects of, 319
awakened, 28, 29–30
cultivating, 72, 193–194
dark side of, 133
embracing Divine Truth and expanding, 275–276
identifying and releasing psychological and emotional barriers, 72
inner work and personal development, 72

innocence of, 79–80
journey of healing and
    transformation, 73–74
resilience, continuous growth,
    divine support, 72–73
seeds of, 155–157
state of consciousness in Kingdom
    of Heaven, 79
unique, 171–173
cornerstone of truth, 221–222

daily practice, 148
'dead' teachings, 37
death, 65–66, 179–180
    transcending, 343–344
dialogue within, 134
discernment
    in acts of kindness, 171–173
    energy of, 80
    and intuitive understanding,
        209–211
    trust and, 130–131
    and vulnerability on spiritual
        journey, 299–301
distractions, navigating, 23–24
diversity in faith, 228–229
Divine, 53–55
    All-Embracing Presence, 227
    All-Loving Presence, 253
    Calling, 213
    Centre, 201
    Creation, 331
    Destiny, 327–328
    embracing divine absence, journey
        of, 141–142
    encounter in desperation,
        243–245
    experiencing Divine Being, 12–14
    expressions, 345
    Gift, 259
    Guidance, 12–14, 15–16, 163–164
    Harvest, 239–241
    Impulse, 337
    Inheritance, 279
    inner emptiness to Devine
        Revelation, 160–161
    Intervention, 118–119

    lessons within, 219–220
    Love's unconditional embrace,
        335–336
    Message, 276
    mystery, 209–211
    Nature, 167, 207
    Provider, 53
    resources, 289–291
    Stuff of God, 89
    Supply, 339
    Teaching, 62
    Transformation, 118–119
    Voice, 273
Divine Abundance, 147–148
    and inner transformation, 265–267
Divine Awareness, 3–4
    awakening to, 203–205
    cultivating, 71–74
Divine Energy, 11, 253
    fleeting experiences of, 129
    rooted in, 145–146
    sixth sense, 272
    spiritual fire, 269–270
Divine Essence, 137–138
    authenticity and, 139–140
Divine Identity, 46
    expressing, 175–177
    living demonstration of growing,
        176–177
    and personal responsibility, 61–63
    power of, 147–148
    vigilance and mindfulness in
        nurturing, 311–312
Divine Oneness, 247
    and self-knowledge, 223
Divine Parentage, 324, 331
Divine Presence, 12–14, 131, 182, 193,
    273
    absence, 141–142
    conventional world, 191
    finding, 253–255
    finding rest and liberation in,
        289–291
    power of love and, 110–111
    within, 101–103
Divine purpose, 333
    choosing to fulfill, 164

embracing, 86–87
of life, 231
Divine Self, 138
   and human, 167
   in others, 117–118
   uniting with our, 197–199
Divine Spirit, 81, 235
   and balancing energies, 183–185
   physical observation of, 271–272
   unity with, 83–84
Divine Truth, 45–48, 143–144, 209, 319–322
   and compassion, 89–92
   embodying, 175–176
   embracing, 159–161
   and expanding consciousness, 275–276
   seeking, 201–202
   soul connections on path to, 317–318
   soul's journey to, 303
   in unexpected places, 219–220
Divine Unity
   journey of, 83–84
   and self-expression, 83–87
Divine Wealth, 265
   within, 339–340
Divine Wisdom
   and authentic self-expression, 90–91
   feast of, 217–218
   and Power, 339
   beyond science to, 114
Divine within, 5–6, 261
   awakening to, 293–295
   hidden, 337–338
   others, 117–119
DNA (Deoxyribonucleic acid), 27
doctor/patient relationship analogy, 117
double helix model, 27
   in spiritual world, 28
dream(s), 85–86
   of oneness, 38–39
   symbols, 85
drive for survival, 207

dual nature, human beings, 163, 207

earthly
   existence, 323
   life, 61
   parentage, 323, 331
ego
   -driven charity, 172–173
   -pride, 20
   and therapy, 48
   unmasking, 76–77
emotional resilience, 203–205
empathy, awakening, 105–108
emptiness
   illusion of, 141–142
   sense of, 141–142
   of the well, 243
energy
   of discernment, 80
   feminine, 184, 350
   masculine, 184, 350
   polarised, 80–81, 350
   of rationality, 80
Enlightenment, 90
Entering the Circle, 69
'enter the wedding chamber', 247
equality and wholeness, 349–350
Esoteric truths, 209
Essence of God, 53
eternal essence of life, 277–278
Eternal Fountain of Life, 243
eternal fountain of Truth, 243
eternal journey beyond death, 277–278
Eternal life, 1
evolution of human psyche, 19
existence, earthly, 323
external human self, 287

false beliefs, overcoming, 134–135
false persona, 221
   removing, 139–140
false prophets, 143–144, 243
false rescuer, 149–150, 172
false teachers, 143–144
false wealth, renouncing, 341–342
Father as One source of life, 55

Father Sylvan, 34
feeling, 85
feminine energy, 184, 350
five senses, 271
freedom and personal responsibility, 325–326
fullness of being, 275–276
fullness of God, 237

genetic code, 197
God, 324, 343
    Essence of, 53
    in every moment, 347–348
    fullness of, 237
    presence in all encounters, 219–220
    Presence within ourselves, 23
    returning to God's embrace, 335–336
    triune nature of, 153–154
    as True Father, 331
Gospel of Thomas, xix–xx, xxii
guidance
    Divine Guidance, 12–14, 15–16, 163–164
    inner guidance, 171–172
    from others, 189–190
    parental guidance, 189

healing
    fragmented psyche, 167–169
    hardship to, 122–123
    inner divide, 168–169
    from journalist to healer of hearts, 261–263
    journey of, 243–245
    journey to healing and transformation, 283–285
    light of compromise, 208
    permanent, 137
    through Restorative Justice, 106–108
    trauma, 250–251
heaven, 37–38, 71
hidden
    city within, 121–123
    kingdom, 347–348
    self. *See* other self
    talents, 307–309
    truths to shared light, 125–127
hidden Divinity, 333
    Within, 337–338
Holy Spirit, 153–154
human
    consciousness, 235
    and Divine Self, 167
    dual nature, 163, 207
    ego, 50
    functioning, 85
    journey, 19–20, 250
    language, 80
    life, 290
    parentage, 331
    self, 167
humanity, 77–78, 345
    interconnectedness of God and, 151–152
    journey of, 105–108
humanness, discovering, 21–22
human psyche evolution, 19
human self, external, 287

ignorance, awakening from, 325–326
illusion of emptiness, 141–142
image, 271
inferiority, sense of, 137
Infinite and Eternal Self, 221
inner
    awakening inner child, 159–161
    Christhood, 159
    conflict, 167
    Divine Self, 44, 167
    Divine Voice, 58–60
    Divinity, 42, 43
    emptiness, 160
    fulfillment path, 266–267
    harmony, 134, 167–169
    healing, 156
    invisible Life Spirit, 287
    Knowing of enduring God-Self, 23
    space, 24
    Spirit awareness, 163
    treasure, 339–340

Truth, 57–58, 231–232, 347
unity, 167
voice, 16
'wounded child', 168–169
Inner Christ, 61–63, 139–140, 320
being, 337–338
embracing, 159–160
inner guidance
awakening to, 171–172
courage to follow, 57–60
Inner Light, embracing, 90
inner pearl, unveiling, 250–251
inner potential, discovering, 21–22
inner Presence, 42, 228
of God, 152
Inner Sacred Self, 277
Inner Self, 225–226
knowing our, 231
inner transformation, 156–157, 163–166
and divine abundance, 265–267
from worldly pursuits to, 261–263
innocence, 187–188
insights and opportunities, 283–285
instincts
animal, 19–20, 21–22
and spirituality, 19–20
intuition, 85, 271
In Tune with the Infinite, 32

James the Just, 41
Jesus, 164
as 'bridegroom', 329–330
criticism of Pharisees, 181, 325
denying Pharisees power and control, 181
description about disciples, 75–76
doctor/patient analogy, 117
healings, 63
inner Christ, 61–63
objections of Jewish faith, 49
parables and symbols, 67–69, 71–74
teachings, 53, 55, 83
Jewish worshipers, 42
journey, 27
of authenticity and completion, 75–78
of authenticity and divine support, 57–60
concept of 'journey's end', 142
from conformity to authenticity, 315
of conscious union, 86–87
of discernment and intuitive understanding, 209–211
of divine unity, 83–84
eternal journey beyond death, 277–278
of faith and resilience, 240–241
of healing and purpose, 243–245
of healing and transformation, 73–74, 110–111, 283–285
of healing, self-discovery, and love, 284–285
of humanity, 105–108
of illumination, 210–211
of liberation, 201–202
into love, wisdom, truth, and beauty, 53–55
mother's journey through persecution and unconditional love, 225–226
parts, 27
of redemption and inner awakening, 244–245
of seeking, 3–4
of self-discovery, 17–18, 214–216, 261–263, 290–291, 293–295
of self-reflection and transformation, 194–195
of self-transformation, 122–123, 261–263
of spiritual discovery, 227–229
of spiritual empowerment, 28–29
of spiritual resonance and inner transformation, 32–35
towards spiritual unfoldment and divine purpose, 297–298
of the strayed sheep, 335–336
of trust and discernment, 130–131
of wholeness, 83–87
within, 320–322
judgements, 97–99, 187–188

Jung, Carl Gustav, 38

keys of knowledge, 143–144
Kharitidi, O., 69
Kingdom
    of God, 347–348
    of Heaven, 5, 71, 79
    within, 79–80
knowing yourself, 223
knowledge
    essence of, 223
    keys of, 143–144
    second-hand, 273
'Know Thyself', 17, 90, 327–328

Large Fish, 23–25
legacy within, 339–340
lie, 16
life, 287
    authenticity in, 221–222
    Divine purpose of, 231
    eternal essence of, 277–278
    earthly, 61
    Eternal Fountain of Life, 243
    Eternal life, 1
    Father as One source of, 55
    finding, 197
    on high principles, 121–123
    as living example, 125–127
    priorities in, 213
    purpose of, 171, 197
    relatedness of all, 261–263
    sacred purpose of, 213
    of transformation, 193–195
'Light of Truth', 126
light within, 175–176
living
    as divine example, 175–177
    as divine expressions on earth, 345
    in light, 253–255
    presence within, 343–344
    in truth, 15–16
    by your own truth, 57–60
Living One within, 201–202
'logos', 33
Lost Christianity, 34

love
    miracles of, 109–112
    and transformation, 38–39

male energy. *See* masculine energy
male phallus, 183
mandala, 84–85
    of self-discovery, 86
masculine energy, 184, 350
material wealth, 237–238
meditation, 58
    groups, 300
miracles of love, 109–112
motivation, 149–150
'Moving Mountains', 333
mustard tree parable, 71–74
Mystery Teachings, 209

Nag Hammadi Scriptures, xix, 351
    ownership, xix–xx
    scientific dating, xx
newness of every moment, seeking, 7–8
new world, 179–180

omnipotence, 54
Omnipresence of God, 5–6, 53
omniscience, 54
One Being, 84
One Divine Energy, 138
One Divine Life, 113
    Force, 38
One Life, The, 208
Oneness, 38–39, 44, 80, 343–344
    within and without, 287–288
    awakening to, 84, 113–115
    of life's journey, 86
    mandala, 84–85
    methods leading us towards, 84
    power of community and, 114–115
    understanding, 113–115
    Within, 207–208
One Omnipresent Energy, 323
One united wholeness, 83–87
other self, 93–96
others, empowering, 149–150
'other-worldly experience', 244–245

parable, 184, 249
  God and life, 151–152
  hidden city within, 121–122
  humanity's story, 77–78
  mustard tree parable, 71–74
  and symbols, 67–69, 151
  of the pearl, 249–251
  of weeds, 193–195
parentage, earthly, 323, 331
parental guidance, 189
'pearl of great price', 249–251
perceptions, 254–255
Perpetual Presence, 347
persona, artificial and cloned, 76
personal control of lives, 8–9
personality, 221
  split, 50–52
personal journey, 197
  into self-awareness, 91
personal power, 164, 265
  reclaiming, 134–135
personal truth, guide to, 32
person of light, 89–92
polarised energies, 80–81, 350
polarities, 80
power
  of living our truth, 231–233
  of perspective, 254–255
power of spirit, 109
  father's love and son's journey, 110
  gratitude and empowerment, 111–112
  manifestation of spirit, 111–112
  power of love and Divine Presence, 110–111
presence of Christ, 61–63
presence of God in all encounters, 219–220
Presence of the Father as One source of life, 55
present, embracing, 213–216
pre-set minds, 7
pretense to authenticity, 16
principles, building life on high, 121–123

projection, 97–98
psychological shadow, 313
psychology, 54
psychotherapy, 54, 300

real self, 289–291
reborn as Child of God, 160
relatedness of all life, 261–263
renewal of world, 31–32
'rescuer', 149–150
'rescuing', 149–150, 172
responsibility, freedom and personal, 325–326
Restorative Justice, 106–108
retreat, 300
  silent retreat, 44
  transformative experience, 38–39
revelations, secret, 45–46
risen Christ, 63

Sabbath, 101–103
Sacredness of Life, 331
Sacred Oneness, 323
sacred self, awakening, 275–276
Sacred Silence, 147
Sacred understanding, 259
Sacred Wholeness, 337–338
sacred wisdom, 209–211
'saviours', 149–150
science, 114
'Science of Mind', 50
scientists, 273–274
'second-hand' knowledge, 273
Secret Book of James, The, 41
secret meanings of wealth and power, 265–267
secret revelations, 45–46
seeds of consciousness, 155–157
seeking, 293–295
  divine truth in present moment, 201–202
  highest awareness within yourself, 121–123
  individual divinity, 201–202
  journey of, 3–4

newness of every moment, 7–8
path of, 297–298, 303
true knowledge and experience, 257–258
within yourself, 243–245
seeking truth, 11–12
in life, 201–202
within myths, rituals and symbols, 183–185
outside of themselves, 159
sense of emptiness, 141–142
with shrewdness and innocence, 143–144
self
awakening, 214–216
-centred animalistic behaviours, 21–22
-delusion, 17
external human, 287
human, 167
-judgment, 97–98
liberating, 32
real, 289–291
realization, 79–82
-reflection and transformation, 194–195
-respect and collective value, 16–17
transcending limited, 281
unifying, 167–169
unveiling, 232–233
-willingness to love all others, 20
self-awareness, 97–99, 327–328
personal journey into, 91
self-belief, 133–135
lack of, 137
self-discovery, 198–199, 214–216
challenges on path to, 77
and divine healing, 290–291
path to, 90
and spiritual transformation, 293–295
self-discovery, journey of, 17–18, 261–263
and transformation, 21–22

self-expression
divine unity and, 83–87
nurturing, 81–82
Self, inner Divine, 167
self-knowledge, 171–172
and Divine Oneness, 223
selflessness, 208
self-proclaimed teacher, 129
self-worth, 265
discovering, 213–216, 250–251
embracing lessons and discovering, 283–285
path to, 137–138
sense of, 16–17
sense of
emptiness, 141–142
inferiority, 137
senses, 271
sensing, 85
shadow, 133, 313–315
psychological, 313
of subjugation, 232–233
silence and connection, 24
'sixth sense', 77, 271–274
Soul, 237, 281, 324, 329
aligning body and, 345
authentic 'inner-tuition', 273
awakened, 42, 329–330
awakening, 4
Awareness, 42
connections on path to Divine Truth, 317–318
conscious development, 272
conscious soul, 272
developed, 250
divine purpose, 281
existence, 323
human parentage, 331
intuition and divine connection, 271–274
Journey, 3
journey to Divine Truth, 303
liberating soul's energy, 315
priceless treasure of, 249–251
purpose of, 42

value, 250
Wholeness of, 349–350
spirit
   of generosity, 305–306
   power of, 109
   wonderment and opulence of, 109–112
spiritual
   awakening challenges, 283–284
   banquet, 217–218
   crop, 239–241
   discovery, 159–161, 227–229
   ego, 49
   encounter and transformation, 24–25
   family, 317–318
   fire, 269–270
   growth, 33
   Identity, 191–192
   leader's downfall, 50–52
   light, 271–274
   perception and divine essence, 67–68
   renewal path, 163–164
   resonance and inner transformation, 32–35
   resources, 239
   seekers, 299
   treasures, 250–251
   truth, 67–68, 343–344, 299
spirituality and instincts, 19–20
spiritual journey
   aloneness, 46
   amidst challenges, 46–48
   discernment and vulnerability on, 299–301
   inspirational, 125–127
   therapy, 42
spiritual path
   caution and authenticity on, 45–46
   daily practice, 148
   uniqueness on, 197–198
Spiritual Wholeness, transcending selfishness for, 207–208
spiritual world
   double-helix model in, 28

split personality, 50–52
Still Small Voice, 44, 60
   of God, 291
   inner, 337
superficiality, 257–258
survival, drive for, 207
symbolic wisdom, 67–68

teacher
   choosing with discernment, 129–131
   self-proclaimed, 129
   true, 130
therapy, 72
   and ego, 48
thinking, 85
Thomas, 45–46
Thomas Merton's influence, 126–127
transcending
   human limitations, 159–160
   mortality, 277–278
Trinity, 153
true
   abundance within, 237–238
   blessings, 259
   giver of life, 323–324
   identity discovering process, 23–24, 279
   kinfolk, 317–318
   poverty, 187–188
   riches within, 341–342
   teacher, 130
   wealth, 265, 341–342
   wealth and power, 265–267
True Self, 75–78
   liberating, 90
truly blessed, 259
trust and perseverance, 147–148
Truth, 45–46, 134, 303
   of death, 277–278
   denied access to, 143
   esoteric, 209
   eternal fountain of, 243
   of life, 197–199, 277–278
   living in, 15–16
   of physical matter, 261

power of living our, 231–233
search for, 297–298
seekers, 297–298
seeking, 11–12, 143–144
and wisdom in inner well, 243–244

unconditional
giving, 305–306
love, 20
unique consciousness, 171–173
uniqueness, 300
on spiritual path, 197–198
unity in fragmented world, 113–115

valuing others, 308–309

wealth, 265
divine wealth within, 339–340
financial, 341
material, 237–238
true, 341–342
'white lie', 16
Wholeness, 80–82, 247
of being, 333
cultivating life of, 155–157
embracing chosen path to, 83–84
and equality, 349–350
journey of, 83–87
path of, 93–96
of Soul, 349–350
of Truth, 187
'Wounded Child, The', 17, 250

www.ingramcontent.com/pod-product-compliance
Lightning Source LLC
Chambersburg PA
CBHW071358300426
44114CB00016B/2101